International Finance in Emerging Markets

Songporn Hansanti • Sardar M.N. Islam •
Peter Sheehan

International Finance in Emerging Markets

Issues, Welfare Economics Analyses
and Policy Implications

Physica-Verlag

A Springer Company

Authors

Dr. Songporn Hansanti
Head of International Business
Department
Kasetsart University
Faculty of Management Sciences
Postmail Box 107
40/852 Prachaniveth 3
Thasai, Muang, Nonthaburi
Thailand 11000
songporn.h@ku.ac.th

Professor Sardar M.N. Islam
Professor and Director
Decision Sciences and Modelling Program
CSES, Victoria University
Melbourne
Australia
Sardar.Islam@vu.edu.au

Professor Peter Sheehan
Professor and Director
Centre for Strategic Economic Studies
Victoria University
Melbourne
Australia
Peter.Sheehan@vu.edu.au

ISBN 978-3-7908-2043-0   e-ISBN 978-3-7908-2044-7

DOI: 10.1007/978-3-7908-2044-7

Contributions to Economics ISSN 1431-1933

Library of Congress Control Number: 2008923470

Cover design: WMXDesign GmbH, Heidelberg

Printed on acid-free paper

9 8 7 6 5 4 3 2 1

springer.com

Preface

This book reviews the contemporary issues in international monetary and financial economics (such as financial liberalisation, crisis, exchange rate determination, capital control, domestic capital market reform, etc.) in an emerging financial market such as Thailand from a welfare economic perspective, highlighting the social welfare implications of these issues. This book also suggests a normative social approach (as formalised in the new[3] welfare economics paradigm) (see Islam 2001a,b; for a discussion of this concept) for analysing and addressing these issues and formulating appropriate policies.

Undertaking the above tasks, the asymmetric information paradigm and other elements of the new[3] welfare economics paradigm are adapted in analysing the international financial issues of Thailand, their causes and economic and social welfare consequences.

The last two decades have been a critical period for Thailand's development. From the mid-1980s to the beginning of the 1990s, the Thai economy performed remarkably well and was a showcase for the world economy. Having achieved a double-digit growth rate for a brief period, Thailand in the late 1980s was regarded as the fastest growing economy in the world by the World Bank and the IMF. With prospects of further rapid economic growth, the Thai government accepted Article VIII of the IMF, which required Thailand to liberalise and deregulate its financial system. Accordingly, Thailand removed most regulations on its financial system from 1989 to early 1994. Consequently, the country enjoyed further economic growth and large volumes of capital began to flow into Thailand's financial market. Unfortunately, the story of Thailand's success was short-lived and soon ended, after the financial liberalisation was completed. Finally, economic growth came to a sudden stop and the crisis erupted in July 1997.

This book investigates the recent issues in International Finance in Thailand, focusing on the major issues such as the contribution of financial liberalisation to the crisis in Thailand, the sequence of financial liberalisation, capital controls, and exchange-rate policy, using the asymmetric information paradigm (market, policy and institutional failures). In addition, this study also examines time-series data and other information to explore the consequences of financial liberalisation for the crisis in Thailand. The book divides the analysis into three parts. Part I reviews the literature on contemporary international financial issues and investigates the financial liberalisation framework that Thailand pursued in opening up its financial system. Part II explores the impact of financial liberalisation on the Thai economy, focusing on the issues of sequencing of financial liberalisation, capital controls and exchange rate policy. Part III reviews financial liberalisation theory and the Thai crisis. In this final part, we present our conclusions about the contribution of financial liberalisation to the financial crisis in Thailand.

The Thai financial crisis was a watershed in Thailand's economic development. The crisis generated considerable analysis, literature and conferences on its cause. However, comparably little work has been undertaken on exploring the development and social welfare implications of the crisis for Thailand's immediate and mid-term future. The most immediate implication of the crisis was the initial drop in income throughout the Kingdom. New numerical estimates that reflect the movements in social welfare resulting from the crisis are developed and presented in this book. It is shown that while the financial crisis had a dramatic negative impact on average income levels, the processes of financial liberalisation and globalisation that preceded the crisis were also having negative impacts on the social welfare levels of Thailand. Conventional measures of social welfare, such as Gross Domestic Product or economic growth provide misleading information on social welfare movements. By adjusting this measure for the net benefits of financial liberalisation, a more intuitively correct measure of social welfare is possible. This study will develop a time series, 1975–1999, which estimates this new adjusted GDP measure of social welfare. It shows that stark differences exist between unadjusted GDP measures of social welfare and financial liberalisation adjusted GDP over this time period. Following this, it is possible to undertake new analyses of the development and social welfare implications. This book explores the opportunities for changes in public policy that can prevent further crises. Various public policy initiatives can now be more fully considered than was possible in the past. This book therefore represents a significant contribution to both development and welfare economic literature.

The study shows that four policy errors in international financial management, especially in the financial liberalisation process, which were caused by the asymmetric information problem, existed in the Thai economy during the study period and contributed significantly to the financial crisis in Thailand. The four errors were inappropriate sequencing of financial liberalisation, too rapid and too extensive liberalisation of capital controls, misalignment of the exchange rate through a basket of currencies dominated by the US dollar and lack of adequate supervisory systems in the face of large scale capital inflows, giving rise to moral hazard problems. These errors contributed to problems of a high level of current account deficit, speculative behaviour, overinvesment, loss of competitiveness, increased short-term external debt and excessive investment in and lending to the domestic markets. These problems resulted in economic instability and disruption, and made the country vulnerable to financial crisis when the expectations of foreign investors were not met.

In addition, a quantitative empirical analysis (by applying cost benefit analysis) of financial liberalisation and the associated processes shows that the cost of financial liberalisation has been higher than its benefits in Thailand in recent years.

This book, therefore, provides an in-depth analysis of some emerging and enduring issues in international finance from a welfare economics perspective, especially the issues of financial liberalisation, exchange rate determination, capital control and financial crisis, which provides an improved understanding of social welfare implications of international finance in an emerging financial market.

There is probably no book currently available which addresses the financial issues discussed in this book from a welfare economics perspective. The theoretical issues are balanced by the application of welfare economics to an emerging market. This book fills that gap. It can be used as a reference book by researchers, academics, practitioners, policy makers, and postgraduate students in the areas of finance, financial economics, monetary economics, and development economics. It can be used a reference or an additional text for a finance subject at the Masters or Doctoral level.

Our special thanks go to Dr. Ruchi Gupta, Dr. Susan Zeidan, Dr. Abdullahi Ahmed and Mrs. Margarita Kummick for their comments and help with editing and proofreading this book.

Thailand   *Songporn Hansanti*
Australia   *Sardar M.N. Islam*
Australia   *Peter Sheehan*

February 2008

Table of Contents

1 Introduction

1.1 Introduction

The most striking feature of the present international financial system in the globalised world is financial liberalisation. A trend toward the global liberalisation of financial systems became widespread in the 1990s, including in developing countries (Ouattara 1998; Siamwalla 2000). According to Hallwood and MacDonald (2000), the purpose of financial liberalisation is to detach the financial sector from its anchorage in the domestic economy and to make it a part of the international financial sector. In other words, the purpose of financial sector reforms is to make the domestic financial sector integrated into the globalised financial system. Brooks and Oh (1999) refer to financial liberalisation as the progressive allocation of resources according to market forces rather than personal relationships or government direction, with the aim of strengthening the competitiveness of the financial system. In his study, Vichyanond (2000a) regards financial liberalisation as the process of opening up a domestic financial system to increasing international capital with the aim of fostering economic growth. According to Alba et al. (1999) and Queisser (1999), financial liberalisation is the process by which individual countries liberalise their capital account by renouncing any controls, taxes, subsidies, or restrictions that affect capital account transactions between residents and non-residents. In principle, then, financial liberalisation is the process whereby a country seeks to increase its competitiveness and growth by freeing up its financial system for international capital through reforming trade, foreign exchange policy, capital controls and the domestic financial market.

Theoretically, financial liberalisation is said to benefit developing countries. Sauve (1999) suggested that there are at least two reasons why a country could benefit from financial liberalisation. First, the opening up of financial markets provides more opportunities for foreign investors to invest, leading to a spillover into savings and investment, which contributes to higher growth and development in the long run. Second, liberalisation can promote innovation and modernisation of the domestic financial system through transfer of capital, technologies and skilled labour, which results in improved services that lead to better quality investments. In addition, Levine (1996) and Claessens and Glaessner (1998) added that liberalising foreign entry increases competition and so lowers the cost of finance for domestic users, who gain easier access to cheaper funds from the external sources.

Rapid financial liberalisation did appear to bring substantial benefits to developing Asian countries, as is indicated primarily by the surge in the volume of international flows to Asia during much of the 1990s (Sheehan 1998a, 1998b; Siksamat 1998). According to Sheehan (1998b), private capital flows to Asian countries rose more than fivefold between 1993 and 1996. At the same time, Asian countries such as Thailand, Indonesia, Malaysia and South Korea experienced high economic growth as a result of increased capital inflows, exports and investments (Siamwalla 2000). A study by Gab (2000) revealed that the value of exports increased rapidly during 1993–1995. For instance, Malaysian exports grew at an average of 18%, with 12% for South Korea and Indonesia and 16% for Thailand. Furthermore, Park (1998) found that real income of Asian countries also rose significantly at the rate of 8.4%, 6%, 5.7 and 6.2% in Indonesia, Thailand, Malaysia and South Korea, respectively, during the period of 1985–1995. Such impressive economic performance led the World Bank (1993b) to regard these countries as 'economic miracles' and declared them the fastest growing in the world. The facts, stated above, and others led Phongpaichit and Baker (1998a) to conclude that the achievements of these Asian economies derived partly from the benefits of liberalising their financial systems.

Unfortunately, the miracle did not last and ended when a crisis surprisingly erupted in Thailand and soon spread to strike the neighbouring countries of South Korea, Malaysia and Indonesia. As the crisis unfolded, questions of what caused this sudden collapse of some of the world's fastest growing economies arose (Queisser 1999). Ironically, the Asian crisis was not a traditional financial crisis caused by poor macroeconomic performance, such as high inflation and large budget deficits (Krugman 1998a). Instead, these Asian countries had been praised for their strong macroeconomic fundamentals, accompanied by low inflation, small budget deficits and high rates of domestic savings and investment (Yoshitomi 1999). The Asian crisis was different to other financial crises and one fact stood out: each of these four countries had implemented financial liberalisation prior to the crisis (BOT 1998b). Recent studies by Siamwalla (1997, 2000), Ryan (2000) and Vichyanond (2000a,b) identified financial liberalisation as a cause of the crisis in Asia. Additionally, Brooks and Queisser

(1999) and Mishkin (1999) argued that the crisis represented a problem of financial liberalisation due to mismatch between the liberalisation of their external economic relations, on the one hand, and the lack of adjustment of domestic institutions, on the other.

Kumar and Debroy (1999) reported that financial liberalisation played a major role in increasing foreign debt, because liberalisation allowed private financial institutions and non-financial corporations to borrow from abroad more freely. Thus, all crisis countries recorded rising lending from international sources and incurred high levels of foreign debt, particularly short-term debt. According to the World Bank (1998), the short-term debt to foreign reserves ratio in Indonesia, South Korea and Thailand was more than 100% by mid 1997. Soon after, investor confidence turned sour when the countries failed to service their debt. This made borrowing difficult and led to a sudden economic stagnation, which resulted in collapse of the economies. Corsetti et al. (1998) argue that the crisis in Asia was due to liberalisation coupled with weak bank supervision, allowing poor investment decisions to develop, which resulted in a problem of excessive lending. In their study, they found that the ratio of bank lending to GDP grew by more than 50% in Thailand and the Philippines, 27% in Malaysia and 15% in South Korea. Moreover, Krugman (1998a, 1998b) and Mishkin (1999) concluded that financial liberalisation gave rise to excessive lending in risky investments, which resulted in huge loan losses and led these countries into a moral hazard problem hinged upon poor risk management behaviour and the weakness of the domestic financial system. Siamwalla (1997), Julian (2000) and Ryan (2000) argue that the recent financial crisis in Asia suggested that the benefits of financial liberalisation were uncertain but the costs of financial crises were obvious. In many quarters, the 1997 Asian crisis has been seen as demonstrating the urgent need to rethink the comprehensive application of financial liberalisation.

The problem this book will address is how financial liberalisation contributed to the financial crisis with specific reference to Thailand, focusing particularly on four main issues: the sequencing of financial liberalisation; the removal of capital controls; the choice of exchange rate policy; and issues arising from asymmetric information. The book will assess and analyse the contribution of financial liberalisation to this crisis.

This introductory chapter lays the foundation of the book. Section 1.2 summarises different views on the financial crisis in the context of international crises and the Asian crisis in particular. Section 1.3 describes the problem and objective of this book. Finally, Section 1.4 presents the structure of the book.

1.2 Recent Issues in International Finance

Financial liberalisation, financial crisis, exchange control, exchange rate determination, absence and failure of international financial markets are some of the contemporary issues in the international financial system. Capital controls and capital account liberalisation are also some issues in liberalisation.

Financial crisis affecting individual countries and even related groups of countries are nothing new (Nava-Campos 2000), and the experiences of crises in the past have caught the attention of both scholars and policy-makers seeking to find the causes and the solutions to prevent them. Sundararajan and Balino (1991), Lindgren et al. (1996) equate crises with episodes where there have been runs or other substantial portfolio shifts, collapses of financial firms, or massive government intervention. Typically, economists distinguish crises into two types: currency crises and financial crises. The first, currency crises, usually involve a sudden movement of the exchange rate and a sharp change in capital flows (Dollar and Dreamer 2000; Nava-Campos 2000). The second, financial crises tend to originate in the banking sector-eventually induce bank insolvency – and are generally accompanied by a collapse in asset prices (Dornbusch et al. 1995; Krugman 1991, 1998b). Kaminsky and Reinhart (1999) added that financial crises usually involve a debt problem in the real sector. In other words, banks and other intermediaries usually do not get into trouble if borrowers can service their debt. Additionally, Nava-Campos (2000) asserts that financial crises can occur without any currency crisis, as witnessed in many cases in Africa and in some transition countries (such as Russia), where the main problem has been the insolvency of the banking system.

1.2.1 Overview of International Financial Crises

Although the world's financial crises occurred in different places and different time periods, they can be characterised into two major episodes, namely, pre and post-World War II crises (Aghevli 1981; Mishkin 1991; Bordo and Schwartz 1996). According to Mishkin (1996) the pre-war crises occurred mainly in the US, while the post-war crises spread to other economies as well, for instance, Chile and Mexico.

The early literature emphasised the study of the major pre-war crises in the US, where there was a long history of financial crises that occurred almost every twenty years, starting from 1857 to 1930. As documented in Mishkin (1991), most pre-war financial crises in the US were associated with a sharp increase in interest rates (resulting from a rise in interest rates abroad, particularly the London market), stock market crashes, an increase in uncertainty following economic recession or failure of major financial or non-financial companies. Bordo and Schwartz (1996) and Mishkin (1996) pointed out that the financial panic of 1857 was to blame for the rising interest rate, the falling of stock market and particularly for the collapse of a leading financial institution, the Ohio Life Insurance and Trust Company. The severe economic conditions and uncertainty in the bank's health stirred up panic among investors. Consequently, they began to withdraw massive amount of funds, causing the bank to collapse and drove the country into crisis. Furthermore, Grilli (1990) and Mishkin (1996) discovered that the origin of US crises after that (occurring in 1873, 1884, 1893, 1907 and 1930), had similar causes to those of earlier crises. That is, the crises erupted because of growing interest rates, a stock market crash and the collapse of major financial companies. However, Bordo and Schwartz (1996) argued that the 1873 crisis was unusual and different from other crises as it was not preceded by a sharp increase in interest rates but originated totally from the financial difficulties of financial institutions. The bank panic began with the failure of the New York Warehouse and Security Company who had made substantial loans to the Missouri, Kansas and Texas railroads. When the railroad companies failed, panic spread nationwide and investors began to withdraw funds from the bank, causing its insolvency.

Some of the most important post-World War II crises differ from those of the pre-war period in one important aspect, namely, the banking system has not been subjected to panic bank withdrawals (Mishkin 1991). Bordo and Schwartz (1996) argued that the post-war crises occurred because of mismatch between fiscal and monetary policies (mainly due to a fixed exchange rate). Some of the major crises that we discuss here include the Chilean crisis (1982), the Mexican crisis (1976, 1982 and 1994), and lastly the European Monetary System (EMS) crisis (1992–1993).

The unfolding of Chile's crisis begins in 1982 with a strategy to peg their currency to the US dollar in order to lower inflation. Practically, this strategy was likely to succeed as long as US inflation remained low (Mishkin 1991; Bundnevich and LeFort 1997). Unfortunately, US inflation rose dramatically at the time when the peso was pegged to the dollar, causing Chilean inflation to rise, and the prices of tradable goods to increase. The attempt to maintain the pegged currency regime also implied that trade sectors lost their competitiveness, as their prices rose relative to foreign goods, and this deepened the trade deficit (Dornbusch et al. 1995). In sum, Chile's crisis is well explained by its loss of competitiveness, its high inflation and huge trade deficits that rose significantly while inflows to finance sector declined, leading to collapse of the economy (Mishkin

1991; Bordo and Schwartz 1996). Consequently, the authorities were forced to sell foreign reserves to settle the current account deficit and finally to devalue the peso by the end of 1982.

Mexico is another country that has been long associated with financial troubles. The country experienced a financial crisis at least once in every decade from the 1970s through to the 1990s. A study by Bordo and Schwartz (1996) argued that financial crisis of 1976, originated from high fiscal deficits caused by high foreign debt, a decline of private investment as a result of the world recession, and the pegged exchange rate that made the real prices of imports decline and led to a surge in dollar value while the real price of exports rose. Accordingly, the current account deficit rose rapidly and capital flight began to occur, forcing the government to enter into negotiations for a bailout from the IMF (Buffie 1990). The second crisis, in 1982, was characterised by a huge increase in public sector expenditure that was not matched by revenue increases, resulting in a fiscal deficit as well as a balance of payment deficit (Mishkin 1991; Bordo and Schwartz 1996). Moreover, trade liberalisation and real exchange appreciation lowered the real prices of imports, which raised the current account deficit (Buffie 1990). Indeed, these factors made the devaluation of the peso appear unavoidable (Mishkin 1991). Accordingly, the Mexican government announced the devaluation of the peso by 40% in January 1982. Finally, a decade later in 1994, financial crisis appeared again. An important factor leading to this crisis was the deterioration in banks' balance sheets as a result of a high level of non-performing loans (NPL) (Mishkin 1991, 1996; Bordo and Schwartz 1996). OECD (1995) pointed out that the Mexican government pursued a fixed exchange rate of the peso to the US dollar in order to lower inflation. However, this action did not succeed in eliminating the inflation differential between the two currencies. Prior to the crisis, inflation in Mexico reached 10% by the end of 1993. Moreover, Bordo and Schwartz (1996) added that political unrest and the assassination of the presidential candidate in March 1994 precipitated capital outflows that drained government reserves. Thus, OECD (1995) reported that the peso was forced to devalue on 20 December 1994 and two days later, on 22 December, the government finally abolished the pegged peso and freed it to float.

Like other post-World War II crises, the European Monetary System (EMS) crisis was a negative impact caused by a fixed exchange rate policy. Germany was the nominal anchor in the European Monetary System, thus, other EMS members pegged their currencies to the Deutschemark (DM) in order lower inflation (Bordo and Schwartz 1996). However, after reunification, the German interest rate began to rise and together with a weak US dollar, drew massive inflows into Germany. Consequently, the

DM began to appreciate, and with the DM as a nominal anchor, other EMS countries had to keep their inflation lower than the German inflation or realign their currencies (Mishkin 1996), which they were reluctant to do. Finally, the market enforced a devaluation (Bordo and Schwartz 1996; Mishkin 1996) with the Italian lira was the first to devalue, followed by the British pound, Finnish markka, Swedish krona and lastly the Greek drachma.

The growing number of financial crises has raised questions for economists as to what are the factors causing these crises and how they occur. Recently, there are two competing interpretations of the crises that have been widely debated among economists. Seminal papers by Krugman (1979) and Flood and Garber (1984a) argue that the crises resulted from speculative attacks on the currency, which were driven by the incompatibility of a pegged exchange rate and expansionary domestic financial policy. Their studies have been extended to explain a number of crises, such as: studies of the 1982 Chilean crisis by Velasco (1987); the Mexican devaluation in 1976 by Blanco and Garber (1986); the attack on Argentina's crawling peg in 1981, studied by Cumby and Van Wijnbergen (1989); and the Mexico's 1994 crisis, as well as the 1982 Chilean and the Finish 1992 crisis, by Dornbusch et al. (1995). A number of studies found that the Krugman theory could not explain the EMS exchange rate crisis of 1992, because the economic fundamentals of most countries involved were healthy and did not appear inconsistent with the pegged exchange rate system. This led Eichengreen et al. (1995), Obstfeld (1995) and Obstfeld and Rogoff (1995) to conclude that Krugman's theory could not applied to all type of crises, as it fails to take into account the impact of the policy-making environment.

In their studies of the EMS crisis, Flood and Garber (1984b) and Obstfeld (1986) questioned Krugman's theory by arguing that a crisis is not necessarily related to the behaviour of fundamentals and the pegged exchange rate, but reflects the effects of self-fulfilling speculative attacks. Their explanation of the EMS crisis is that these speculative attacks occurred because the devaluation of the pegged currency was anticipated in the event of high inflation, increasing interest rates and instability of the banking system. Obstfeld (1995) explains the attack on the Italian lira by the fact that speculators were expecting the lira to devalue because of a high domestic interest rate and the government's ability to pay its short-term debt. Similarly, the attacks on the Swedish krona occurred because of high interest rates, high unemployment and banking instability. Ozkan and Sutherland (1994) assert that the crisis in Germany was due to rising interest rates following reunification, which triggered attacks on its currency.

1.2.2 Views on the East Asian Crises

Despite the usefulness of the models introduced by Krugman (1979) and Flood and Garber (1984b) in explaining many past crises, the Asian crises represent a new type of financial crisis, whose causes, consequences and remedies cannot be explained by these two traditional views (Brustelo 1998). According to Krugman (1998b), the Asian crises seem to have differed from the previous crises in four fundamentals.

First, none of the fundamentals that drive "first-generation" crisis models seem to have been present in any of the affected Asian economies. Prior to the crisis, all of the governments were in fiscal balance. In addition, their inflation rates were relatively low by international standards. Second, although there had been some slowdown in growth in 1996, some of the countries were not experiencing high unemployment when the crisis began. In other words, there did not seem to be the kind of incentive to abandon the fixed exchange rate to pursue a more expansionary monetary policy that is generally held to be the cause of the EMS crises (1992) in Europe. Third, there was a boom-bust cycle in the asset markets that preceded the currency crisis: stock and land prices soared, and then plunged in all of the affected countries. Lastly, financial intermediaries seem to have been central players in all of the countries. For instance in Thailand a crucial role was played by finance companies (non-bank intermediaries) that borrowed short-term money, often in dollars, then lent that money to speculative investors (Krugman 1998b; Siamwalla 2000). In the case of South Korea more conventional banks were involved, but they too borrowed short-term funds extensively and lent to speculative investors who invested in highly leveraged corporations (Young 1999; Yoon 2000).

Brustelo (1998) and Krugman (1998b) argue that the Asian crisis is best seen not as a problem caused by fiscal deficits, as in "first-generation" models, nor as one caused by macroeconomic temptation, as in "second-generation" models, but it is best seen as a problem brought on by financial excess followed by financial collapse.

Unlike other crises, the East Asian one did not exhibit traditional fundamental economic weaknesses. A study by Kumar and Debroy (1999) asserts that the macroeconomic elements of the East Asian were strong. For instance, the budget deficits and inflation were low, while investments, savings and growth rates were high. Thus, the East Asian crisis exposes the need to reinterpret the traditional views on crises.

Prior to the crisis, East Asian economies were performing well in terms of GDP growth and this performance was regarded as a striking phenomenon. According to Dollar and Driemeier (2000), the East Asian countries of Thailand, Malaysia, Singapore, Indonesia, Hong Kong and South Korea had registered the most impressive economic growth rates in the world with an average GDP growth of 6–9% during 1980–1989. It was the process of financial liberalisation recommended by the external agencies that changed the Asian economies, which mostly opened up their financial markets lured by the prospect of future growth (Ouattara 1998). Proponents of liberalisation assert that the deregulation of financial markets provided the Asian economies with increased opportunities for investment and savings as international financial capital freely flowed in. A study by Ouattara (1998) pointed out that East Asian countries experienced an unprecedented investment boom following financial liberalisation. For instance, annual gross domestic investment grew with an average of 16.3% in Indonesia, 16% in Malaysia, 15.3% in Thailand and 7.2% in South Korea, during 1990–1996 (BOT 2001).

Prior to the crisis, the Thai economy had performed impressively, with economic growth averaging 7.6% from the late 1970s to early 1990s (Siamwalla 2000). This strong growth required large amounts of investment funds, which prompted the Thai government and the Bank of Thailand (BOT) to liberalise its financial system in the early 1990s (Vajragupta and Vichyanond 1998). Soon after, international capital flows surged into Thailand, fuelling an investment boom (BOT 1998b; Siamwalla 2000). However, as a study by Wiboonchutikula et al. (1999) found, a high proportion of foreign funds were allocated to investment projects in non-tradeable sectors, which were not generating foreign exchange earnings to service the foreign debt. The BOT (1998a,b) added that poor regulation gave rise to misallocation of funds and overinvestment in non-tradable sectors, which led to the creation of an asset price bubble. Furthermore, a savings guarantee by the Thai authorities and weak supervision created a problem of moral hazard, which resulted in excessive lending in the financial system (BOT 1998b; Kumar and Debroy 1999).

The free flow of capital mobility can benefit all countries involved only if these funds are used efficiently within a competitive environment that encourages innovation, and most importantly, affords better returns to investors. However, financial liberalisation can sometime involves risks. Corsetti et al. (1998,1999), in their study of the Asian crisis, argued that policy mistakes heightened the risks associated with financial liberalisation along with weak financial institutions, and problems in corporate and public governance. Similarly, Brooks and Queisser (1999) and Kamin (1999) argue that the Asian crisis can be interpreted as a result of the ongoing process of globalisation that reflects a mismatch between the liberalisation of external economic relations, on the one hand, and the adjustment of domestic institutions, on the other. Clearly, Julian (2000) and Ryan (2000) argue that financial liberalisation is the driving force behind the recent financial crisis in East Asia. Indeed, Vajragupta and Vichyanond (1998), Limskul (2000) and Siamwalla (2000) concluded that the crisis, which was sparked in Thailand with currency devaluation of 38.7% in July 1997, has been seen as a showcase demonstrating the urgent need to rethink the comprehensive implementation of financial liberalisation.

1.3 Statement of the Problem and Objectives of the Study

Thailand has a well integrated international financial system with its own characteristics, issues and agenda, the most crucial ones being related to financial liberalisation, and financial crisis, Despite the fact that the process and implications of financial liberalisation for different countries have been widely debated in economic literature, little empirical research has been done to analyse its effects on Thailand's economy. Past studies have often focused on the implications of globalisation and financial liberalisation for the world economy as a whole.

The primary focus of this book is to present a specific discussion regarding the impacts of financial liberalisation in terms of efficiency (in terms of market and institutional failure asymmetric information paradigm) and functioning of the Thai economy and social welfare changes on Thailand's financial crisis. It aims to present a critical review of a broad range of relevant aspects of financial liberalisation, while remaining focused on the Thai economy. It will document and analyse the implications of financial liberalisation in the context of the contemporary theory in financial crises which includes the sequencing of financial liberalisation, the use of capital control, the choice of exchange rate policy and issues arising from asymmetric information.

1.3.1 Objectives of the Study

The objective of this research is to investigate and discuss the impacts of financial liberalisation on the crisis in Thailand. It aims to document and analyse the global forces that affected the Thai economy in the light of contemporary issues in financial crises. It presents a specific discussion of the impact of financial liberalisation on Thailand's economy and the financial crisis.

The specific aims of this study are as follows:

- To review the literature on international finance with an emphasis on financial liberalisation, focusing on Thailand's economy in particular;

- To present and review contemporary theories of financial liberalisation, including the sequencing of financial liberalisation, the use of capital controls, the choice of exchange rate policy and issues arising from asymmetric information (including market, policy and institutional failures) for efficiency and social welfare maximizing management of international finance using a welfare economics framework;
- To identify and discuss the impact of financial liberalisation on Thailand's economy, crisis and social welfare;
- To assemble appropriate time-series data to analyse the contribution of these contemporary issues in international finance to understand the occurrence of crisis in Thailand; and
- To undertake a social welfare analysis (by applying cost benefit analysis) of the Thai financial liberalisation experience and its associated consequences by undertaking a quantitative empirical analysis of financial liberalisation and the associated processes to show the social welfare implications of financial liberalisation in Thailand.

1.3.2 Finance and Welfare Economics

An emerging methodological approach in economics and finance is that economic and financial issues should be studied within a welfare economic framework with a math-disciplinary approach and an explicit consideration of social welfare implications of financial sector resource allocation and policies (see for example Islam 2001b; Islam and Oh 2003; Hausman and McPherson 1996; Sen 1999). One such issue, which is a central problem in finance, is to find a normative framework for analysing and social decision-making to determine the socially desirable state of the financial sector of the economy.

The objective of this book is to apply a new paradigm in welfare economics, (new)[3] welfare economics (Islam 2001b), which has the characteristics of classical economics and recent positive developments in welfare economics. The main postulate of the new[3] welfare economics is that it is possible to make normative social choices about or analysis of alternative states of the economy, policies and economic organisations on the basis of the some acceptable principles and methods of welfare economics. It has the following tenets:

- Measurability and interpersonal comparison based on subjective and objective information, which is approximate but acceptable;
- Possibility of social choice based on an explicitly revealed social welfare function;

- Incorporation of welfaristic and extra-welfaristic elements of welfare in social welfare analysis;
- Consideration of market non-existence and imperfections, asymmetric information, incomplete contracts, unequal exchange and other social and institutional factors (as these factors make a social choice problem a constrained social optimisation problem making the resultant optimum lower than full potential social welfare (Stiglitz 2003));
- A system approach which incorporates the relevant system of human behaviour and activities, such as economic, social, legal, ecological system in welfare economic studies;
- Operationalisation of social choice theory by adopting developments in mathematical modelling and computation;
- Normative social choice theory in which individual choices (preferences, costs and benefits) are added or considered, along with scientific information, expert opinions and social value judgments (derived from constitution and public policy statements) in making social choices; and
- An operational social welfare function with a set of extended welfare criteria incorporating extra-welfare elements of welfare (the extended welfare criteria includes efficiency, rationality, equity, liberty, freedom, capabilities and functioning) can define a desirable social state.

The arguments in favour of these principles and methods may be in any text on welfare economics such as Arrow, Sen and Suzumura (2003); Boadway and Bruce (1983) and Islam (2001a,b).

To apply the above principles of new[3] welfare economics (Islam 2001a,b) for analysing the issues and developments in the finance sector of the Thai economy from a social perspective, the following exercises will be undertaken in this book:

1. The paradigm of asymmetric information (Stiglitz 2003) will used to analyse the issues in international finance in Thailand within a social welfare context; and
2. An applied welfare economics study (Chap. 8) will be undertaken to estimate the costs and benefits of financial liberalisaiton and globalisation to investigate the social welfare implications of these changes in the Thai economy.

1.4 Book Outline

This book is delineated into three parts. Part A presents a review of the literature. Part B is a study of the consequences of financial liberalisation in Thailand. Finally, Part C is an analysis of the contribution of financial liberalisation to the Thai crisis and social welfare and conclusions.

This book is composed of nine chapters:

1. Introduction

Part A: Literature Review – The Emerging Issues

2. Recent Issues in International Finance: A Literature Review

3. Overview of Thailand's Approach to Financial Liberalisation

Part B: The Thai Experience

4. Analysis of Sequencing Financial Liberalisation in Thailand
5. Capital Controls: Consequences of Financial Liberalisation
6. Exchange Rate Policy and Its Consequences

Part C: Welfare Economics, Economic Theory and Policy

7. Review of Financial Liberalisation Theory and the Thai Crisis
8. Welfare Economic Analysis of Emerging Issues
9. Conclusion and Policy Implications

Part A of this book is covered in Chaps. 2 and 3. In Chap. 2, we provide a literature review on contemporary theories in financial liberalisation, including the sequencing of financial liberalisation, the use of capital control, the choice of exchange rate policy and issues arising from asymmetric information. The first section begins with an overview of the sequencing of financial liberalisation, and then discusses the appropriate sequence of financial liberalisation suggested by the literature. The second section documents the argument for the use of capital controls to prevent and deal with financial crises. We focus our discussion on controls on capital outflows and inflows. The next section reviews the issues of exchange rate policy. First, we highlight factors influencing the choice of exchange rate, and then discuss the main features of an exchange rate regime by focusing on fixed and flexible exchange rates. The last section details the issues in financial crises arising from the theory of asymmetric information. The two main issues of asymmetric information discussed in this section include adverse selection and moral hazard. Asymmetric information is interpreted in a broad sense in this study as it is reviewed to give rise to market, policy and institutional failures, incompatibility and inconsistencies depending on the society where it is applied (see also Arnott and Stiglitz 1988).

Chapter 3 portrays the framework of financial liberalisation pursued by Thailand in liberalising its financial system. The chapter starts with a review of Thailand's economic developments that includes the six National Development Plans and briefly discusses the history of its economic growth. Then, it further explores the factors that influenced financial liberalisation in Thailand, focusing on external and internal factors. The final section provides a detailed discussion of Thailand's financial liberalisation framework. In this section, we review the key financial liberalisation strategies and provide an outline of the order of its occurrence. The financial liberalisation framework of Thailand includes transformation of trade patterns through interest rate deregulation, relaxation of exchange rate and capital controls, and establishment of new financial institutions.

Part B is found in Chaps. 4–6 and contains a study of the impacts and consequences of financial liberalisation on the Thai economy. Chapter 4 attempts to make an assessment of the sequence of Thailand's financial liberalisation. This chapter analyses and outlines the order of the sequence and compares it with the sequence and order described in the literature. The sequence of Thailand's financial liberalisation comprises four steps. As the first step in liberalising its financial system, Thailand undertook the reform of foreign trade, which included the implementation of several *National Development Plans,* aiming to promote the country's export and industrial sectors. The second step was to maintain a sound macroeconomic component. Theoretically, it is suggested that in order to avoid economic instability which may be caused by free flows of capital, a country should ensure that the three main macroeconomic aspects: fiscal or budget deficit, current account and foreign reserve, are well-maintained prior to the implementation of financial liberalisation. In this second section, we detail three key macroeconomic components: fiscal deficit, current account balance and foreign reserves, respectively. The third step was deregulation of the exchange rate and capital controls. We delineate into three episodes between the period of 1989 to early 1994. The final step was domestic financial reforms that normally involved the development of supervisory and monitoring program as described in the literature. However, Thailand pursued a different approach in reforming its domestic market by establishing the two new financial institutions, the Bangkok International Banking Facilities (BIBF) and the Export-Import Bank (EXIM). In this last section, we explore the immediate impact of such reform, focusing on the movement of capital of the BIBF and EXIM bank.

Chapter 5 analyses the impacts of the deregulation of Thailand's capital controls. To accommodate financial liberalisation, Thailand removed most controls on both capital outflows and inflows. For the inflows, Thailand has always welcomed investments from foreign sources; however, foreign investors were allowed to invest more freely in private and equity sectors. In terms of outflows, Thailand has always placed heavy controls on outgoing capital and required prior approval from the Bank of Thailand (BOT) before funds could be transferred out of the country. With financial liberalisation, the Thai government gradually removed controls on capital outflows to allow both local and foreign transfer of funds out of the country. This chapter concerns consequences of capital controls deregulation resulting from financial liberalisation. Firstly, the chapter presents a chronology of capital controls reform and discusses the overall pattern of net private capital flows from the 1980s up to the crisis year in 1997. The next section details the characteristics of capital flows in Thailand, and divides them into two main sections: capital flows to banking and non-bank sector. For the banking sector, we explore the movement of capital flows of commercial banks and the BIBF. The main discussion in the non-bank sector emphasises four types of capital flows: foreign direct investment (FDI), foreign loans, portfolio investment and non-resident accounts.

Chapter 6 analyses the consequences of the exchange rate policy on the financial liberalisation process particularly that pursued by Thailand as part of the financial liberalisation framework. Under the banner of financial liberalisation, the Thailand implemented a basket of currencies, pegging the baht to the US dollar, which dominated the basket. This was to ensure that the country would benefit from the pegged exchange regime, by attracting more inflows into the country in order to service economic growth and investments. This chapter analyses the consequences of this exchange rate regime and is composed of three sections. First, we provide an overview of the basket of currencies. The second section studies the development of the basket of currencies. The third section explores the consequences of the basket of currencies for the Thai economy. In this section, the study is divided into two main parts. First, we focus on the contribution of the basket of currencies to the growth of trade. Then, we further study the role of the pegged exchange rate in contributing to the surge in of foreign capital to Thailand's financial market, focusing on the commercial banks and the BIBF.

Part C is the last part of this book and comprises the three final chapters, Chaps. 7, 8 and 9. This part focuses on the social welfare and public policy issues arising from asymmetric information resulting in market, policy and international failures. Chapter 7 analyses the consequences of applying contemporary theories of financial liberalisation (the sequencing of financial liberalisation, the use of capital control, the choice of exchange rate policy and issues arising from asymmetric information) to explain the impact of liberalisation on the Thai crisis. The discussion in this chapter centers around four main issues. Firstly, we analyse the sequencing of financial liberalisation in Thailand. We observed an inappropriate sequence of liberalisation where there was a mismatch of the sequence described by the literature and Thailand's sequence. That is, libcralisation implemented when current account was imbalanced widened the deficit, foreign exchange rate and capital control reforms were implemented prior to domestic financial reform led to a significant trade of currency and high level of outflows, causing problems currency speculation and weakness to macroeconomic fundamentals, and to establish the offshore banking (BIBF) rather than reforming the domestic market with supervisory and monitoring system caused problem of overinvestment. Secondly, we explore controls of capital after financial liberalisation and found that the controls were too loose, resulting in large inflows were directed to risky projects with poor returns. Thirdly, the fixed exchange rate in Thailand has reduced the country's competitiveness when the US dollar appreciated and increasing external debts, particular the short-term one as a result from rapid increase of foreign capital which normally came in as lending to domestic market. Lastly, we explore the issues of asymmetric information and found that various aspects of financial liberalisation caused a problem of moral hazard with the expectation of a stable exchange rate and guaranteed loans, resulting in excessive investments and lending which finally sparked the financial crisis in the end.

The Thai financial crisis was a watershed in Thailand's economic development. The crisis generated considerable analysis, literature and conferences on what caused the crisis. However, comparatively little work has been undertaken on exploring the development and social welfare implications of the crisis for Thailand's immediate and mid-term future. The most immediate implication of the crisis was the initial drop in income throughout the Kingdom. New numerical estimates are developed and presented in this book that reflect the movements in social welfare resulting from the crisis. It is shown that whilst the financial crisis had a dramatic negative impact on average income levels, the processes of financial liberalisation and globalisation that preceded the crisis were also having negative impacts on the social welfare levels of Thailand. Conventional measures of social welfare, such as Gross Domestic Product or economic growth provide misleading information on social welfare movements. By adjusting this measure for the net benefits of financial liberalisation, a more intuitively correct measure of social welfare is possible. Chapter 8 by Islam and Clarke will develop a time series, 1975–1999, which estimates this new adjusted-GDP measure of social welfare. It shows that stark differences exist between unadjusted GDP measures of social welfare and financial liberalisation adjusted GDP over this time period. Following this, it is possible to undertake new analysis on the development and social welfare implications. Chapter 8 explores the opportunities for changes in public policy that can prevent further crisis. Various public policy initiatives can now be more fully considered than was possible in the past. Chapter 8 therefore represents a significant contribution to both development and welfare economic literature.

Chapter 8 presents a social welfare analysis of the Thai financial liberalisation experience and its associated consequences by undertaking a quantitative empirical analysis (by applying cost benefit analysis) of financial liberalisation and the associated processes to show the social welfare implications of financial liberalisation in Thailand in recent years.

The final chapter, Chap. 9, summarises the contributions and consequences of financial liberalisation to the crisis in general with specific reference to Thailand. In our study, we concluded that the crisis in Thailand was not caused by any single factor, in fact its origins are to be found in various policy mistakes and poor management of the financial system itself. The inappropriate sequence of financial liberalisation resulted in a growing current account deficit, speculative behaviour and weakness of macroeconomic fundamentals, caused by failure to reduce the current account deficit prior to financial liberalisation, foreign exchange trade by foreign commercial banks and rapid increase of capital outflows. Capital control reform by allowing foreign capital to flow freely caused high levels of risky investment toward unproductive sectors. The pegged exchange rate that strictly tied the baht to the US dollar did not enhance growth and investments, but on the contrary, weakened the country's competitiveness when the value of the dollar began to appreciate, causing a decline of exports, investments and economic growth. Additionally, we also found that the pegged exchange regime has encouraged more foreign capital, which generally came in as short-term lending, hence the external debts of the country grew dramatically. Finally, moral hazard problem derived from the pegged exchange rate regime and establishment of the BIBF, causing the expectations of guaranteed value of currency and loans, which led to excessive investment, and lending in the domestic market. We conclude, the financial crisis in Thailand was a showcase of inexperienced international monetary policy and mismanagement of financial liberalisation by Thailand with an inappropriate sequence of financial liberalisation, loose controls over the capital accounts, misalignment of the currency and lack of moral hazard management and the existence of some adverse socio-economic and institutional factors.

It is hoped that the findings of this book are used to formulate better policies and strategies, which may assist in avoiding future crises and help Thailand and other countries to cope with financial liberalisation. Lastly, we also point out possible policy recommendations and areas for future research that the next study can extend this study.

PART A: Literature Review – The Emerging Issues

2 Recent Issues in International Finance: A Literature Review

2.1 Introduction

The purpose of this chapter is to overview the main issues in international finance such as financial liberalisation, focusing on the process as a possible cause of financial crisis. The rest of this chapter is organised as follows. Section 2.2 provides an overview and review of literature on the sequence and order of financial liberalisation. Section 2.3 reviews capital controls, and focuses on two types of controls, namely, controls on capital outflows and inflows. Section 2.4 gives a brief discussion of factors that influence the choice of exchange rate policy, and presents an overview of both fixed and flexible exchange rates, and presents a social choice approach for choosing an appropriate exchange rate regime. Further, Sect. 2.5 first gives an overview of asymmetric information, before reviewing theories of adverse selection and moral hazard. Section 2.6 finally, summarises the chapter.

2.2 Financial Liberalisation: Sequence and Order

In the new age of global capital markets, developing countries have been popular destinations for international investment funds. As a result, financial liberalisation in developing countries is now seen by many to be an irresistible trend (Rajan 2001a,b). The integrated capital market has been regarded as a necessity for developing countries to benefit from globalising capital markets. But it has been also claimed that some developing countries have become economically vulnerable from financial market integration (Lane et al. 1999; Gab 2000) and financial liberalisation. Indeed, it has been argued that the economic and financial crisis that followed this integration has highlighted an incorrectly ordered and perhaps hasty process of financial liberalisation, and has demonstrated the necessity of an appropriate and correct sequence of financial liberalisation (Hallwood and MacDonald 2000).[1]

2.2.1 Overview

A study by Gab (2000) concluded that financial liberalisation generates both benefits and disruption to developing countries. A study by Sauve (1999) reported that high economic growth in Asia, led by high trade and investments, is a prime example of the benefits from financial liberalisation. While Brooks and Oh (1999) argue that the recent crisis in Asia revealed risks associated with financial liberalisation, for instance high external debts, over-investments and so on. Other views (Goldstein and Turner 1996; Caprio et al. 1997; Demirguc-Kunt and Detragiache 1997a, 1997b; Honohan 1997; Williamson and Mahar 1998; Chirathivat 1999) hold that high capital flows imply the international capital market is fundamentally unstable and disruptive, suggesting the need for tight capital control to stabilise emerging financial markets. High capital flows can be followed by a financial crisis accompanied by large shifts in interest rate spreads between emerging markets and world financial centres and by sharp movements in exchange rates. On the other hand, the proponents of high capital flows say that speculative capital flow has a stabilising effect that raises efficiency in the economy. Traditional views (Jung 1986; Gelb 1989; DeGregorio and Guidotti 1992; King and Levine 1993) supporting high capital flows say that a potential positive role of high capital flows is to provide incentives for policy makers who are politically opportunistic to follow efficiency-increasing economic policies. Recent intermediate views (Arestos and Demetriades 1999; Brooks and Oh 1999; Ariff and Khalid 2000) of the public choice approach argue that the discipline effect from international capital flows is not sufficiently farsighted, and that the

---

[1] For discussion of this view, see for example Williamson (1982), McKinnon (1982), Edwards (1984, 1986), Corbo and deMelo (1987), Edwards and Edwards (1987), Kahkonen (1987), Fry (1988), World Bank (1989a,b), Collier and Gunning (1992), Falvey and Kim (1992), Williamson and Mahar (1998), Rajan (2001a,b) and Rajan and Bird (2001). On the other hand, Siamwalla (2000) argues that the recent crisis in Asia was not entirely due to an inappropriate sequence of financial liberalisation, but highlighted poor management of the financial market. While, Aoki (1997) and Mishkin (1997, 1999) concluded that the crisis was due to problems of asymmetric information, Valdes-Prieto and Soto (1998) blamed it on a lack of capital controls and Pantusane (1998) views the mismanagement of exchange rate policy as a cause of the crisis.

inherent short-sightedness of this discipline effect can explain the recent crises (Ito 1998; Gab 2000).

Recent empirical studies have concluded that inappropriately sequenced financial liberalisation has been an important contributory factor to the boom and crash cycles in emerging economies (Williamson and Mahar 1998). Gourinchas et al. (1999) studied lending boom episodes across ninety-one countries during the period 1960–1996, and concluded that the probability of experiencing a financial crisis was significantly greater following a lending boom, linking this to financial liberalisation. Empirical studies by Demirguc-Kunt and Detragiache (1998) and Hutchison and McDill (1999)[2] found that a financial crisis was more likely in a liberalised financial system, particularly when the institutional support was weak. Kaminsky and Reinhart (1999) concluded that in eighteen of the twenty-six banking crises in their sample, the financial sector had been liberalised some time during the previous five years (Rajan 2001).

2.2.2 Sequence and Order of Financial Liberalisation: A Literature Review

According to Sundararajan (1999), orderly liberalisation often requires implementation of critical and massive reforms simultaneously. What is needed is a package of reforms involving different components of the financial sector, such as aspects of banking supervision, money markets, monetary operations and central banking. He argues that, at the least, this is necessary for financial stability reasons, and to be able to be effective in implementing stabilisation policies.

The influential views on the sequence of liberalisation of Edwards (1989a) and McKinnon (1993) assert that domestic financial market liberalisation and current account liberalisation should be implemented first, followed by capital account liberalisation. Moreover, early literature on the optimal sequencing of economic reform also suggests the importance of capital controls during the process of development.[3] In this view, liberalisation of the capital account should not be undertaken until the end of the process; freeing up capital flows prematurely before domestic and trade

---

[2] Samples in Demirguc-Kunt and Detragiache (1998) include a panel of fifty-three countries for the period 1980–95 and ninety-seven countries for the period 1975–97 by Hutchison and McDill (1999).

[3] Burkett and Lotspeich (1993) argue that financial liberalisation should not take place until both fiscal and monetary controls are established. Also see Wihlborg and Willet (1997) and Whitt (1999) for discussion of this view.

liberalisation could lead to economic instability (McKinnon 1973, 1993; Edwards 1984; Balassa 1990; Glick and Hutchison 2000).

McKinnon (1993) and Burkett and Lotspeich (1993) argue that there are at least two reasons why capital account liberalisation should be delayed until the end of the reform sequence. First, if inflows occur prior to the completion of trade reforms, the domestic allocation of foreign savings may not be efficient. Second, whether or not trade reforms are initially in place, a rapid inflow of capital will cause real appreciation of the exchange rate, which makes it difficult for domestic tradeable producers to adjust to the removal of protection. Thus, a massive influx of capital at the time liberalisation occurs, finances an unusual increase in imports while decreasing exports and gives out the wrong long-run price signals to private market participants (Edwards 1984). In addition, other elements of a supporting policy package for orderly capital account liberalisation are restructuring weak and insolvent banks. Indeed, where banks are weak or insolvent, one would want to restrict their access to international capital flows, and so there may be a case for imposing controls on selective capital movements. Furthermore, there would be a need to strengthen auditing, accounting and disclosure practices (Sundararajan 1999).

McKinnon (1993) has attempted to account for institutional capabilities and weaknesses, with 'the optimal order of economic liberalisation'. It is thus argued that:

> ...how fiscal, monetary, and foreign exchange policies are sequenced is of critical importance. Government cannot, and perhaps should not, undertake all liberalising measures simultaneously. Instead, there is an – 'optimal' order of economic liberalisation, which may vary for different liberalising economies depending on their initial conditions. (McKinnon 1993, p. 77)

McKinnon elaborates by suggesting that the speed of adjustment is sluggish in the goods markets, and faster in the financial markets. Thus, financial markets could not be reformed in the same manner and at the same time as other markets, without creating awkward difficulties. Recognition of these problems has led to the proposition of sequencing in financial reforms. Successful reform of the real sector is seen as a prerequisite to financial reform. Thus, financial restraint would have to be maintained during the first stage of economic liberalisation. Furthermore, different aspects of reform programs may work at cross-purposes, disrupting the real sector in the process. This is precisely what Sachs (1989) labelled as 'competition of instruments'. Such conflict can occur when abrupt increases in interest rates cause the exchange rate to appreciate rapidly thus damaging the real sector. Sequencing becomes important again. It is thus suggested that liberalisation of foreign markets should take place after liberalisation of domestic financial markets. In this context, proponent views on financial liberalisation suggest caution in sequencing in the sense of a gradual process of liberalisation emphasising the achievement of macroeconomic stability and adequate bank supervision as preconditions for successful financial reform. It is also argued by proponent views of financial liberalisation that the authorities should move more aggressively on financial reform in good times, and rather slowly when borrowers' net worth is reduced by negative shocks, such as recessions and losses due to changes in the terms of trade (World Bank 1989b; Arestos and Demetriades 1999).

Falvey and Kim (1992) and Caprio et al. (1994) have reviewed financial reforms in a number of countries, primarily developing countries, and studied the experience of six countries at some length. They conclude that appropriate sequencing along with favourable initial conditions of financial markets and macroeconomic stability are critical elements in the successful implementation of financial reforms.

In the light of the poor results that followed the Latin American financial liberalisation in the 1970s and early 1980s, many economists now recognise that financial liberalisation in developing countries is most successful when it is gradual (Kahkonen 1987; McKinnon 1989; Villanueva and Mirakhor 1990b). In principle, the order of liberalisation now accepted by some economists is the following sequence (see Fig. 2.1).

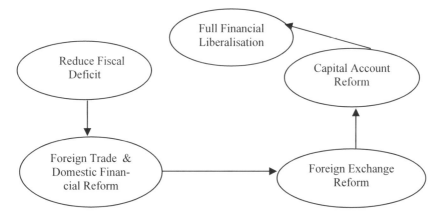

Fig. 2.1. Sequence of financial liberalisation

Source: Adapted from Hallwood and MacDonald (2000).

A study by McKinnon (1993) has reviewed the three prerequisites for successful reform which are the establishment of macro-financial control by lowering government deficits, the correct sequencing of domestic financial market reforms including reductions in trade restrictions and deregulation of external capital flows, and prudential regulations on bank activities to prevent financial market instability from derailing the liberalisation process. Hallwood and MacDonald (2000) argue that there are five major areas where financial liberalisation measures need to be taken. The five areas include reduction of the fiscal deficit, liberalisation of domestic financial system, liberalisation of foreign trade, liberalisation of foreign exchange control, and exchange rate management. Additionally, Caprio et al. (1994) argue that successful liberalisation will depend on the speed of implementation of the process of financial liberalisation, which should be done gradually. In this gradual process a sequencing of financial liberalisation (Edwards 1986, 1989a; McKinnon 1993; Johnson et al. 1997) is recommended, emphasising the achievement of stability in the broader macroeconomic environment and adequate bank supervision within which financial reforms were to be undertaken (McKinnon 1988; Cho and Khatkhate 1989; Sachs 1989; Villanueva and Mirakhor 1990a,b). Employing credibility arguments, Calvo (1988), Rodrik (1987) and Arestos and Demetriades (1999) suggest a narrow focus of reforms with financial liberalisation left as last. In principle, it is widely agreed that a gradual process is recommended for successful financial liberalisation and the appropriate sequencing of financial liberalisation consists of reductions of deficits, foreign trade and domestic financial reforms, foreign exchange rate reforms, and capital account reform, left to the last.

2.3 Capital Controls

Capital control is another important issue in international monetary economics. The window of opportunity offered by capital controls has been abused by certain powerfully-connected business interests, not only to secure publicly funded bail-outs at public expense, but even to consolidate and extend their corporate domination, especially in the crucial financial sector. Capital controls have been part of a package focused on saving friends of the regime, usually at the public's expense (Jomo 2001, p. 55).

Currency controls are a risky, stopgap measure, but some gaps desperately need to be stopped. (Krugman 1998b, p. 1)

The volume of foreign capital transactions has increased dramatically in recent years both for developed and developing countries. The forces of globalisation have pushed both investors and borrowers into international financial markets.[4] The liberalisation of financial markets has also presented crucial challenges for policymakers in controlling the flows of capital (Dooley 1996; Cardenas and Barrera 1997). Neely (1999) defines capital controls as any policy implemented to limit capital account transactions. Bakker (1996) argues that this broad definition makes it difficult to generalise the issues of capital controls as they can take many forms and can be utilised for various purposes.[5] Furthermore, Edwards (1999) suggests that the series of crises has demonstrated the need for controls over capital. Recent studies on the new international financial theories have focused on two types of capital controls, namely, controls of capital outflows and inflows (Edwards 1999; Neely 1999).

2.3.1 Controls on Capital Outflows

A number of academic economists have argued that controls on capital outflows have been one of the solutions to deal with a financial crisis (Edwards 1998, 1999). In most cases, controls on capital outflows are applied to postpone a choice between devaluation and tighter monetary policy (Neely 1999). In his article, Krugman (1998a) argued that controls on capital outflows are useful, at least to prevent a speculative attack from both domestic and international sources. In essence, Edwards and Edwards (1987) has delineated the two major types of controls on capital outflows, 'preventive controls' and 'curative controls', which are discussed in the following section.

2.3.1.1 Preventive Controls on Capital Outflows

Generally, these are employed when a country is facing a balance of payments deficit, but has not yet suffered currency devaluation (Edwards 1999). Preventive controls include taxes on funds remitted from international transactions, dual exchange rates with a more depreciated rate applied for capital transactions, and outright prohibition of fund transfers (Yoshitomi and Shirai 2000). The main objectives of these types of control are to slow down the drain of foreign reserves, and at the same time,

---

[4] Edwards (1999) argues that globalisation gives rise to capital mobility and has created a highly unstable international financial system. Mussa (2000) reveals the danger of high openness to international capital flows, especially short-term flows to countries with weak or inconsistent macroeconomic policies or inadequately capitalised and regulated financial system.

[5] See Alesina et al. (1994) and Grilli and Milesi-Ferrentti (1995) for empirical studies of factors associated with capital controls.

provide authorities with time to implement corrective policies, while fending off speculation (Edwards 1999; Yoshitomi and Shirai 2000).

According to Edwards (1999) and Yoshitomi and Shirai (2000), some earlier empirical evidence suggests that preventive controls are likely to be ineffective. Studies by Edwards (1989b) and Edwards and Santaella (1993) showed that the private sector would find ways to circumvent the controls in the months prior to a devaluation crisis. Results from their studies reported that almost 70% of the cases where the controls on outflows were applied as a preventive approach resulted in a large increase in capital flight at the end. Similarly, a study by Cuddington (1986) on the determinants of capital flight in developing countries came up with the same conclusion. Kaminsky and Reinhart (1999) found that the authorities tried unsuccessfully to avoid currency collapse by introducing controls on capital outflows. Additionally, Edwards (1999) and Yoshitomi and Shirai (2000) argue that capital controls often give a false sense of security that encourage complacent and careless behaviour on part of the authorities.

Some economists believe that these types of controls have been far less successful. Edwards (1999) argues that controls of capital outflows introduce corruption, as international investors bribe local authorities to move their money out of a country facing prospective financial crisis (Yoshitomi and Shirai 2000). Under these circumstances, the authorities usually fail to implement a credible and effective program after the controls are in place (Yoshitomi and Shirai 2000). In other words, preventive controls are unlikely to help improve macroeconomic disequilibrium. Rogoff (1999) believes that preventive controls are too costly to run, as their disadvantages outweigh the benefits.

2.3.1.2 Curative Controls on Capital Outflows

In contrast to preventive controls, curative controls are usually imposed when a country is already experiencing a crisis. Krugman (1998a) argues that a country facing a major crisis can benefit from imposing temporary controls on capital outflows. For instance, it can help a crisis-country to lower the domestic interest rate and encourage domestic demand (Krugman 1998a; Edwards 1999; Yoshitomi and Shirai 2000). These controls also allow a country in crisis, additional time to put their financial sector back in order. However, once a country's financial sector is back on its feet, controls need to be removed (Edwards 1999).

Edwards (1999) concluded that the usefulness of curative controls on outflows is not conclusive. Yoshitomi and Shirai (2000) argue that these types of controls in a post-crisis period have not been helpful. For instance, an empirical study by Edwards (1989b) reported that 50% of sample countries had unsuccessfully attempted to avoid the crises by imposing curative controls, which failed to improve the balance of payments. Two-thirds of the countries experienced unsatisfactory GDP growth after the financial crisis. While, only 35% of the countries that did not apply curative controls went through an economic slowdown.

Additionally, Latin American countries such as Argentina, Mexico and Brazil that implemented controls on outflows in the 1980s crisis, experienced a long-term economic slowdown, high unemployment and high inflation (Edwards 1999; Yoshitomi and Shirai 2000).

2.3.2 Controls on Capital Inflows

In the aftermath of the East Asian crisis, there has been increasing support for the imposition of controls on capital inflows, as a way of preventing future currency crises (Eichengreen 1999). Controls on inflows are expected to protect emerging countries from international speculation, while at the same time allowing them to undertake an independent monetary policy (Edwards 1999). Furthermore, Khor (1998) concluded that controls on capital inflows are imposed for two reasons: first, as part of macroeconomic management to reinforce or substitute for monetary and fiscal measures; and second, to attain long-term national development goals, for instance, to put in place regional controls ensuring residents' funds are locally invested or that certain types of activities are reserved for residents.

Theoretically, controls on capital inflows can be under taken in two forms, administrative (directly) and market-based (indirectly) (Moreno 2001). Administrative or direct controls involve outright prohibitions on certain transactions, minimum maturity or stay requirements, or other methods. Market-based or indirect controls attempt to discourage particular capital movements by making them more costly, and involve direct or indirect taxes, including, unremunerated reserve requirements (URR)[6] or regulatory and reporting requirements. Similarly, however, Neely (1999) concluded that capital controls can be distinguished by price mechanisms (including taxing certain inflows transactions) and quantity controls (involve quotas or outright prohibitions on incoming capital). In principle, taxing capital inflows can be helpful in curbing an excessive temporary increase in economic activity, particularly in private consumption, that is being financed to a large extent by capital flows (Reinhart and Smith 2001). Crotty and Epstein (1999) stressed that the most efficient way to control

---

[6] See for example, DeGregorio et al. (2000) for empirical work of URR on capital inflows.

capital inflows is to rely on taxation. The two tax mechanisms that have gained support in the economic literature are URRs and the Tobin tax.

Taxation of capital inflows in the form of URRs has been one of the most frequently used controls.[7] Banks, and non-banks dealing on their own account, are required to deposit at zero interest with the central bank an amount of domestic or foreign currency equivalent to a proportion of the inflows or their net position in foreign currency. URRs may be used to limit capital inflows for particular types of transaction. For instance, Chile during 1991–1998 required foreign investors to leave a fraction of their short-term bank deposits with the central bank, earning no interest. The Chilean reserve requirement applied not only to bank deposits, but also to many types of capital inflows. As the deposits earn no interest and allow the central bank to buy foreign money market instruments, the reserve requirement effectively functions as a tax on capital inflows (Edwards 1998).

Another type of tax mechanism that has gained support in the literature is the 'Tobin' tax, proposed by James Tobin in 1972. The Tobin tax charges participants a small percentage of all foreign exchange transactions (ul Haq et al. 1996; Kasa 1999). Advocates of such a tax argue that it diminishes foreign exchange market volatility by curtailing the incentive to switch positions over the short term in the foreign exchange market. It has also been argued that there are many potential problems with a Tobin tax. The tax might reduce liquidity in foreign exchange markets or be evaded easily through derivative instruments. It is uncertain who would collect the tax or for what purposes the revenue would be used. Lastly, a Tobin tax would have to be enacted by widespread international agreement to be successful.

2.4 Exchange Rate Policy

The choice between fixed and flexible exchange rates has long been one of the most fundamental issues in international finance (Collignon et al. 1999). Furthermore, the debate between fixed and flexible exchange rates is often phrased as a choice between absolutes. However, the early literature introduced by Mundell (1961) and McKinnon (1963) concluded that one choice cannot be right for all countries. According to Hossain and Chowdhury (1996), most developed countries are open economies and follow exchange rate policies that can be characterised as a fixed or flexible

---

[7] See Bundnevich and LeFort (1997), Laurens and Cardoso (1998), and Valdes-Prieto and Soto (1998) for studies examining the effects of the URR on capital inflows.

foreign exchange regime. We will first review the factors behind the choice of exchange rate policies in Sect. 2.4.1. Then, Sect. 2.4.2 provides an argument between fixed and flexible exchange rates.

2.4.1 Factors Influencing a Choice of Exchange Rate Policy

The exchange rate is said to be the most important single price in the economy (Kenen 1994). There may be good reasons for either fixing it or for letting it float, depending on the structure of an economy and its trade pattern. Decisions concerning the choice of future exchange rate regimes, however, need to be internally and logically consistent. The authorities may pursue various decision criteria in choosing an appropriate exchange rate system (Visser 2000).[8] Frankel et al. (1991) argue that the final choice by the authorities depends on three main factors: the structural characteristics of an economy, the need to reinforce the credibility of monetary policy, and the existence of a regional cooperation agreement. On the other hand, Hallwood and MacDonald (2000) argue that five factors are likely to be relevant concerning a choice of exchange rate policies: the country's size, its degree of openness, its degree of international financial integration, its inflation relative to the world average, and its trade pattern.

Indeed, the question of whether developing countries are better off with a fixed or a flexible exchange rate system is a difficult one. In sum, the optimal management of the exchange rate depends on the underlying socio-economic and institutional set up, the policymakers' social and economic objectives, the source of shocks to the economy, trade policy, international agreements on financial cooperation and the structure of the economy (Rusidy and Islam (2007); Frankel et al. 1991; Hallwood and MacDonald 2000; Mussa et al. 2000). Rusidy and Islam (2007) argue that the choice of an appropriate exchange rate regime is essentially a normative social choice problem (Arrow et al. 2003). Like social choice problems in other areas, this social choice problem in the choice of an appropriate exchange rate regime that depends on the underlying socio-economic and institutional conditions, social value judgments and preferences of that country (Hipsher et al. 2007).

---

[8] See Edwards (1996) for a theoretical study on a choice between fixed and flexible exchange rate regimes.

2.4.2 Overview of Fixed and Flexible Exchange Rate

Should countries adopt fixed or flexible exchange rates? One way to tackle this age-old question is to consider which exchange rate regime provides more discipline against loose monetary policies, high fiscal spending, or excessive wage demands. Recent conventional wisdom within the economics profession holds that fixed rates provide more discipline (Aghevli et al. 1991; Frankel et al. 1991). Tornell and Velasco (1995) concluded that fixed rates induce more fiscal discipline because adopting lax fiscal policies must eventually lead to an exhaustion of reserves and an end to pegging the rate.

Fixed exchange regimes have been adopted as part of the macroeconomic stabilisation programs employed by different countries in different times (Hansanti 2005). This diversity of circumstances makes it unlikely that there is any consistent pattern in the outcomes of these stabilisation attempts (Rebelo 1997). Krugman (1979) stresses that a fixed exchange rate regime establishes important links between fiscal policy and monetary policy. Governments with large fiscal imbalances may have to resort to the monetization of the deficit, which leads to a gradual loss in reserves and renders vulnerable to speculative attack (Hansanti 2005).

Following a pegging of exchange rates, developing economies tend to experience an increase in GDP, a large expansion of production in the non-tradeable sector, a contraction in tradeable productions, a current account deterioration, an increase in the real wage, a reduction in unemployment, a sharp appreciation in the relative price of non-tradeable, and a boom in the real estate market (Rebelo 1997). Similarly, Vegh (1992) suggests that after fixing the exchange rate, the economy tends to experience the following.

- There is an economic expansion: consumption rises, real wage increases, the rate of unemployment falls, and there is often a boom in the real estate market. Investment increases in many causes, but not as strongly or as consistently as consumption.
- The relative price of non-tradeable goods + services increases rapidly, slowing down the decline in the rate of inflation.
- The current account and the trade balance deteriorate.
- Production in the tradeable sector often falls relative to trend.
- There is initially a large fiscal adjustment of temporary programs.
- The initial expansion in economic activity tends to be followed by a slowdown.

According to Branson and Papefstratiou (1981), a country's choice of currency peg should be determined by the geographic structure of its foreign trade. In particular, if its foreign trade is mainly with a single partner, it should peg to that country's exchange rate, this will help to stabilise relative prices by constraining exchange rate fluctuations (Hansanti 2005, 2006).

There are several arguments in favour of a fixed exchange rate. Pegging to a low inflation currency can provide a credible anchor for restraining domestic inflation expectations, as long as expectations that the fixed exchange rate will not be abandoned are credible. Another argument for a peg is that it fosters fiscal or monetary policy discipline by curbing the temptation to follow excessively stimulatory macroeconomic policies that would lead to an exhaustion of foreign exchange reserves and an end to the peg.[9] At the micro level, a fixed exchange rate may also reduce transaction costs and exchange rate risks, which can discourage trade and investment (Glick 2000; Visser 2000).[10]

According to Glick (2000), the main cost of a fixed exchange rate is the loss of macroeconomic flexibility in the response to shocks, particularly those that affect the equilibrium real exchange rate.[11] Giving up an escape clause to exercise devaluation, during times of severe global downturn, may be undesirable, if the short-term cost of defending the peg exceeds the long-term benefit of maintaining it. The loss of the domestic central bank as a lender of last resort can also be costly. Lastly, fixed rates lacking credibility leave countries open to speculative attacks on their currencies, and serve as a 'lightning rod' for concerns about broader debt and banking problems as well as government macroeconomic policies, and may spawn crises that greatly amplify the costs of adjustment.

In addition, fixing currencies has the advantage of reducing the average fluctuation of the domestic currency to other currencies, thus, reducing the risk for those who have to take an open position in various currencies. In other words, a peg implies that all traders would bear no exchange rate risk (Hansanti 2005). A country without well-developed financial markets may find it advantageous to peg to a single major currency and thereby

---

[9] However, Tornell and Velasco (1995) argue that flexible rates may provide more fiscal discipline through the more immediate effects of lax policies on the exchange rate and the price level.

[10] Eichengreen and Hausmann (1999) argue that emerging market economies could benefit from a fixed exchange rate as countries can borrow for the long-term in local currency either from abroad or domestically, creating a match between assets and liabilities.

[11] Edwards and Savastano (1999) argue that fixed exchange regimes may give rise to real overvaluation of a currency and increase inflation.

effectively expand the domain of its currency by allowing market participants to take advantage of services available for that major currency (Mussa et al. 2000).[12]

In regard to a flexible exchange rate, it is argued that floating exchange rates insulate a country from external shocks or terms of trade movements (Hansanti 2005). For instance, if there is a large balance of payments deficit due to an external shock such as an increase in oil prices, money supply will decline under a fixed exchange rate system in the absence of sterilisation. This will have a contractionary impact on the domestic economy. However, under the floating exchange rate system, the exchange rate will depreciate in response to balance of payments deficits without any contractionary impact on money supply and the domestic economy (Hossain and Chowdhury 1996).

Frankel (1995) argues that the advantages of flexible rates include, being freed of the obligation to keep the exchange rate fixed and monetary policy can respond independently to disturbances. When a country opens up its financial market to international capital flows, this point becomes more compelling. Monetary policy becomes a powerful instrument. A monetary expansion under floating exchange rates has much of its effect via the international channel a depreciation of the currency and the resulting stimulus to net foreign demand, supplementing the traditional channel of a lower real interest rate and resulting stimulus to domestic demand.

A seminal paper by Glick (2000) provides an argument in favour of a flexible exchange rate. At the macro level, flexible exchange rates allow a country to have an independent and discretionary monetary policy as a tool for responding to shocks, particularly to aggregate demand. In addition, flexible rates provide a faster and less costly adjustment mechanism to change relative prices, in response to shocks necessitating an adjustment in the real exchange rate, particularly when nominal goods prices change slowly.

A flexible exchange rate and discretionary monetary policy usually come at the cost of some loss of credibility that can lead to an inflation bias. At the microeconomic level, higher exchange rate variability creates uncertainty and discourages international trade and investment (Glick 2000). Also, a floating exchange rate regime has been found to come under speculative attacks, making the foreign exchange market more volatile. As a result, fluctuations in exchange rates have been larger than could be explained either by variations in inflation rates or by perceived structural changes among countries (Hossain and Chowdhury 1996).

---

[12] See for example Aghevli (1981) and Williamson (1982) for a discussion of these views.

The insulation property of a flexible exchange rate regime can also be questioned on three grounds (Hossain and Chowdhury 1996). First, developing countries experience domestic supply shocks such as crop failure, more often than external shocks. Second, sharp and continuous depreciations of domestic currency may be intolerable politically, making a floating exchange rate ineffective against external shocks. Third, if there is currency substitution, as one would expect in the absence of exchange controls, it is reasonable to believe that a rational holder of money balances will diversify his portfolio of currencies, and the dealers in foreign exchange in developing countries must have access to world currency and capital markets for a variety of monetary services, but the volatility of currency increases the risk of access to those markets. For Thailand, a study by Bird and Rajan (2001) argue that internationalisation of the financial system has contributed to financial crises for two reasons. Firstly, internationalisation of the financial system did increase the supply of foreign funds into the country. Secondly, capital account liberalisation did generate demand for bank credit in the domestic market. Thus, these two factors coupled with poor reform of domestic financial sector led the country into crisis.

It is argued that for a developing economy like Thailand, a managed floating regime is appropriate (Grossman and Stiglitz 1980; Stiglitz 1994, 2003). Also shadow price models can be adopted to determine the appropriate exchange rate (Chao and Yu 1995). These shadow price models should also incorporate underlying market conditions of the national and global economy. The initial exchange rate derived from the shadow price model should be adjusted according to the market, economic and institutional conditions which change over time.

Rusidy and Islam (2007) argue that for a developing economy, a managed floating regime with market adjustments is appropriate (Stiglitz 1994) and a shadow price model can be adopted to determine the initial appropriate exchange rate (Chao and Yu 1995) which should also incorporate underlying market conditions of the national and global economy. In this approach, the initial exchange rate derived on the basis of a shadow price model needs to be adjusted following developments and changes in the market, economic and institutional conditions of the economy.

2.5 Asymmetric Information

The new trend in international capital markets, namely globalisation, has made global investment more accessible to all investors (Frankel and Schmukler 1997). Mishkin (1997, 1999) argues that globalisation enables funds to move from economic agents who lack productive opportunities to those who have such opportunities. In the light of an asymmetric view of financial crises, Mishkin (1992a, 1996, 1997) defines a financial crisis as 'a disruption to financial markets in which adverse selection and moral hazard problems become much worse, so that financial markets are unable to efficiently channel funds to those who have the most productive investment opportunities'. According to Mishkin (1997), asymmetric information leads to two basic problems in the financial system, they are adverse selection and moral hazard. The literature discussed in this section draws heavily from the study by Mishkin (1992a,b, 1996, 1997) and Aoki (1997). This section will present a review of asymmetric information theory and it proceeds in the following manner. Section 2.5.1 is an overview of the concept of asymmetric information. A literature review of adverse selection and moral hazard is provided in Sects. 2.5.2 and 2.5.3 respectively. Finally, Sect. 2.5.4 reviews the roles asymmetric information and financial crises.

2.5.1 Asymmetric Information: An Overview

Asymmetric information has been widely discussed in the finance and related literature (Frankel and Schmukler 1997). Some examples include Akerlof (1970), Grossman and Stiglitz (1980), French and Poterba (1991), Lang et al. (1992) and Gehrig (1993). Asymmetric information characterises a situation where for a given amount of information, one side of the market has better information than the other (Van-Ees and Garretsen 1993). Asymmetric information can lead to market, policy and institutional failures and incompatibilities (Grossman and Stiglitz 1980) given the underlying socio-economic conditions.

Frankel and Schmukler (1997) argue that asymmetric information can show up in different ways. First, domestic investors may have access to locally available information that foreign investors do not receive. Perhaps foreign investors can obtain the same information, but must bear an extra cost to get it. Second, foreign investors may have the same information, but interpret it in a different way. Third, there may be leaks in information which domestic investors are able to obtain first. Fourth, foreign fund holders might lack information on how the fund is being managed. Even though there is an information disadvantage, global investment may still look attractive as a consequence of high-expected returns and diversification benefits (especially from emerging markets).

Asymmetric information in financial markets creates two main problems known as adverse selection and moral hazard. In the case of adverse selection, a 'lemons problem' arises if lenders cannot determine the quality of borrowers (Akerlof 1970). Lenders will only sign contracts that reflect the average quality of the pool of loan applicants. As a result, good borrowers are kept out of the market. In the case of moral hazard, a higher contractual rate of return induces lenders to undertake more risky investment projects. Hence, both adverse selection and incentive effects cause the mix of loan applicants to change adversely with an increase in the contractual rate of return on loans, which negatively affects the lenders' profits (Van-Ees and Garretsen 1993). In essence, adverse selection and moral hazard in financial markets frequently derive from government regulation and informational obstacles that result in perverse incentives (Devaney 2000).

2.5.2 Theory of Adverse Selection

Adverse selection (hidden information) problems arise from the asymmetry of information about the riskiness of investment projects before investment occurs. Financial intermediaries may be able to cope with such problems by accumulating expertise in project evaluation and credit analysis (Aoki 1997).

Similarly, Mishkin (1997) argues that adverse selection is an asymmetric information problem that occurs before the transaction. This problem exists when the parties who are the most likely to produce an undesirable (adverse) outcome are the most likely to be selected for a loan. Borrowers who want to take on big risks are likely to be the most eager to take out a loan because they know that they are unlikely to pay it back. Since adverse selection makes it more likely that loans might be made to bad credit risks, lenders may decide not to make any loans, even though there are good credit risks in the marketplace. According to Mishkin (1997), this outcome is a feature of the classic 'lemons problem' that was first introduced by Akerlof (1970).[13]

This paper by Akerlof analysed the market for used cars by applying his 'lemons problem' theory to illustrate the importance of informational asymmetries. The scenario is quite simple in that the seller of a used car usually knows more about it than the buyer does. They know, for instance, how well it runs on the highway, in the snow, when it's hot outside, and so on. The buyer knows relatively little. So if a seller offers to sell the car for, say, $5,000, the buyer should be suspicious, since, if the car were worth

---

[13] See Chap. 8 in Ivan (1998) and Chap. 17 in Pindyck and Rubinfeld (1998) for case studies and discussion of this view. Also see Chap. 8 in Mishkin (1992b) for a detailed discussion of adverse selection and the 'lemons problem'.

more than 5,000, the owner would not be selling it at that price. In this case, Akerlof showed, the market may break down completely. In other words, he shows that when sellers know the true quality of a good, but buyers know only little about the quality, markets may not exist. Essentially, a buyer's best estimate of the quality of any individual seller's good is the market average, and sellers of high quality goods are unable to command a price consistent with the quality of their good. In long run, low quality drives out high quality until no market exists. This argument was later extended in a number of studies.

Genesove (1993) extends Akerlof's argument by allowing buyers to gain information concerning the 'types' of sellers in the market. He considers a buyer in search of a good apple. While only the seller is able to discern the true quality of apples, the buyer is able to distinguish between two distinct types of sellers: one who has a large orchard and hates apples and a second who has a small orchard and loves apples. From whom should he purchase? Obviously, the purchase should be made from the seller with the large orchard who hates apples. This seller takes all her apples to market, good and bad. The seller who loves apples is unlikely to take good apples to the market. The buyer can improve on the estimate of the average apple by incorporating information on seller type. If the market incorporates this information, the seller who hates apples will receive a premium for the sale of her apples.

Myers and Majluf (1984) and Greenwald et al. (1984) pointed out that a lemons problem occurs in debt and equity markets when lenders have trouble determining whether a borrower is a good risk (has good investment opportunities with low risk) or a bad risk (has poor investment opportunities with high risk). In this situation, a lender will only be willing to pay a price for securities that reflect the average quality of firms issuing the securities at a price below fair market value (the net present value of the expected income streams) for high-quality firms but above fair market value for low-quality firms. Owners or managers of high quality who know their quality also know that their securities are undervalued and will not want to sell them in the market. Low-quality firms, however, are willing sellers because they know that the price of their securities is greater than their value. Since asymmetric information prevents investors from determining the quality of firms, high-quality firms will issue few securities and credit markets will not work as well since many projects with a positive net present value will not be undertaken (Mishkin 1997). Several studies have examined markets where asymmetric information leads to price differentials based on seller type. Gibbons and Katz (1991) apply the model to post-displacement wages, finding that individuals displaced by layoffs earn lower wages in their next job than do individuals displaced by plant closings. Greenwald and Glasspiegel (1983) examine historical data from pre-civil war slave auctions in New Orleans. Because of the different types of crops grown in the new and old South, similar slaves have a higher marginal value in the new South. Sellers bringing slaves from the old South to the new South are found to receive a premium over similar slaves sold by locals. Genesove (1993) is able to identify two seller types in auctions for new-car dealers and used-car dealers. It is expected that used-car dealers prefer to keep their best-used cars and take only their low-quality used cars to auction. New-car dealers are expected to receive a price premium for an otherwise similar used car. By regressing the final price of autos sold in the auction as function of seller type and controls for the visible characteristics of the auto, limited support for the hypothesis is found.

Stiglitz and Weiss (1981) demonstrated that information asymmetry can lead to credit rationing in which borrowers are arbitrarily denied loans (a public failure). This occurs because a higher interest rate leads to even greater adverse selection: the borrowers with the riskiest investment projects will now be the likeliest to want to take out loans at the higher interest rate. If the lender cannot discriminate who are the borrowers with the riskier investment projects, he may want to cut down the number of loans he makes, which causes the supply of loans to decrease with the higher interest rate rather than increase. Thus, even if there is an excess demand for loans, a higher interest rate will not be able to equilibrate the market because additional increases in the interest rate will only decrease the supply of loans and make the excess demand for loans increase even further. Indeed, Mankiw (1986) concluded that a small rise in the riskless interest rate can lead to a very large decrease in lending and even a possible collapse in the market.

2.5.3 Theory of Moral Hazard

Contrary to adverse selection, moral hazard is an asymmetric information problem that occurs after the transaction and when a principal commission -an agent to act on his behalf, but the agent engages in shirking, pursues self-interest to the detriment of the principal's interest, or indulges in dishonest or immoral behaviour (Mishkin 1997).[14] Aoki (1997) refers to moral hazard as a hidden action problem arising because investors cannot distinguish the effects of events that management cannot control from the

---

[14] See Chap. 17 in Pindyck and Rubinfeld (1998) for case studies and discussion of moral hazard.

effects of management actions taken in implementing an investment project. Financial intermediaries may be able to reduce these problems by monitoring management activities (interim monitoring). Moral hazard is a disposition on the part of individuals or organisations to engage in riskier behaviour, than they otherwise would, because of a tacit assumption that someone else will bear part or all of the costs and consequences if the incurred risk turns out badly (Wolf 1999). Moral hazard is defined in the economics literature as 'actions by economic agents in maximising their own utility to the detriment of others in situations where they do not bear the full consequences of their actions' (Ivan 1998; Pindyck and Rubinfeld 1999).

Moreover, moral hazard occurs because the borrower has incentives to invest in high-risk projects where the borrower does well if the project succeeds but the lender bears most of the loss if the project fails. The borrower also has incentives to misallocate funds for personal use, for instance, to undertake investment in unprofitable projects that increase the borrower's power or stature. The conflict of interest between borrower and lender, stemming from moral hazard or the agency problem, implies that many lenders will decide that they would rather not make loans, so that lending and investment will be at sub-optimal levels (Mishkin 1997).[15] Sandmo (1999) and Wolf (1999) concluded that insurance is a major cause of moral hazard, where insurance companies have to realise that an insurance policy may change the behaviour of the insured in a way which makes the event covered by the insurance policy more likely to happen. For instance, fire insurance may make homeowners exercise less care to prevent fires, unemployment insurance may cause workers to exercise less care in holding on to their jobs. It is difficult for the insurance company to determine, once a fire has occurred, whether it was due to an exogeneous event or to negligence. Another application of the concept is to agency problems, where agents enter into a contract requiring the agent to exert themselves in the best interests of a principle. The principle is only able to observe the result, and cannot determine the extent to which this is due to the agent's effort or to some exogeneous cause. Similarly, Peake (2000) argues that moral hazard is where one party to a contract has an incentive to change behaviour after an agreement is reached. In automobile insurance, for instance, information on how carefully and defensively the

---

[15] Mishkin (1997) argues that asymmetric information is not the only source of moral hazard. Moral hazard can also occur if high enforcement costs make it too costly for the lender to prevent moral hazard even when the lender is fully informed about the borrower's activities.

insured person drives is private information. Once the contract is entered, the insured no longer faces the prospect of financial loss and thus has less incentive to continue to drive carefully. This lack of incentive raises the potential costs to the insurer, who is unable to monitor the insured to determined whether or not the person is driving safely (Sandmo 1999; Wolf 1999; Peake 2000).

On the other hand, Arnott and Stiglitz (1988) advocate that moral hazard occurs whenever risk is present and a problem arises not only in insurance markets, but also for insurance provided by governments, through social institutions or in principal-agent contracts (institutional failures). The severity of the institutional failure depends on the nature of underlying socio economic conditions. In emerging/developing economy like the Thai economy, this problem can be more severe compared to a developed economy with efficient institutions and social structure.

Corsetti et al. (1999) stresses that moral hazard becomes a source of crises when there is over-investment, excessive external borrowing and current account deficits in a poorly supervised and regulated economy. According to Ely (1999), moral hazard leads to financial crises in three situations. First, bad management (poor internal control, self-dealing, bad lending and investment decisions, and excessively rapid expansion) is the main cause of isolated or non-contagious financial failures. Second, an economic contagion, almost always triggered by a decline in the market value of assets, causes the financial sector to fail when in normal economic times it would not. Third, government restrictions on asset and geographical risk dispersion limit the ability of individual banks or financial institutions to diversify their asset risk in order to protect themselves against contagious events such as a regional asset deflation made worse by asset fire sales. In effect, asset and branching restrictions magnify contagion losses by increasing the number of bank failures and financial crises.[16]

2.5.4 Financial Crises and Asymmetric Information

Financial crises and banking crises have become a worldwide phenomena occurring in both developed and developing countries. A number of studies (Mishkin 1991, 1996, 1999; Corsetti et al. 1998; Goldstein 1998) have used asymmetric information theory to explain financial and banking crises, and severe asymmetry problems caused by financial liberalisation, which were common in most recent crises in Mexico and Asia (Mishkin

---

[16] See also Chap. 11 in Mishkin (1992b) for further discussion and case studies on moral hazard and financial crises.

2000).[17] The root of the Mexican crisis in 1994 begins with financial reforms implemented by the administration of President Carlos Salinas in 1988, which led to a lending boom, over-investment and massive loan losses (Tower 1997). Bordo and Schwartz (1996) argue that when the liberalisation took place in the early 1990s, the expertise of the Mexican banks in managing financial inflows and making loans was very limited. For instance, there were no official credit bureaus to monitor loans to make sure borrowers were not taking on excessive risk. Mishkin (1996) found that loans to the private sector rose rapidly after liberalisation, from 10 per cent of GDP in 1996 to over 40% of GDP in 1994. This confirms that the Mexican financial crisis was a direct impact from asymmetric information problems. Lenders failed to distinguish between good and bad borrowers, resulting in heavy investment in risky and non-performing assets. Indeed, this led to deterioration in banks' balance sheets and further worsened asymmetric information problems, making the Mexican economy ripe for a serious financial crisis (Tower 1997). Finally, the crisis erupted at the end of 1994 and the government was forced to accept financial assistant from the US and the IMF.[18]

On the other hand, several studies (McKinnon and Pill 1997; World Bank 1998; Pilbeam 2001) agreed that the crises in Asia share a similarity with the earlier crisis in Mexico. One key factor stood out: financial liberalisation led to asymmetric information problems which worsened and caused deterioration in banks' balance sheets. Mishkin (2000) argues that there are two reasons why the deterioration of banks' balance sheets led East Asian countries into financial crisis. First, the deterioration in the balance sheets of banking firms led them to restrict their lending in order to improve capital ratios or even led to a full-scale banking crisis which forced the banks into insolvency, thereby directly removing the ability of the banking sector to make loans. Second, the deterioration in bank balance sheets can promote financial crisis because it makes it difficult for the central bank to defend its currency against a speculative attack. Any rise in interest rates to keep the currency from devaluating can harm the banking system, because the rise in interest rates occurs as a result of the maturity mismatch and exposure to increased credit risk when the economy deteriorates. In other words, the banking system may collapse if the central bank

---

[17] See also Diaz-Alejandro (1985), Krugman (1998b), Radelet and Sachs (1998) and Kamin (1999).
[18] Mexico receipted a total of US$50 billion in an emergency package where US$20 billion came from the US government and the rest from the IMF.

chooses to raise interest rates to defend its currency when speculative attack on the currency occurs. Once investors realise that a weak banking system makes it unlikely that the central bank will successfully defend the currency, this provides greater incentives for the investors to attack the currency because the anticipated profits from selling the currency will rise with each increase in interest rate.

Moreover, Pilbeam (2001) argues that financial liberalisation yields new lending opportunities as well as new opportunities for financial institutions to take on risk. McKinnon and Pill (1997) state that financial liberalisation results in excessive borrowing because it sends over-optimistic signals regarding the future economy to the non-bank private sector which increases loan applications to domestic banks who in turn increase lending expecting that they will be protected from risks by the government. Accordingly, the inflows (mostly in the form of lending) and credit extensions to the Asian countries grew at far higher rates than GDP (Corsetti et al. 1998). Johnson (1998) argues that lending to Asian countries after financial liberalisation expanded too rapidly, resulting in excessive risk taking which led to huge loans losses later. In his study, Goldstein (1998) found that the share of non-performing loans losses to total loans rose from 15 to 35% during 1993–1996. This led Siamwalla (2000) to conclude that a rapid increase of inflows at the time when the supervisory system was weak gave rise to problems of asymmetric information ending in financial crisis.

In addition, several studies (Tower 1997; Calomiris 1998; Johnson et al. 1998; Pilbeam 2001) argue that the Mexican bailout helped fuel the Asian crisis because international lenders thought the IMF would insulate them from losses if a crisis occurred. According to Meltzer (1998) and Vasquez (1999), one aspect of asymmetric information holds that the more governments or the IMF bail out institutions suffering from financial crises, the more lenders and borrowers are willing to engage in excessive lending and borrowing as they expect the government or the IMF will come to the rescue in the face of a crisis. Krugman (1998a) argues that with guaranteed liabilities, the owners of financial companies know that while they can earn the excess return in the good times, they can walk away from the institution at no personal cost in the case of bankruptcy. McKinnon and Pill (1997) state that financial liberalisation sends over-optimistic signals regarding the future economy to the non-bank private sector and because domestic banks expect that they will be protected from risks by the government, this results in excessive borrowing. In principle, government or IMF bailouts actually make crises more likely than if they did not intervene.

2.6 Summary

This chapter provides a review of the issues in financial liberalisation and crises, covering the sequence and order of financial liberalisation, capital controls, exchange rate policy and asymmetric information.

Having reviewed the above issues, we conclude that domestic financial reform needs to be considered first, and capital account liberalisation is best left to the last stage. Moreover, it is widely accepted that the appropriate sequence and order of liberalisation involves four steps: reduction of deficit, reform of finance and trade domestically, reforms to put in place the appropriate exchange rate policy, and finally liberalising the capital accounts. Capital controls are divided into two main types: controls of capital outflows and inflows. Controls of capital outflows, on one side, involve preventive controls that are applied when a country is facing fiscal deficit but not yet experiencing a crisis. On the other side, curative controls on capital outflows are applied when a country is already enduring a crisis. Controls on capital inflows are said to insulate a developing economy from financial crisis and also to provide extra time to correct monetary policy. According to the literature reviewed in this chapter, the choice between a fixed and flexible exchange regime varies from one country to another, depending on the nature of the economy, trade pattern of each country, monetary policy and degree of financial integration. On the one hand, some economists provide arguments in favour of a fixed exchange regime as it can result in economic expansion, increasing investments and lowering inflation. On the other hand, several studies argue that a flexible exchange rate provides more discipline and allows the country to have an independent monetary policy, avoiding external shocks and providing a faster adjustment process in response to the shocks. Finally, asymmetric information involves the theory of adverse selection and moral hazard. Major differences between these two branches of asymmetric information theory are that adverse selection is an asymmetric problem and causes an adverse decision before the investment takes place, while, moral hazard arises after the investment and is a problem of inability to distinguish the actions taken by an economic agent in implementing investment projects. In the light of financial crises, a number of studies concluded that financial liberalisation has further worsened the problem of asymmetric information. The two most recent crises in Mexico and Asia are prime examples. In both cases, financial crises occurred shortly after full financial liberalisation causing asymmetric information problems of excessive risk taking, lending booms, deterioration of banks' balance sheets and massive loans losses, which drove the countries into deep financial problems.

The next chapter is the last section of Part A (literature review) of this book. It portrays past actions taken by Thai authorities in introducing financial liberalisation. It provides a detailed discussion of strategies and frameworks in the early days of the financial liberalisation process. Firstly, it explores the developments and behaviours of Thailand's economy from early 1960 up to the period prior to financial liberalisation in the early 1990s. Secondly, a brief history of Thailand's economic growth is discussed. Thirdly, it surveys the influential factors behind Thailand's financial liberalisation. Finally, it presents an overall framework for financial liberalisation in Thailand.

3 Overview of Thailand's Approach to Financial Liberalisation

3.1 Introduction

As mentioned in the previous chapters in order to successfully integrate the domestic economy with the global economy it is important to follow a certain set of financial sector reforms. In order for the liberalisation process to take off it is important to introduce a range of reforms like trade reforms, foreign exchange policy reforms, capital controls and the domestic financial market reforms.

The objective of this chapter is to provide an analysis of the strategies and policies adopted in the financial liberalisation process as implemented by Thailand. It begins with an overview of Thailand's economic development, including a review of the history of Thai economic growth prior to the financial liberalisation period in the 1990s and then analyses the internal and external factors that influenced Thailand's decision to liberalise its financial system. Furthermore, it portrays the framework of financial liberalisation pursued by Thailand.

The chapter proceeds in the following manner. Section 3.2 presents a summary of the six Development Plans that Thailand implemented during the period of 1961–1991. Additionally, a brief analysis of the economic performance of Thailand during each plan is also provided in this section. Section 3.3 reviews the background of Thai economic growth, focusing on the period before financial liberalisation was implemented. Section 3.4 analyses the factors that influence Thailand's financial liberalisation. The factors discussed in this section are internal and external. Section 3.5 provides an overview of the framework of the financial liberalisation. Lastly, a summary is given in Sect. 3.6.

3.2 Thailand's Economic Development

3.2.1 The Six National Development Plans

In his study, Pakhasem (1972) regards the Thai economy in the 1950s as unbalanced, uncoordinated and disrupted. During the period of 1955 to 1960, Thailand began to reorganise its economy after recommendations from international agencies to implement development plans and policies to attract foreign assistance for furthering its economic development process (Siksamat 1998).[1] Under the World Bank recommendation, the official reform of the trade patterns in Thailand took place in the early 1960s, alongside the establishment of the National Economic Development Board (NEDB).[2]

The NEDB acted as the government's economic planning agency to develop strategies to transform the Thai economy into a global economy. As soon as it was established, the NEDB implemented the *First National Development Plan* (1961–1966), which aimed to encourage industrialisation and economic growth in the private sector with a target of 6% GDP growth per year for the period of 1961–1966. The plan was carried out well with an average growth rate of 8.1%, (exceeding the target rate), while inflation was also low at 1.3% (see Table 3.1). According to Parnwell (1996), the success of the first plan was due to two main factors. First, at that time world demand was favourable toward Thai products. Second, the US government's military spending in Thailand provided support to the economic development.[3]

The *Second National Development Plan* (1967–1971) was a continuing plan carried forward from the first plan. The objectives of the second plan remained the same as those of the first but with greater emphasis on rural developments. Overall, the performance of the Thai economy during this period was disappointing. The average real GDP growth declined from 8.1 to 7.7%. Similarly, the average fiscal balance experienced a further deficit of more than 2%. Lastly, the average percentage of foreign debt also indicated a huge increase by at least 6% (see Table 3.1).

---

[1] See Chap. 1 in Warr (1993) for a discussion of this view.
[2] NEDB is now called the National Economic and Social Development Board (NESDB).
[3] See Chap. 2 in Siksamat (1998) for a more detail discussion.

Table 3.1. Thailand's selected economic indicators, selected years

Year	GDP growth [%]	Inflation rate [%]	Per capita [Baht]	Fiscal balance [% of GDP]	Foreign debt [% of GDP]
1961–1966	8.1	1.3	2,466	−0.68	8.1
1967–1971	7.7	0.3	3,634	−2.98	14.3
1972	4.1	4.9	4,420	−4.29	14.9
1973	9.9	15.4	5,623	−2.93	13.1
1974	4.4	24.3	6,916	0.72	12.8
1975	4.8	5.3	7,328	−2.46	13.6
1976	9.4	4.2	8,136	−4.66	14.4
1977	9.9	7.6	9,234	−3.10	17.1
1978	10.4	7.9	10,858	−2.60	20.3
1979	5.3	9.9	10,296	−2.23	23.5
1980	4.8	19.7	13,980	−3.90	27.1
1981	5.9	12.7	15.673	−2.81	25.3
1982	5.4	5.2	17,281	−4.89	27.6
1983	5.6	3.8	18,538	−2.48	28.0
1984	5.8	0.9	19,512	−3.36	30.6
1985	4.6	2.4	20,483	−3.69	37.8
1986	5.5	1.9	21,548	−3.01	37.1
1987	9.5	2.5	24,329	−0.68	34.7
1988	13.3	3.8	28,710	−2.31	29.0
1989	12.2	5.4	33,635	3.52	26.9
1990	11.6	6.0	39,149	4.90	29.4
1991	8.4	5.7	44,314	4.30	34.0

Source: Adapted from Siksamat (1998).

Notes: The data for 1961–1966 and 1967–1971 are average.
            Growth rate of GDP at 1988 constant prices.

The *Third National Development Plan* was covered the period of 1972–1976. The plan was drafted with the objective of generating economic growth, while focusing on the distribution of income to rural areas. During this period, the Thai economy experienced economic difficulties and a slowdown resulting from a sharp increase of the world oil price, reduction of the US military budgets and the world economic recession (Warr 1993). According to Table 3.1, GDP growth fluctuated from the beginning of the plan. In 1972, GDP reached its lowest point at 4.1%, but increased to 9.9% in 1973. However, it later declined to 4.4 and 4.8% in 1974 and 1975, respectively. Inflation grew significantly especially in 1973 and 1974, tripling from 4.9% in 1972 to 15.4% in 1973 and peaking at 24.3% in 1974. A sharp increase of inflation can be explained by two main factors, namely those of supply and demand.[4] On the supply side, Thailand suffered from high oil prices during the oil crisis of 1973. Consequently, costs of Thai products became higher resulting in an increase in prices and reduced export competitiveness in the international market. On the demand side, national economic expansion was limited by the decline of US military spending in Thailand, as well as the recession of the world economy (Siksamat 1998). These factors caused budgetary problems for the Thai government that led to economic recession and an increased current account deficit at the end of the period.

The *Fourth National Development Plan* (1977–1981) had the objective of redesigning economic adjustments to rescue the Thai economy from crisis. During this period, Thailand experienced economic disruption and instability derived from external sources, for instance, the second oil crisis of 1979–1980, high interest rates and declining demand for Thai exports. In spite of these unfavourable external conditions, the Thai economy performed reasonably well. Real GPD growth expanded at an average of 7.3% (see Fig. 3.1). This achievement resulted partly from a public investment expansion despite low levels of domestic savings (Warr 1993).[5] On the down side, Thailand confronted problems of fiscal deficit, foreign debt and inflation. The fiscal deficit grew at an average of 3% compared to 2.6% in the previous period. During the second oil crisis, foreign debt rose by 23.5% in 1979 and 27.1% in 1980, and inflation also increased from 9.9 to 19.7% in the same period. In principle, all these problems occurred due to a widened domestic investment-saving gap resulting from insufficient income to compensate the deficit.

As a result of previous economic instability, the *Fifth National Development Plan* (1982–1986) was drafted to encourage economic stability and economic restructuring, as well as, lower inflation, reduction of the current account deficit and lower foreign debt. During this period, the Thai economy was affected again by continuing increases of the world oil price. From Fig. 3.1, GDP growth for this period was 5.4%, declining approximately 2% from the previous period. Fiscal deficit was relatively high compared to the previous period at 4.9% of GDP. Moreover, foreign debt rose continuously throughout the period 1982–1986, with average debt increase more than 10% of GDP from previous period, reaching the highest debt of 32.8% in 1986.

---

[4] See Parnwell (1996) for discussion of this view.
[5] See also Chap. 2 in Siksamat (1998).

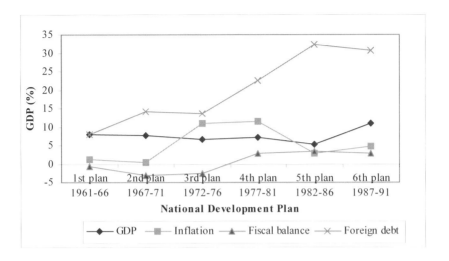

Fig. 3.1. Key economic indicators during the National development plan

Source: Adapted from Bank of Thailand, various issues.

The *Sixth National Development Plan* (1987–1991) aimed to promote economic growth and reduce the current account deficit via an export-led growth strategy.[6] In order to enhance export competitiveness, the Thai government decided to devalue the currency, and reform taxes and regulations for the export sector. Consequently, GDP rose by double-digit rates of 13.3%, 12.2% and 11.6% from 1988 to 1990, respectively (see Table 3.1). Additionally, the GDP growth average of 11% was double that of the previous period. In terms of Thailand's outstanding foreign debt, there was relatively high level of debt of 34.7% of GDP in 1987 and 34% in 1991 (see Table 3.1), however, average debt was lower compared to the previous period in 1982–1986 (see Fig. 3.1).

3.3 History of Thailand's Economic Growth

After a decade of zero growth rates in the 1950s, Thailand's economy has transformed from one of the poorest to the fastest growth economy in the world during the following four decades (Warr 1993; Phongpaichit and

---

[6] Warr (1993) argues that export-led growth policy was concentrated on the manufacturing sector.

Baker 1995, 1998a).[7] Growth peaked during the second half of the 1980s, when exports grew rapidly at the rate of 20% a year and real GDP grew at double-digit rates for many consecutive years (Wiboonchutikula et al. 1999). For instance, Thailand recorded double-digit GDP growth during 1988–1990, reaching a peak of 13.2% in 1988 (Falkus 1995). As a result of this rapid economic growth, many economists considered Thailand to be 'the fifth tiger of Asia' (Bhongmakapat 1990b; Patmasiriwat 1995; Warr and Nidhiprabha 1996).

Thailand's economic performance from 1987–1990 was extremely impressive. According to Chaiyasoot (1995), real GDP growth was 9.5%, 13.3%, 12.2% and 11.6%, from 1987 to 1990, respectively (see Table 3.1). This growth resulted primarily from a boom in the manufactured exports sector. From 1980 to 1990 annual average growth rates of sectoral contributions to GDP were, agriculture 4.1%, industry 9.0% and services 7.8% (Siamwalla et al. 1993).[8]

While Bhongmakapat (1990a) advocates that there were several forces that tended to hinder Thailand's economic success, Warr and Nidhiprabha (1996) assert that there were three major forces behind the Thai economic boom: the depreciation of the US dollar, foreign investment from newly industrialised countries (NICs), and the continuing low international petroleum prices in relation to those of Thailand's export commodities.

Thailand became one of the leading destinations for private capital investment after the depreciation of the U.S. currency in the mid 1980s (Bhongmakapat 1999) made Thai exports more competitive internationally (Warr and Nidhiprabha 1996). Furthermore, the Thai economic boom took off as the baht remained pegged to the dollar during its depreciation relative to other currencies, especially the yen and those of the NICs (Johnson 1991). Japan took advantage of its appreciating yen by relocating its production sites in Thailand to lower production costs, and soon other NICs followed for the same reason (Patmasiriwat 1995). Yoshida (1990) added that the reduction in oil prices in 1985 were favourable to Thailand's economic growth and enhanced its competitiveness. Limskul (2000) concluded that during this period, Thailand experienced private investment growth of 20–30% and export growth of 29%. The domestic market grew considerably as a result of income expansion in export-oriented activities.

Falkus (1995) argues that the rapid and unexpected growth during the mid 1980s changed the structure of the Thai economy forever. Also, the

---

[7] A study by Manarungsan (1989) of Thailand's GDP from period of 1870 to 1950 found zero growth per capita over this period.

[8] Falkus (1995) argues that industry exceeded agriculture in its contribution to GDP for the first time in 1986.

World Bank (1993b) regards Thailand as one of the so called High Performing Asian Economies (HPAEs), while its economic performance has been hailed by the IMF as 'an excellent example of successful development and growth' (Chowdhury 1999).

The high growth and stable macroeconomic environment from the late 1980s, provided enough confidence for Thailand to open to the international financial market (Wiboonchutikula et al. 1999). In essence, the Thai government implemented a comprehensive financial reform program in the early 1990s, which included the liberalisation of its financial sector and the integration of its economy with global financial and product markets (Alba et al. 1999). According to Wibulswadi (1995), the stated objectives of the financial reform program of the Thai government were 'coordinating and synchronising several aspects of the reform with the ultimate objectives to enhance competitiveness, flexibility, efficiency, and stability of the financial sector'. Moreover, Allison and Suwanraks (1999) added that financial liberalisation was undertaken with the following purposes: to strengthen competition in the domestic financial system, to give more resilience to financial institutions as preparation for the worldwide liberalisation of trade and services, and to expand the role of Thailand to serve as a regional financial centre.

3.4 Forces Influencing Financial Liberalisation in Thailand

The dynamism behind financial liberalisation can be derived from various sources. They can come in the form of self-driven or global forces. This section provides an overview of the forces of financial liberalisation that are delineated into two broad categories, namely, internal and external.

3.4.1 Internal Forces

3.4.1.1 Export-Led Growth Policy

Thai government policy had paid attention to exports since the *Third National Economic and Social Development Plan* in the 1970s, however, greater emphasis was given in the 1980s, especially from 1985 onward (Suphachalasai 1995). According to Warr and Nidhiprabha (1989, 1996), the Thai government aimed to promote export-led economic growth to at least 5% per year in real terms and to continue liberalising its state enterprises and the whole economy from 1987 onward.

In the early 1990s, the Thai economy was at the turning point of becoming more industrialised (Ratanakomut et al. 1995; Ratanakomut 1999). In general, the government sought industrial and export-led economic growth through a largely liberal, market-oriented approach, within a framework of economic stability and conservative monetary policy (Falkus 1995).

The main thrust of industrialisation in Thailand has been reliance on the private sector to generate economic growth within the framework of a free-market economy (Dhiratayakinant 1995). The rapid expansion of the Thai export sector has, to a large extent, been the result of an increase in local competitiveness, and to a lesser extent commodity composition and growth in demand for Thai exports in overseas markets (Ariff and Hill 1985; Strunk 1997; Haggard and Kim 1999).

However, the Thai economy faced a greater degree of competition in its traditional export markets in the early 1990s. The grouping of countries into trading areas represents a greater potential for, as well as a threat to, the growth of Thailand's exports (Dhiratayakinant 1995). Higher economic growth induced by an inflow of direct foreign investment strengthened the momentum towards export activity and further industrialisation, and convinced the government of the importance of export-led growth (Patmasiriwat 1995). This growth required a huge source of investment finance, which Thailand could not finance with its own savings (Limskul 2000). Thus, to achieve its export-led growth plan, Thailand needed to open its doors to welcome foreign funds by liberalising its financial system (Hipsher et al. 2007).

3.4.1.2 Acceptance of the IMF Article VIII

In the early 1970s, the IMF had set the scene for a more market-oriented approach in the global arena as well as providing advice and finance for developing economies (Chatterjee 1999). From 1985 to 1988, its perspective of financial systems had changed under US leadership, which recommended structural changes derived from financial liberalisation. This meant a significant industrial growth potential and improvement of capital inflow into countries (Aglietta 2000).

The overall economic policies of Thailand changed significantly after the devaluation of its currency in 1984.[9] Phongpaichit and Baker (2000) argue that the 1984 currency devaluation demonstrated the need for technocrats' skill to manage the transition from agriculture to export-oriented

---

[9] Pantusane (1998) asserts that the devaluation of the Thai baht in 1984 was pressured by the slowdown of its economy as a result of a sharp increase in the world oil price and Thai government foreign debt.

industrialisation.[10] Many of these technocrats had been educated in the US and were drawn to free-market policies (Phongpaichit and Baker 1998a, 1998b, 2000). They argued that the potential of the Thai economy was restricted by oligopolies and particularly by the power of the banking cartel. Furthermore, they encouraged the Thai government to pursue the World Bank and IMF project to liberalise financial markets. As a result, the Thai government agreed to accept the Article VIII of the IMF by the end of 1980s, which required Thailand to deregulate and reform its financial system (see Appendix A). The Thai government began to reform its financial system in 1989. By the beginning of 1994, the Thai financial system was fully liberalised with the role of the financial sector greatly broadened (Phongpaichit and Baker 2000).

3.4.1.3 A Sound Fiscal Condition

The performance of the Thai economy has been hailed as an economic phenomenon. From 1965 to 1990, Thailand's GNP grew consistently at the rate of 4.2% (compared to an average of 2.5% for low and middle income countries) (Warr 1993; Warr and Nidhiprabha 1996). Krongkaew (1995) reports that Thailand experienced a positive economic growth from the early 1960s. Indeed, during 1988–1990 Thailand was the fastest growing economy in the world with an impressive average growth of 11.8%.

Moreover, Thailand's fiscal cash balance and international reserves also performed exceptionally well. According to Table 3.2, Thailand achieved its first cash balance surplus in 1988, after having years of fiscal deficits. International reserves were growing dramatically. Vajragupta and Vichyanond (1998) advocate that these much more than sufficient international reserves enabled Thailand to cover all necessary expenses. Thus, the condition of the Thai economy was strong and ready for any changes to take place. Overall, the condition and performance of the Thai economy provided confidence for Thailand to open its economy for further development, especially in the financial sector via liberalisation.

---

[10] The majority of the technocrats were executives of the Bank of Thailand.

Table 3.2. Thailand's fiscal balance and international reserves

	Fiscal cash balance[11] [% of GDP]	International reserves[12] [Months of imports]
1987	−1.4	4.7
1988	1.9	4.3
1989	3.2	5.0
1990	4.7	5.3
1991	4.9	5.8
1992	3.1	6.3
1993	2.2	6.8
1994	1.8	6.8
1995	1.0	6.3
1996	2.2	6.5

Source: Vajragupta and Vichyanond (1998).

3.4.2 External Forces

3.4.2.1 Opening of Neighbouring Economies

At the beginning of the 1990s, Thailand faced major trade competition from the new industrialised Asian countries of China and Vietnam. These newcomers competed with Thai exports especially in textiles, garments and shoes (Haihong 2000). Limskul (2000) concluded that these neighbouring countries became Thailand's competitors as they were also striving to achieve export-led growth. However, the crucial competitor for Thailand is China (Bhongmakapat 1990a, 1990b; Dhiratayakinant 1995).

China started to liberalise its economy in 1986 by granting permission for the operation of wholly foreign owned companies throughout the country (Chai 1997). The foreign exchange rate controls were also relaxed to allow foreign firms to convert their Chinese currency earnings into foreign exchange at the swap markets (Chen 1997). Tax concessions were also provided to FDI to attract more capital inflow (Haihong 2000).

The steady devaluation of the Chinese yuan towards the end of the 1980s further decreased the competitiveness of neighbouring countries. Furthermore, China devalued its currency by 40% in 1994 (Chen 1997; Haihong 2000). This made Chinese goods very cheap compared with those from Thailand. In essence, Thailand would loose its competitive and com-

---

[11] Cash balance is the difference between import and export.
[12] International reserves include forward rate.

parative advantages against China without further economic strategies to liberalise its financial system.[13]

Another influence on Thailand's financial liberalisation was the opening up of the Indochinese countries. Since the 1980s, Vietnam, Laos and Cambodia have opened their countries to foreign investment. At the beginning of the 1990s, they further opened their economies and began to move toward the emerging global economy (Vajragupta and Vichyanond 1998). With the potentials of these newly opened economies, Thailand saw the need to liberalise its financial system and broaden its financial structure in order to accommodate increased trade and investment, and more importantly, to gain the advantage of being the financial centre between the Indochinese region and the rest of the world.

3.4.2.2 The Trend Towards Globalisation of the Financial System

The trend of financial globalisation was reinforced by the loose monetary policies of developed countries, especially during the early 1980s. Financial liberalisation was a western objective for the Asian developmental model (Higgott and Phillips 1999). In the early 1990s, there was also a period of heightened euphoria over the prospect of developing East Asian economies, making them a principal destination of much of the global flow of funds (Yoshitomi 1999). These international financial market trends of the 1990s contributed to the large inflow of financial capital to East Asian developing economies including Thailand.

Moreover, regional integration extended beyond linkages based on trade and FDI in the early 1990s. International financial integration greatly promoted dramatic increases of capital flows to emerging Asian markets (Queisser 1999). As a result, FDI was no longer the dominant source of financing for external deficits of Southeast Asian economies. Other forms of capital inflows such as foreign portfolio investment and bank loans became dominant. This was a consequence of domestic financial deregulation and capital account liberalisation in Southeast Asian countries (Yoshitomi 1999).

Since the 1980s many developing countries have liberalised their capital markets, often in the face of pressure from developed countries and the IMF. Thailand also followed the trend of financial globalisation, which had been set by the IMF (Limskul 2000). As a member of the WTO and having accepted Article VIII of the IMF, Thailand was required to provide access to and equal treatment of foreign financial institutions. Since Thailand would gradually have to open not only its industrial and agricultural

---

[13] See McKibbin (2000) for a discussion of globalisation and comparative advantage.

markets but also its financial markets, it was thought reasonable for the country to start liberalising its financial sector at the earliest possible moment to prepare for greater competition from abroad in the future (Vajragupta and Vichyanond 1998). Growing trends of trade and investment in an increasingly integrated world economy, however, made it difficult for Thailand to maintain growth and development without further financial liberalisation.

3.5 Financial Liberalisation Framework

Limskul (2000) reported that Thailand's financial liberalisation consisted of two phases. The first phase started during 1990–1992 by encouraging and reforming trade patterns via interest rate deregulation. The second phase was the establishment of new banking facilities to serve as international financial intermediates. Similarly, BOT (1998b) argues that the key actions taken by Thailand in liberalising its financial system were interest rate liberalisation, exchange control deregulation, and the establishment of the Bangkok International Banking Facilities (BIBF). Moreover, a study by Vichyanond (1994, 1995) reached the same conclusion, with the addition that the implementation of new banking facilities also included the establishment of the Export-Import Bank (EXIM Bank) as another aspect of the framework. In this section, we delineate the financial liberalisation framework of Thailand into three main components, namely, trade reforms and interest rate liberalisation, exchange rate control reform and establishment of new financial institutions.

3.5.1 Trade Reforms and Interest Rate Deregulation

In general, the objective of interest rate liberalisation is to promote savings and efficient investment and to deepen financial markets (World Bank 1989a,b). Positive real interest rates favour financial over non-financial savings, leading to the deepening of financial markets. In fact, greater financial intermediation tends to ensure economic growth by promoting financial deepening and improving the productivity of investment (Tseng and Corker 1991).

Deregulation of interest rates was a compulsory component of the financial reforms implemented by almost all liberalising countries including Thailand (Tseng and Corker 1991). Historically, the Thai financial system was highly regulated and financial operations were subjected to interest rate ceilings on both deposits and lending. However, with the continuous economic expansion resulting from the export-led growth policy, Thailand saw the need for funds from external sources, particularly when it was evident that total deposits had not expanded in line with borrowing needs (Vichyanond 1994). In other words, there was indeed an urgent need to increase foreign funds to fill the saving and investment gaps, and these funds played a major role in the future economic development of Thailand by helping the transformation from an agricultural to industrial based economy. With the aim to encourage future trade and economic development, the Bank of Thailand (BOT) implemented the three-year interest rate liberalisation plan during 1989–1992, as the first step in liberalising its financial system to promote and encourage the country's trade and development through increasing saving and investment (Hipsher et al. 2007).

Among the most important actions included in the reform program was the dismantling of interest rate controls over the period 1989–1992 (Alba et al. 1999). As a result, interest rate ceilings on long-term time deposits were abolished in June 1989 (Vichyanond 1994, 1995, 2000a; Allison and Suwanraks 1999).[14] Thus, interest rates on long-term deposits increased from 9.5% in 1988 to 10.5–11.0% in 1989. Furthermore, the remaining ceilings on short-term deposits (time deposits of less than one year) were removed on 16 March 1990 (Vichyanond 1994, 1995; BOT 1998a; Allison and Suwanraks 1999; Alba et al. 1999). In June 1992, interest rate ceilings on finance and credit companies' deposit and lending rates, and on commercial banks' lending rates were removed (Vichyanond 1994; Alba et al. 1999; Allison and Suwanraks 1999). In essence, Thailand's interest rate was fully liberalised by the end of 1992.

In addition, after interest rate liberalisation, Thai authorities also put forward some requirements to ensure its transparency. From October 1993 onward, the Bank of Thailand (BOT) required that banks should disclose their minimum loan rate (MLR is the rate on term credits to large customers) and minimum retail rate (MRR is the rate on small customers) (Vichyanond 1994, 1995; Vajragupta and Vichyanond 1998; BOT 1998a, 1998b). Also, the wider margins charged above these rates had to be declared to the public (Alba et al. 1999). In sum, the liberalisation of interest rates in Thailand was one aspect of a comprehensive approach to economic and financial liberalisation.

---

[14] Long-term deposits are defined as deposits with maturities of more than one year.

3.5.2 Relaxation of Exchange Rate and Capital Controls

Having accepted Article VIII of the International Monetary Fund, Thailand held an obligation to liberalise its current account by relaxing the foreign exchange control. According to Chaiyasoot (1995), the objective of liberalising Thailand's exchange control was to enhance confidence of investors and entrepreneurs (both international and domestic), as well as, to ensure the sanctioning of Thailand's credit in international markets. Moreover, Vichyanond (1994, 1995) Vajragupta and Vichyanond (1998) and BOT (1998a, 1998b) advocate that Thailand also aimed to provide increased access to international capital, and to help cope with the trend in globalisation of its economic and financial systems. In order to liberalise the exchange control, Thailand undertook three main steps during 1990–1994 (Vichyanond 1994, 1995; Chaiyasoot 1995; Alba et al. 1998; BOT 1998a, 1998b; Limskul 2000).

Step I was announced on 17 July 1989 to allow the public to lend in foreign funds and make outflows for a purpose of dividend, interest or principle transactions (Vichyanond 1994, 1995; Chaiyasoot 1995). On 21 May 1990, the BOT further allowed commercial banks to process the purchase of foreign exchange relating to international transactions without prior approval (Alba et al. 1998; BOT 1998a, 1998b). In addition, Vichyanond (1994, 1995) and Chaiyasoot (1995) added that the limit on foreign exchange transactions was increased, as well as, approval given to commercial banks to process the repayment of foreign loans and remittance of securities sales in foreign currency. The first step toward the liberalisation of exchange controls was expected to benefit the public as a whole, as most of the main restrictions were abolished (Hansanti 2005, 2006).

Step II of the exchange control liberalisation was announced on 1 April 1991. The government amended the *Exchange Control Act, B.E. 2485* (1942) and the Ministerial Regulation No. 13, B.E. 2497 (1954) to allow the public more freedom in selling and buying of foreign exchange from the commercial banks. Chaiyasoot (1995) reported that the BOT allowed repatriation of investment funds, dividends and profits, loan repayments and interest payments without prior approval. Vichyanond (1994) stated that the public were also free to purchase foreign exchange for current account transactions without prior authorisation. On the export front, the BOT further liberalised the exchange control on 1 May 1992. Thai exporters could now receive payments for business transactions in foreign currency and transfer those foreign currency receipts to pay for imports or foreign loans. Moreover, to facilitate foreign currency transfer, commercial banks were free to withdraw funds from their accounts or to receive deposits from government departments and state enterprises (Vajragupta and Vichyanond 1998).

Step III was announced on 10 January 1994 and aimed to promote Thailand as a regional financial centre among Indochinese countries. The BOT increased the maximum limit on the baht to be carried to neighbouring countries from 250,000 to 500,000 baht. The amount permitted to transfer for overseas investments also increased from US$5 million to US$10 million (Vichyanond 1994; Vajragupta and Vichyanond 1998).

3.5.3 The Establishment of International Financial Facilities

3.5.3.1 The Establishment of the Bangkok International Banking Facilities (BIBF)

According to the government policy promoting Thailand as a regional financial centre, the offshore banking business was launched in Thailand with the establishment of the Bangkok International Banking Facilities (BIBFs) in March 1993 (Vichyanond 1995; BOT 1998a, 1998b; Vajragupta and Vichyanond 1998; Alba et al. 1999; Limskul 2000). The establishment of the BIBF was aimed to serve the increasingly sophisticated needs of international trade and investment and enhance the capacity of the domestic banking business in preparation for competition in the global financial market (BOT 1998a).

The BIBF operations included taking deposits or borrowing in foreign currencies from abroad, lending in foreign currencies in Thailand (out-in lending) and abroad (out-out lending), non-baht cross-currency foreign exchange transactions, giving guarantees against any debts denominated in foreign currencies to persons residing abroad, undertaking financial transactions which involved international trade where buyers and sellers resided abroad, seeking loans from foreign sources, as well as acting as fund managers in arranging loans. In addition, the BIBF engaged in other investment banking services such as provision of financial information, undertaking investment feasibility studies, providing financial advisory services, an advisory service for business acquisition and take-over or mergers, and arranging or underwriting debt instruments for selling abroad (Chaiyasoot 1995; BOT 1998b; Shirai 2001).

To enable financial institutions operating the BIBF to compete with financial institutions in other financial centres, the authorities granted the following privileges: a reduction in the corporate income tax rate, from 30 to 10%; exemption from special business tax (including municipal tax) which was currently at 3.3% of total turnover; exemption from withholding tax on interest income from deposits or lending for out-out transactions with non-Thai residents; exemption from stamp duties; and reduction of withholding tax on interest on foreign loans for countries without a double-taxation agreement with Thailand from 15 to 10% (Vichyanond 1994; BOT 1996; Chaiyasoot 1995). Finally, unlike other deposit or deposit type instruments, short-term (under 12 months) BIBF monetary instruments were not subject to the 7% cash reserve requirements favouring a short-term maturity structure (BOT 1996).

In January 1995, the authorities expanded the offshore banking business further by granting 37 licenses for the Provincial International Banking Facilities (PIBFs) to 22 commercial banks in order to operate in areas outside Bangkok. At the end of 1997, 30 PIBF offices had begun operations. These offices were located in five provinces: Chiang Mai in the northern region, Chonburi and Rayong in the eastern region, Ayutthaya in the central region, and Songkhla in the southern region. The PIBF's funding had to be from overseas as in the case of the BIBF. However, the PIBF could extend credits both in Thai bahts and in foreign currencies, while the BIBF could extend credits only in foreign currencies (BOT 1996).

In December 1996, seven new foreign banks were granted permission to establish BIBF offices in Thailand following the upgrading of seven BIBF units to fully-licensed branches. Recently, there were 48 BIBFs comprising 12 Thai banks, 17 foreign bank branches in Thailand and 19 foreign banks (BOT 1996, 1998a).

As of December 1997, 52 financial institutions held licenses to operate offshore banking businesses. However, only 48 BIBF offices were in operation, of these 15 belonged to Thai commercial banks, 18 to foreign bank branches already operating in Thailand, and 19 to other foreign banks. BIBF credits to domestic businesses amounted to 1,411.4 billion baht, accounting for 23.6% of total domestic credits extended by the banking system (BOT 1998a).

3.5.3.2 The Export-Import Bank

The Export-Import Bank of Thailand (EXIM Bank) was established under the *Export-Import Bank of Thailand Act* B.E. 2536 (1993) which became effective on 7 September 1993. A few months later, the EXIM Bank officially started its operations on 17 February 1994 with the aim of providing financial services to strengthen the competitive edge of Thai businesses in the world market. In addition, the EXIM Bank was a financial institution wholly owned by the Royal Thai Government under the Ministry of Finance's supervision. Under the *Export-Import Bank of Thailand Act*, the EXIM Bank was empowered to engage in various business undertakings. They could offer short-term as well as long-term credits, either in domestic or overseas markets, in Thai or any foreign currency denominations. In mobilising funds, EXIM Banks could borrow from local or overseas financial institutions, as well as issue short-term or long-term financial instruments for sale to financial institutions and the general public, both domestically and internationally (BOT 1998a). In other words, EXIM Banks can currently engage in any financial activities customary to commercial bank practices, except for accepting deposits from the general public. The activities of the bank include supporting the export of goods and services for foreign currency earnings, as well as, providing services to facilitate imports or investments that enhance export capability and to help promote foreign direct investment (FDI) (Hipsher et al. 2007).

In promoting exports, the EXIM Bank avoided facilities already well served by commercial banks, while focusing on services not presently available or insufficiently furnished to exporters by commercial banks such as long-term credit for export of capital goods, financial facilities for overseas contracts, export credit insurance and export financing for small, medium and new exporters (BOT 1996, 1998a). In addition, the EXIM Bank was committed to providing new services in foreign currencies to help address problems relating to balance of payments and the export sector such as the Merchant Marine Financing Facility and the Term Loan for Machinery Upgrading and Pre-Shipment Financing Facility (Vichyanond 1994; BOT 1998a). For Thai investors abroad, the EXIM Bank was prepared to support their investment projects through medium and long-term credit facilities. Additionally, in order to strengthen their position, it was able to joint-invest in their ventures through equity participation (Vichyanond 1994).

To accommodate emerging economies, the EXIM Bank also provided financial support to investment projects in neighbouring countries provided these projects would bring benefits to Thailand. For instance, supported projects included machinery or raw materials from Thailand, and those engaging Thai contractors or producing raw materials or energy for sale to Thailand (BOT 1998a).

In compliance with the liberalisation policy, some areas of EXIM operations incur high risks such as export credit insurance and financing facilities for investment projects in neighbouring countries. BOT (1998a) argues that any loss incurred from business transactions in accordance with the government policy or resulting from export credit insurance, would be compensated by the Ministry of Finance.

In short, the establishment of the EXIM Bank was part of Thailand's financial liberalisation framework to promote Thailand as a regional financial centre. The EXIM Bank represented a new element of the Thai financial infrastructure and is now proving essential amid current trade liberalisation trends.

3.6 Summary

This chapter presents an overview of Thailand's policies and frameworks as adopted in its financial liberalisation programme. It first discusses the development of the Thai economy, where we focus our study on the six National Development Plans from 1961 to the period before the financial liberalisation of the 1990s. Secondly, it gives a brief history of the economic miracle in Thailand, prior to financial liberalisation. Thirdly, it provides a discussion of the factors behind Thai financial liberalisation derived both internally and externally. Finally, it presents an analysis of the financial liberalisation framework implemented by Thailand.

Prior to the 1960s, Thailand was invariably seen as one of the slowest economies with a growth of zero per cent. Accordingly, the World Bank strongly suggested that Thailand should undergo a series of reforms and place more emphasise on investment in the private sector in order to foster economic growth. Having accepted advice from the international organisations, Thailand began to reorganise its economy by establishing an economic planning institution called the National Economic Development Board (NEDB). The First Development Plan was implemented in 1961 followed by five more to make a total of six plans prior to financial liberalisation in the early 1990s.

As a result, Thailand gradually transformed from an agricultural to an industrial based country, whose economy began to grow and performed well, especially during 1988–1990 when double-digit growth rates were recorded. The unexpected growth provided enough confidence for Thailand to further develop its economy into the emerging global economy. The factors that drove Thai financial liberalisation fall into two main categories, namely, internal and external forces. The internal forces are the government's export-led growth policy, the free-market policy that come with accepting the IMF Article VIII and a good fiscal position. On the other hand, external forces derived from the need to be competitive with emerging neighbouring economies and the pressure toward liberalisation coming from the global financial system. The financial liberalisation framework pursued by Thailand included transformation of trade through interest rate deregulation, exchange rate control reform and the establishment of BIBF and EXIM Banks.

Interest rate deregulation was the first action taken in June 1989 when the interest rate ceiling on long-term deposits was lifted. Exchange reform came second and involved three main steps implemented in May 1990, April 1991 and January 1994, respectively (see Appendix B). Finally, two new financial institutions were established to enhance capital inflows. They were the BIBF (March 1993) and the EXIM Bank (February 1994).

The next part of this book, Chaps. 4 to 7, is an assessment of the financial crisis theories (reviewed earlier in Chap. 2) applied to the financial sector in Thailand. In addition, time-series data are employed to analyse the effect of financial liberalisation on the Thai financial crisis.

PART B: The Thai Experience

4 Analysis of Sequencing of Financial Liberalisation in Thailand

4.1 Introduction

In order for financial liberalisation to lead to financial and economic growth and to increase the presence of financial agents in the economy it is important that the state adopt a certain set of policy reforms so as to strengthen the domestic economy. Liberalising the domestic financial sector and easing cross border flows of capital can be beneficial if the reform process is sequenced in the right order. The following chapter traces out the reforms process as adopted by Thailand in its liberalisation process.

The traditional view on sequencing of financial liberalisation states that a certain order of financial liberalisation should be implemented to ensure benefits are derived from free flow of capital while at the same time avoiding economic disruption (McKinnon 1982; Williamson and Mahar 1998).[1] While, some economists believe that the sequence of financial liberalisation can be varied from one country to another, depending on the nature and conditions of each economy, a significant number of economists now accept that the sequence of financial liberalisation is reduction of deficits, trade and domestic financial reform, foreign exchange rate reform, with capital account reform left to last (Villanueva and Mirakhor 1990b; Hallwood and MacDonald 2000).[2] Having explored financial liberalisation frameworks in the previous chapter, we now analyse the sequence of financial liberalisation that Thailand pursued, by assessing the sequence that it undertook against the order described in the literature, which was reviewed earlier in Chap. 2. Thus, the chapter is organised as follows. Section 4.2 focuses on Thailand's foreign trade pattern reforms and their consequences for the economy. Section 4.3 discusses the reduction of deficits and

---

[1] See for example Edwards (1984, 1986) for discussion of this view.
[2] See also Kahkonen (1987), McKinnon (1989), Gab (2000) and Hallwood and MacDonald (2000) for discussion of this view.

maintain of foreign reserves. Section 4.4 studies foreign exchange and capital control reforms undertaken in three main episodes between 1989 and 1994. Section 4.5 analyses the domestic financial reforms that involved the establishment and operations of two new financial institutions, the Bangkok International Banking Facilities (BIBF) and Export-Import Bank (EXIM). Section 4.6 provides a summary of the chapter.

4.2 Reforms of Foreign Trade Pattern

In order to ensure the benefits of free capital flows, it is recommended that the country pursuing financial liberalisation, first reforms its foreign trade (Arestos and Demetriades 1999). McKinnon (1993) argues that a successful trade reform prior to other financial reforms can lead to an efficient domestic allocation of foreign funds, which results in further economic growth and development. In other words, inflows occurring after the foreign trade reform can be channeled properly to the tradeable sector, producing further foreign income, which results in economic growth and development through a positive feedback effect.

Historically, as an agricultural country, the nature of Thailand's trade had relied mainly on agricultural exports (Warr 1993). As stated in Chap. 3, Thailand started reforming its foreign trade pattern with the first national development plan, as suggested by the World Bank from the early 1960s. However, a significant change in its trade pattern began in 1986 when the Thai government placed particular emphasis on an export-led growth policy through various reforms, for instance, with low levels of taxation and a fixed exchange rate policy to attack foreign capital inflows, generate domestic savings and encourage the country's trade. Consequently, Thai trade patterns changed from agriculture based to manufacturing and industry export oriented post 1986.

Figure 4.1 is a comparative study of foreign income earnings from agriculture, industry and manufacturing as a percentage of GDP from the 1960s to the 1990s. It shows that the agricultural sector was initially the major source of foreign income for Thailand with an average contribution of 40% in the 1960s, 33% in 1970s and 31% during 1980–1985. In contrast to agriculture, the industrial sector was on a trend of steady growth 18% in the 1960s, 25% in the 1970s, and 28% during 1940–1985. During 1986, agriculture was overshadowed by the industrial and manufacturing sector as the biggest foreign income earner with a sudden jump to 34% of total GDP, compared to only 16% for agriculture. From then on, income from the industrial and manufacturing sector continued to grow dramatically, peaking at 40% in 1990.

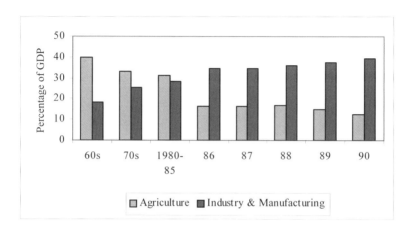

Fig. 4.1. Thailand's trade patterns, selected years

Source: Authors' calculations from The Bank of Thailand Yearly, various issues.

Moreover, high income generated from the industrial and manufacturing sector had had a direct impact in enhancing economic growth. According to Fig. 4.2, we observe that GDP in baht grew rapidly after Thailand's foreign trade was dominated by the industrial and manufacturing sector in 1986 and almost doubling to 38 million baht in 1990. Thai GDP grew from 15 million baht in 1981 to 20 million baht in 1986. The Thai economy experienced difficulties resulting from the decline of the global economy and the domestic banking crisis from the early 1980s. Consequently, Thailand's GDP growth rate fluctuated from 6.3% in 1981 to 4.1% in 1982 and hit the lowest at 3.5% in 1985. Indeed, the growth of the industrial and manufacturing sector helped the economy to recover and expand from 1986 onward. For instance, GDP rose from 5% in 1986, to record double-digit growth for three consecutive years of 13.2%, 12.2 and 11.6% during 1988–1990. GDP also rose significantly from 20 million baht in 1986 to 27 million baht in 1988, peaking at 38 million baht in 1990.

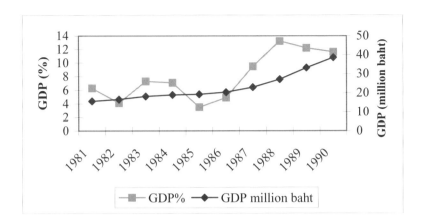

Fig. 4.2. Level and growth of Thailand's real GDP, 1981–1990[3]

Source: The Bank of Thailand Yearly, various issues.

Since the First Development Plan was implemented in the 1960s, the pattern of Thailand's foreign trade gradually transformed from being agricultural based to industry and manufacturing oriented. Year 1986 marked a significant change of foreign trade pattern for Thailand with an export-led growth policy featuring reduced tax and a pegged exchange rate. As a result, the pattern of foreign trade was completely transformed when the agricultural exports that once dominated foreign incomes were overshadowed by exports from the industrial and manufacturing sector. Soon after, the Thai economy expanded rapidly and achieved the first ever double-digit GDP growth in 1988. Indeed, this successful foreign trade transformation in Thailand proved the economy was in good health and that the country was ready to liberalise its financial system in order to generate more foreign funds to service further economic expansion and growth. Accordingly, the Thai government began deregulation by lifting the ceiling on long-term interest rates in June 1989. Almost a year later, the ceiling on the short-term interest rate was removed. Finally, in June 1992 all interest rate ceilings were abolished. The consequences of interest rate deregulation will be explored later in Chap. 6 of this book.

---

[3] Level of Real GDP at constant 1988 prices.

4.3 Reduction of Deficits and Maintaining Foreign Reserve

In order to prevent economic instability and currency speculation, the traditional view of sequencing financial liberalisation states that prior to financial reform a country should reduce its fiscal[4] and current account deficits and maintain sufficient levels of foreign reserves (McKinnon 1973, 1993; Sundararajan 1999; Glick and Hutchison 2000). In this section, we analyse the position of Thailand's fiscal and current account deficits and foreign reserve prior to financial liberalisation. A further aim of this section is to assess whether or not Thailand successfully reduced deficits and maintained high foreign reserves before financial liberalisation and to examine how these elements impacted on the financial crisis in 1997.

Thailand had a long period of fiscal imbalance beginning with national economic reforms of the early 1960s. During the first decade of the reform, the fiscal balance of Thailand was in deficit at an average of –1.83% of GDP. In the following decade, the imbalance worsened, reaching an average of –2.72% as a result of the first oil shock and the world economic recession (Warr 1993; Siksamat 1998). However, this lengthy period of fiscal imbalance finally ended when Thailand turned fiscal deficit into surplus for the first time in nearly thirty years in the late 1980s.

Figure 4.3 shows that the Thai economy remained in deficit from 1981 to 1987, with the oil shock of the late 1970s still impacting its performance in the early 1980s. In 1981, Thailand experienced a deficit of –2.3% of GDP or US$–17.5 billion. The fiscal imbalance worsened when the financial crisis caused by the world economic slump deepened and in 1982, the deficit rose more than double the 1981 figure from US$–17.5 billion to US$–42.5 billion (or –5.1% of GDP). From 1983 to 1986, the fiscal deficit was stable, ranging from –2.9% in 1983 to –3.5% in 1984, –3.3% in 1985 and –3.5% in 1986. However, in the latter period, the Thai economy showed signs of improvement. GDP stood high at 9.5%, and exports grew by 28.5%; thus the fiscal deficit declined to –1.4% in 1987.[5]

---

[4] We refer to fiscal balance as government budget, which is the difference between the actual revenue and expenditure of the government from both budget and non-budget allocations.

[5] For a discussion of Thailand's export growth see Chap. 6 of this book.

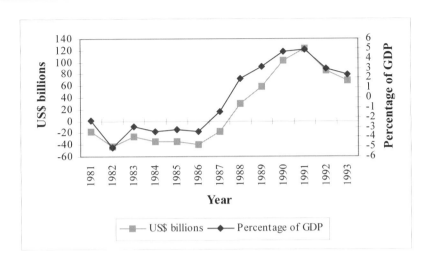

Fig. 4.3. Fiscal balance of Thailand, 1981–1993 (percentage and US$ billions)

Source: Authors' calculations from The Bank of Thailand Yearly, various issues.

With an export-led growth policy, Thailand achieved fiscal balance for the first time in 1988 with a surplus of US$30.2 billion or 1.9% of GDP. Furthermore, the Thai economy was able to maintain the surplus throughout the 1990s, for instance, the fiscal surplus increased from 1.9% of GDP in 1988 to 3.2% in 1989 and 4.7% in 1990. At the beginning of the financial reform between 1991 and 1993, Thailand continued to achieve economic growth and reached a fiscal surplus of 4.9%, 3.0 and 2.2% during 1991–1993 (see Fig. 4.3).

Similar to its fiscal position, Thailand experienced a current account deficit beginning with the transformation of economic policies and trade patterns in the 1960s. Like most developing economies, Thailand was affected by economic shocks derived from both internal and external sources (Warr 1993; Chaiyasoot 1995). Internally, Thailand had been ruled by authoritarian military governments that caused continued political and social unrest throughout the 1970s, leading to economic disruption and instability. On the external side, it experienced the two oil shocks of 1973–1974 and 1979–1980, as well as the global economic recession at the end of 1970s to early 1980s. In general, these factors were the prime obstacle to investment and economic growth and led to problems of current account imbalance in the 1980s and early 1990s.

Figure 4.4 exhibits an averaged current account balance from 1981 to the financial liberalisation era in the early 1990s. As a result of the oil shock in the late 1970s, Thailand began the 1980s with a record high current account deficit of US$–2.6 billion which was equivalent to –7.4% of GDP in 1981. During the first financial crisis of 1982–1985, the current account worsened and fluctuated. Despite the reduction of the current account deficit in 1982, the deficit rate rose by –2.8% to –7.2% in 1983. Following the export-led growth policy implemented in 1986, BOT (1998b) argues that Thai exports grew at a rate of 23.9% of GDP and the current account deficit became a surplus of 0.7% of GDP for the first time in 1986. Unfortunately, the surplus was short lived and only lasted for a year. Thailand's current account headed back into a deficit of –0.6%, –2.4% and –3.3% in 1987, 1988, and 1989, respectively. The most serious deficit problem, perhaps occurred during the financial reform between 1990 and 1993. Thailand reached its highest deficit ever recorded of –8.3% in 1990. Afterwards in 1991, the deficit stood at –7.5%, then declined by 2% to –5.5% in 1992. In the last stage of financial liberalisation in 1993, the deficit was at –5%, BOT (1998b) argues that this was considerably high by international standards.

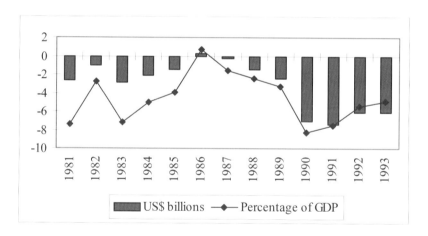

Fig. 4.4. Thailand's current account, 1981–1993

Source: Authors' calculations from The Bank of Thailand Yearly, various issues.

Lastly, we study the behaviour of Thailand's foreign reserves, presented in Fig. 4.5. According to the figure, Thailand's foreign reserves were considerably low from 1981 to 1985. This is because the Thai economy suffered from two major external shocks; the oil shock and the financial crisis. Consequently, Thailand's foreign reserves were relatively low during this period at 2.8 million baht, 2.7 million baht, 2.6 million baht, 2.7 million baht and 3.0 million baht from 1981 to 1985, respectively. According to Warr (1993), the low reserves in 1981 were a consequence of the global oil shock carried forward from 1979. On the other hand, the case of low reserves during 1982 to 1985 was due to the first financial crisis. In other words, these factors resulted in economic slowdown and discouraged investment from international markets especially capital investment (Siksamat 1998).

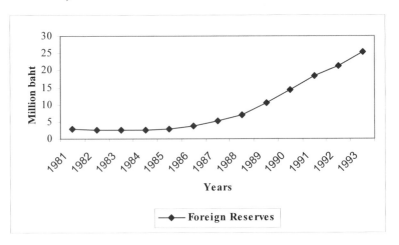

Fig. 4.5. Thailand's foreign reserve, 1981 to 1993 (million baht)

Source: Adapted from Vichyanond (1994) and The Bank of Thailand Monthly (2000).

Having accepted the recommendation of a growth strategy from international organisations, the Thai government began to place greater emphasis on the export sector from 1986 onwards. As we discussed earlier, the economy grew rapidly, owing to a significant increase of industry and manufacturing exports, which continued until their percentage share of exports to GDP overtook agriculture for the first time in 1986, and led to an increase in the country's foreign revenue. Thus, Thailand's reserves grew dramatically from 3.8 million baht in 1986 to 5.2 million baht in 1987, 7.1 million baht in 1988 and 10.5 million baht in 1989. At the beginning of financial liberalisation in the early 1990s, Thailand's foreign reserves continued to increase dramatically, from 14.3 million baht in 1990 to a relative peak of 25.4 million baht in 1993 (see Fig. 4.5).

Suphachalasai (1995) and Vajragupta and Vichyanond (1998) argue that the unexpected growth of the Thai economy in the late 1980s indeed provided a positive sign of a successful financial reform. Furthermore, we found that Thailand successfully turned fiscal deficits to surplus and was able to maintain a high level of foreign reserves prior to the financial liberalisation. This impressive performance suggested strong economic growth and generated confidence for further liberalisation of its financial system.[6] However, the literature on the sequencing of financial liberalisation, such as Edwards (1989a) and Sachs (1989) state that a country should reduce its current account balance prior to the implementation of financial reform. Burkett and Lotspeich (1993) suggest that if financial liberalisation occurs prior to the reduction of current account deficits, then the country may experience a problem of widening deficits, which could spiral out of control and result in economic instability. In other words, liberalisation of the financial system while the current account deficit is high, is likely to generate economic instability rather than provide benefits. In the case of Thailand, we found high level of current account deficits as high as −8.3% in 1990 when Thailand pursued financial liberalisation. The suggestion is that although foreign reserves and fiscal balance were well maintained, financial liberalisation at a time when current account deficits were high could lead to economic disruption. Indeed, the financial liberalisation in Thailand when current account deficits were high, is seen as inappropriate in the eyes of sequencing liberalisation theorists.

4.4 Foreign Exchange and Capital Control Reforms

Having reformed its trade pattern and maintained sufficient reserves, Thailand further removed its control of foreign exchange and capital controls during the period of 1989 to early 1994. As reviewed earlier in Chap. 3, the official reform of foreign exchange and capital control deregulation by the Thai government can be categorised into three main episodes. The first episode began on 17 July 1989 by granting members of the general public access to foreign capital, and allowing them to transfer out larger amount of capital for purpose dividends, interest and principal repayments. From 21 May 1990 onward, commercial banks were allowed to make purchases or sales of foreign exchange (especially for the purpose of export and loan repayments) without prior approval from the BOT. The second episode began with the amendment of the Ministerial Regulation No. 13, B.E. 2497 (1954) and the *Exchange Control Act*, B.E. 2485 (1942), allowing commercial banks further freedoms in purchasing and selling foreign exchange. On April 1991, the BOT officially announced episode two of the exchange control reform by allowing commercial banks

---

[6] See also Chaiyasoot (1995) and Vichyanond (1994, 2000a) for a detailed discussion of this view.

to purchase and sell foreign exchange to private businesses and the general public without prior approval. On 1 May 1992, the government further allowed the public to receive payments in foreign currencies and transfer them abroad, while commercial banks were allowed to withdraw funds from their account and use them freely. The last episode of the exchange control reform was officially declared in January 1994. This episode comprised of two main aspects. First, the limit of Thai baht allowed out of the country was raised from 250,000 baht to 500,000 baht. Second, Thailand allowed maximum foreign currency transfers out of the country to reach million to US$10 million up from US$5 million. Consequently, the volume of foreign exchange trade by the commercial banks and capital outflows increased dramatically.

Table 4.1. Commercial banks' trade of foreign exchange (million baht)

	1989	1990	1991	1992	1993	1994	1995	1996
Purchases								
US$	809,297	1,100,335	1,521,480	1,995,666	3,882,089	8,044,379	13,206,671	23,626,402
Yen	26,799	54,199	62,409	66,277	89,311	83,367	102,193	134,709
DM	18,857	22,650	20,831	22,041	24,125	25,476	28,244	26,253
Pound Sterling	8,184.20	10,598	9,487	10,553	12,498	10,896	10,183	11,444
S$	7,291	8,433	10,044	8,571	9,841	11,599	11,315	11,096
HK$	8,934	8,087	7,948	10,835	11,793	11,018	11,264	10,323
M$	2,877	2,343	1,950	2,038	2,525	3,419	4,714	4,778
Other Currencies	19,459	23,650	23,045	25,705	21,196	28,520	39,593	37,839
Total	907,698	1,230,296	1,657,194	2,141,686	4,053,378	8,218,674	13,414,177	23,862,844
Sales								
US$	615,176	926,739	1,256,636	1,792,748	3,470,084	7,799,008	12,830,990	23,378,849
Yen	83,150	114,740	139,936	138,759	171,293	188,688	224,929	229,628
DM	27,761	38,305	44,366	51,121	62,046	66,069	85,432	82,407
Pound Sterling	12,170	17,816	15,211	19,574	20,066	22,449	24,301	29,123
S$	12,321	16,420	18,552	21,635	22,670	28,446	29,294	28,682
HK$	7,674	8,011	9,965	14,683	16,047	16,851	13,712	14,222
M$	3,509	5,446	6,245	12,593	25,712	28,939	17,003	13,732
Other Currencies	41,683	48,956	54,775	51,711	59,163	76,837	77,674	80,035
Total	803,444	1,176,432	1,545,686	2,102,824	3,847,081	8,227,287	13,303,335	23,856,678

Source: The Bank of Thailand Monthly, various issues.

Table 4.1 demonstrates the major foreign currencies traded by commercial banks in Thailand during 1989–1996. According to the table, the total trade volume of foreign exchange by commercial banks rose immediately following the declaration of official exchange rate and capital control reforms in 1989. The reforms allowed the public to engage in foreign capital flows and commercial banks were able to trade on foreign exchange currency without approval from the BOT. Thus, the volume of foreign exchange sold by the commercial banks grew from approximately 803 billion baht in 1989 to 1,176 billion baht in 1990, while the purchasing of foreign exchange also increase from 908 billion baht to 1,230 billion baht during the same period of time.

During the second stage of reform, the total volume of trade of foreign exchange grew even more rapidly when the government further amended the *Exchange Control Act* allowing the public to purchase or sell foreign currency from the commercial banks more freely and also permitting them to receive or transfer foreign currency for the first time. As a result, the total volume of foreign exchange traded by the commercial banks rose more than twofold in both purchasing and selling transactions during 1991–1993.

Perhaps, the most significant increase of foreign exchange transactions occurred in the last stage of the reform in 1994. At this time, the government raised the limit on baht taken out of the country from 250,000 to 500,000 baht, while the amount of inflows and outflows for the purpose of international investments also increased from US$5 million to US$10 million. Hence, the total trade of foreign exchange rose more than twofold from 1993 to 1994. From then on, foreign exchange trade by commercial banks grew rapidly to a relative peak of 23,863 billion baht in purchasing and 23,857 billion baht in selling in 1996.

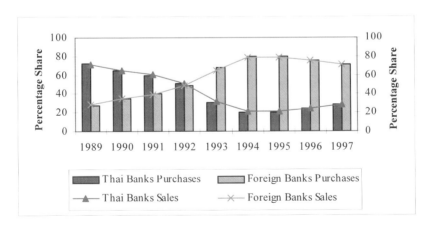

Fig. 4.6. Percentage share of foreign exchange commercial banks

Source: Authors' calculations from The Bank of Thailand Yearly, various issues.

In general, a fast growing trend of foreign exchange trade implies that most of these transactions were by processed commercial banks operating from within the country. Vichyanond (1994) points out that the foreign exchange and capital control reforms in Thailand did not distinguish between: Thai-owned and foreign commercial banks operating in Thailand. Therefore, the reforms benefited both Thai and foreign commercial banks. According to Fig. 4.6, the foreign commercial banks' percentage share of total foreign exchange trade rose dramatically from approximately 28–35% in both purchasing and selling during the first episode of the reform in 1989 and 1990, respectively. When the *Exchange Act* was amended in the second episode, the role of foreign commercial banks increased from 40% in 1991 to 49% 1992 and they became the main trader of foreign exchange in Thailand in 1993 with a total share of 65% of all transactions. The foreign commercial banks' trade of foreign exchange rose even more significantly after the last episode of reform was implemented in 1994 when their percentage share reached almost 80%. After this, they continued to dominate with more than 79, 75 and 70% of total transactions in 1995, 1996 and 1997, respectively.

Table 4.2. Thailand's capital outflows, 1985–1994 (US$ millions)

	1985	1986	1987	1988	1989	1990	1991	1992	1993	1994
FDI	215	137	135	188	286	488	1,667	3,189	906	1,129
Foreign Loans	1,827	1,961	1,697	1,604	2,179	2,747	7,957	11,701	20,640	23,283
Portfolio Investment	8	20	167	653	1,089	2,960	2,140	2,846	6,107	7,885
Non-resident	84	45	30	143	86	235	9,919	20,920	74,278	229,198
Total	2,134	2,163	2,029	2,588	3,640	6,430	21,683	38,656	101,931	261,495

Source: The Bank of Thailand Yearly, various issues.

Another important consequence of capital control reform was severe capital outflows from Thailand. We provide a summary of Thailand's major outflows made for purposes of FDI, foreign loans, portfolio investment and non-residential accounts (see Table 4.2). Our study here focuses only on the immediate outcomes of the reform, while further detailed analysis of capital outflows will be conducted later in Chap. 5 of this book.

Prior to the reform, the Thai government had placed much emphasis on capital outflows, often requiring approval from the BOT before any outward movement could be made. Thus, the capital outflows in Thailand were stable and low during 1985–1988. The important changes in capital outflows occurred with the capital control reform from 1989 onward. In the first stage of the reform in 1989, the public were allowed to transfer funds out for the first time, resulting in a rapid increase of outflows that grew from US$2.5 billion in 1988 to US$6.3 billion and US$6.4 billion in 1989 and 1990, respectively. Thailand experienced a further surge of capital outflows in the second stage of the reform from 1991 to 1993, which allowed the public to be involved in foreign exchange transactions and provided more freedom in transferring capital outflows. Consequently, capital outflows from Thailand escalated very rapidly with an extraordinary increase of outflows made for foreign loans and non-residential account. For instance, non-resident outflows alone rose by more that 4,000% from US$235 million in 1990 to US$9,919 million in 1991 and rose more than twofold in 1992 and 1993, reaching US$21 billion and US$74 billion, respectively. The limit of outflows was raised in the last stage of reform in early 1994, propelling Thailand's capital outflows to a high of US$261 billion. This was indeed a significant increase of outflows compared with the maximum of US$2.6 billion in 1988 prior to the reform. One could argue that high level of outflows alone is not necessarily a problem. In fact, we argue that capital outflows have direct role in offsetting capital inflows, hence net inflows. In the extreme case, the problem could occur as a result form loss of confidence and panic among the investors when the economy fails to perform, causing a sudden stop of inflows and rapid withdraw of capital which in turn widening current account and reducing balance of payment and foreign reserve. Indeed, the combination of these factors is likely to lure the country into financial crisis.

The traditional view on the sequencing of financial liberalisation asserts that the reform of capital controls needs to be undertaken gradually in order to prevent economic instability that may be caused by a rapid increase of capital flows (Edwards 1984; Balassa 1990). In this context, it seems that the loosening of capital controls in Thailand was on the right path since it had gradually removed controls during the period of 1989 to early 1994. However, the World Bank (1998) and Arestos and Demetriades (1999) argue that the country needed to first reform its domestic financial institutions before the deregulation of foreign exchange and capital controls. This is to ensure the domestic institutions are prepared to cope with the eminent massive inflows. While, Sundararajan (1999) argues that the decision to totally free up controls on capital could lead to a problem of speculation on the currency. Thus, it is recommended that a country should at least maintain a minimum of controls such as, controls on selective capital movements and so on, to avoid economic disruption and at the same time to ensure the effectiveness of funds allocation to the right users.

In our study, we noted that foreign exchange and capital control liberalisation in Thailand were not carried out in the order suggested by the literature. Thailand pursued liberalisation of the foreign exchange and capital controls prior to the reform of domestic financial institutions, resulting in economic instability in at least two areas. First, Thai commercial banks lost most of their foreign exchange trade to foreign commercial banks, making the speculative attack on the currency easier. Second, there were severe immediate increases of capital outflows. High levels of outflows could lead to problem of current account deficit, reduction of balance of payment and foreign reserve, resulting in economic disruption in the end. Clearly, these consequences indicate the weakening of the financial system caused by an inappropriate reform of foreign exchange and capital controls in Thailand. Indeed, the reform of Thailand in this manner exposed the country to speculative attack and economic disruption, which led to a financial crisis in the end.

4.5 Domestic Financial Reforms

It is known that domestic financial reforms is one of the crucial requirements needed for a successful financial liberalisation and it must be carefully implemented in order to ensure economic stability (World Bank 1989b; Arestos and Demetriades 1999). The implementation of domestic reform can come in various forms. Sundararajan (1999) argues that at least a country should develop supervisory program to assist domestic financial institutions the way to cope with a high level of foreign capital, which could occur from financial liberalisation. McKinnon (1988) and Sachs (1989) argue that if a country failing to do so could face a problem of misallocation of funds and cause the financial system to collapse. Moreover, Sundararajan (1999) added that it is also essential to monitor the operation of domestic financial institutions in order to avoid problem of insolvency by strengthening auditing, accounting and disclosure practices. Indeed, a successful financial liberalisation could not be achieved without a proper reform of domestic financial system through implementation of supervisory and monitoring program to monitor the activities of financial institutions.

As reviewed earlier that sequencing financial liberalisation can be varied from one country to another, depending to its objectives, policies and economic conditions. Thailand undertook domestic financial reforms as the last step in liberalising its financial system. This final stage reform included the establishment of two new financial institutions called the BIBF and the EXIM bank in 1993 and 1994, respectively.[7] This section aims to study the operation of these two institutions by focusing on the first year of their operation.

The BIBF was established on March 1993 with two main purposes involved: seek and receive funds from external sources and lend them out to domestic markets (out-in lending) or international markets (out-out lending). Within nine months after beginning operation, the BIBF had received foreign funds totally US$7,655 million, the highest inflow in comparison to other sector. For instance, foreign inflows to the BIBF in 1993 alone were greater than the combined inflows to four major non-bank investment sectors such as FDI, foreign loans, portfolio investments and non-resident accounts (see Chap. 5).

Table 4.3. BIBF's lending in 1993 (million baht)

	Mar	Apr	May	Jun	Jul	Aug	Sep	Oct	Nov	Dec
Out-In	1,405.8	34,081.0	61,019.8	91,341.9	109,061.3	125,693.4	144,015.3	157,260.7	173,335.4	197,024.4
Out-Out	0.0	33.4	520.8	1,483.7	1,840.2	11,877.2	20,880.0	2,130.9	2,886.1	3,789.2

Source: The Bank of Thailand Yearly, various issues.

Table 4.3 exhibits the lending behaviour of the BIBF from the beginning of its operation in March 1993 to December of the same year. In March, out-in lending totaled 1,406 million baht, which jumped by more that 2,000% reaching 34,081 million baht in the next month period of April. The total amount of out-in lending continued to increase for the rest of the year, with 91,342 million baht in June, 125,693 million baht in August and 197,024 million baht in December. Looking at out-out lending, the BIBF began to extend funds abroad to the amount of 33 million baht in April. Like out-in, out-out lending also rose rapidly throughout the year, increasing by 1,560% from April to May (33 to 521 million baht), extending to 1,484 million baht in June, 11,872 million baht in August and 3,789 million baht in December. We see the BIBF extended most of its funds within the domestic market, which had a percentage share of more than 90% higher than the international market.

The Export-Import Bank of Thailand (EXIM Bank) was established on September 1993. However, its operations did not officially taken place until March 1994. The EXIM bank was allowed to engage in lending and borrowing from both local and international financial institutions. The EXIM bank borrowed and loaned relatively massive amount of funds as soon as it started operating. Table 4.4 presents a summary of the EXIM

---

[7] See also Sect. 3.5.3 in Chap. 3 for discussion of the BIBF and EXIM Bank.

bank lending and borrowing in the first year of its operations from March to December 1994.

Table 4.4. EXIM bank borrowing and lending, selected months 1994 (million baht)

	March	Jun	Sept	Oct	Nov	Dec
Borrowing						
BOT	5,430	15,890	13,580	14,180	15,500	14,000
Commercial Banks	18	89.6	45.7	38.2	52.3	26.8
Non-resident	–	–	250	250	250	250
Lending						
Commercial Banks	3,568	1,030	791	712	740	684
Private Business	3,673	16,707	14,668	15,362	16,690	15,213
Non-resident	–	–	250	250	250	250

Source: Adapted from the Bank of Thailand Monthly Report, various issues.

The EXIM bank started its operations with financial support from two sources, namely, the BOT and commercial banks. However, the BOT was the main source of funds with 5,430 million baht in March, while only 18 million baht came from commercial banks. In June, the amount of borrowing from both sources rose rapidly from 5,430–15,890 million baht for the BOT and from 18 to 89.6 million baht for commercial banks. Over the year, lending from the BOT was steady remaining approximately between 13.6 and 15.6 billion baht, while borrowing from commercial banks declined dramatically. Foreign funds were also another source of funds. The EXIM bank began to borrow abroad in September starting with 250 million baht and remaining the same throughout the year. On the lending side, the EXIM bank loaned 3,568 million baht in March to commercial banks, and 3,673 million baht to the private business and household sector. Lending to commercial banks declined in June to 1,030 million baht and continued to decline for the rest of the year. On the other hand, lending to the private business and the household sector rose significantly from 3,673 in March to 16,707 million baht in June. Moreover, this sector received steady amount of loans from the EXIM bank, of approximately between 14,600 and 16,700 million baht from June to December of 1994. Similar to borrowing, the EXIM bank began lending overseas in September with 250 million baht, with the amount staying the same for the rest of the year. In short, the EXIM bank followed a trend of borrowing funds mainly from the BOT and rolling them out within domestic markets to the private business and household sector.

In summary, the showcase of high capital flows following financial reform was the BIBF, with a massive influx of foreign capital pouring in as soon as it was established. On the contrary, foreign investors paid little attention to investing via the EXIM bank where our study showed that foreign capital flows were only minor compared to funds to the BOT. The reasons why foreign flows to the BIBF skyrocketed in a very short period of time seem to lie with the capital controls reform. Just prior to establishing the BIBF, the Thai government liberalised capital controls allowing freer flows of foreign capital. In addition, as we reviewed in Chap. 3, to ensure high foreign capital mobility for the BIBF, the Thai government had provided several tax benefits for foreign investors with the BIBF. Consequently, foreign capital poured into the BIBF in just a very short period of time.

Theoretically, the reform of domestic financial institutions should be carried out first before foreign exchange and capital controls liberalisation. According to Sachs (1989) and McKinnon (1993), capital controls deregulation should not be implemented prior to the domestic financial institutions reform as they believed this could lead to problems of misallocation of funds and excessive lending, which damage economic growth. Our findings confirmed the fact that capital controls reform before domestic financial reform caused a massive influx to the BIBF. Furthermore, we observed that high inflows to the BIBF stirred up domestic demand for lending. Our study shows that the BIBF loaned most of its funds within the domestic market, which in turn created excessive lending with potential loan losses if these loans were poorly managed. Most importantly, our study also reveals one crucial implication regarding lack of appropriate reform of domestic financial institutions. Thailand pursued a different approach in reforming its domestic financial market where the establishment of the BIBF and the EXIM was implemented rather than reforming the domestic institutions with supervisory and monitoring system. The direct impact of this mistake is witnessed in the high level of out-in lending that is likely to generate problems of misallocation of funds that could result in overinvestment in the domestic market. Indeed, this element exposes the risk and creates precondition for severe case of financial crisis to occur. In short, the sequence of financial liberalisation in Thailand exhibits another error with domestic financial reform left to the last and without adequate reform of domestic financial institutions. The consequences of capital controls reform to the BIBF will be discussed in greater detail in Chap. 5 of this book.

4.6 Summary

This chapter presents an analysis of the sequencing of financial liberalisation in Thailand. The issue of what is the proper sequencing is widely debated by economists who follow two main schools of thoughts. On the one hand, some argue that there must be a stereotype sequence in financial liberalisation that will maximise the benefits and at the same time minimise economic instability. On the other hand, others argue that there is no particular sequence of financial liberalisation that best suites all countries. In this view, the sequence of financial liberalisation is determined by the nature of the economy and the objectives of reform in each country. However, it is generally accepted now that the country should first transform its foreign trade patterns and reduce deficits before other actions are taken. Most importantly, the country must reform its domestic financial institutions before deregulating control on foreign exchange or capital, failing to do so can result in economic disruption instead of growth.

For Thailand, the country successfully transformed foreign trade from and agriculture base to being industrial and manufacturing export oriented prior to the financial liberalisation. The transformation of foreign trade patterns was carried out from the early 1960s with the development of the national development plans and continued to 1991. Prior to full liberalisation in 1994, Thailand had developed a total of six national plans.[8] However, a major change in Thailand's trade pattern occurred with the Sixth National Plan during 1986 and 1987 when the government placed more emphasis on an export led growth policy by reducing taxes and a pegged exchange rate policy. Accordingly, the Thai economy successfully transformed from an agriculture base to a industrial and manufacturing export base and as a result the economy grew rapidly with double-digit GDP growth rates (see Figs. 4.1 and 4.2). This suggests that the first action of financial liberalisation in Thailand was correctly chosen and successfully executed.

From a theoretical point of view, the country needed to reduce fiscal deficits to surplus before financial liberalisation was implemented. According to our findings, Thailand performed well in reducing fiscal deficits and maintaining high levels of foreign reserves. The Thai economy reversed a long period of persistent fiscal deficit in 1988 and foreign reserves grew after the successful reform of foreign trade in the second half of the 1980s (see Figs. 4.3 and 4.4). These factors provided confidence so that a successful financial liberalisation could be undertaken. However, the current

---

[8] For a detailed discussion and analysis of the National Development Plans see Chap. 3.

account deficit was an important element that had been overlooked. We discovered that the current account deficits of Thailand were as high as −8.3% of GDP at the first stage of financial liberalisation in 1990 (see Fig. 4.5). Ideally, it is not recommended that a country liberalise its financial system while deficits are high because the deficits may increase and lead to economic instability in the future.

Another crucial policy error occurred with the reverse order of financial reform when the foreign exchange and capital control deregulation was taken before the domestic financial was fully reformed. This created several problems that disrupts the economy of the country. We found that there were significant increases of foreign exchange trade by foreign banks (see Table 4.1 and Fig. 4.6). This implies that foreign investors under controlled trade of the Thai currency and the problem may arise when economic conditions of the country were weak, providing the opportunity to speculate on the currency. In addition, we observed that outflows of Thailand rose massively after the reform started, particularly outflows made by non-resident and foreign loans. High level of outflows could leads to economic disruption as it has an impact in reducing net inflows, hence macroeconomic fundamentals such as current account balance, foreign reserves and balance of payments.

Domestic financial market reform was the last step Thailand undertook in liberalising its financial system by establishing the BIBF and the EXIM Bank rather than reforming domestic institutions with supervisory and monitoring system to monitor the operation. The impact of this poor reform could damage to economy with problems of misallocation of funds and overinvestment.

Although there were two institutions established as part of domestic reform, however it was the BIBF that proved to be the most crucial institution that highlighted consequences of high foreign capital flows. Foreign investors preferred to invest more with the BIBF, while the EXIM bank relied on the BOT. The BIBF received massive amount of funds from international markets (borrowing) as soon as it was established and loaned them out as out-in lending to domestic markets not international markets (see Table 4.3). High foreign flows alone were not a problem but lending these funds to the domestic market, in turn stirred demand for lending, created an excessive lending problem.

In essence, from the Thai experience we found obvious errors in the sequencing of financial liberalisation with high current account deficits and the deregulation of foreign exchange and capital controls occurring before appropriate domestic financial reforms were in place. Lastly, these errors exposed Thailand to speculation on the currency, widening current account deficits, overinvestment and weakness of macroeconomic fundamentals.

All these problems were likely to generate economic instability and disruption rather than benefits.

Having analysed the sequencing of financial liberalisation in Thailand, the next chapter discusses the issue of capital controls and their consequences after financial liberalisation.

5 Capital Controls: Consequences of Financial Liberalisation

5.1 Introduction

The issues of capital controls and financial crises have been widely debated in economic literature. Some economists argue that controls on capital are becoming difficult to maintain, especially in a liberalising financial system. Coy et al. (1998) argue that capital controls are unlikely to work well in a world moving toward financial liberalisation, as the controls will have a negative impact on the investment atmosphere. Cooper (1999) advocates the deregulation of capital controls as he believes that financial liberalisation aims to allow unrestricted movement of capital among free economies, and people should also be able to place their assets wherever they prefer. In other words, financial liberalisation aims at promoting comparative advantages and development by attracting foreign investment funds.

Capital controls may have different meanings to different people. Khor (1998) and Crotty and Epstein (1999) refer to capital controls as any policy designed to limit or redirect capital account transactions. Bakker (1996) defines it as any government measures to restrict or bar the sending of capital outside a country. Neely (1999) argues that these broad definitions suggest that it will be difficult to generalise about capital controls because they can take many forms and may be applied for various purposes. Edwards (1999) argues that the use of capital controls does not restrict only the export of capital but also includes a limit on incoming funds from foreign sources. In other words, he argues that capital controls imply prohibitions on the export of capital by either residents or non-residents as well as to a variety of controls on financial and investment processes applicable to residents and non-residents. In principle, we define capital controls as any policy or restriction prohibiting residents and non-residents from freely moving financial capital and investment into or out of a country. Examples of capital controls include outright prohibitions on certain types of foreign investment, quantitative restrictions on foreign ownership of domestic firms, limits or prohibitions on holdings by firms or individuals of foreign exchange-denominated assets, and requirements that capital entering the country must remain for a specified time.

As discussed earlier in Chap. 3, Thailand decided to release its controls on both capital outflows and inflows in the financial reforms process during 1990–1994. This chapter aims to analyse the consequences of those reforms on capital controls and it proceeds as follows. Section 5.2 reviews the pattern of net cross-border flows of Thailand from the beginning of the capital controls reform in 1990 through to 1997 when crisis occurred. Section 5.3 explores the characteristics of Thailand's capital flows by focusing on capital flows to bank and non-bank sectors, separately. For the banking sector, we explore the pattern of net cross-border flows of two main financial institutions, commercial banks and the BIBF. In terms of the non-bank sector, we analyse net cross-border flows for: FDI, loans, portfolio investment and non-residential accounts. Finally, Sect. 5.4 provides a summary of the chapter.

5.2 Pattern of Net Private Capital Flows

Traditionally, capital inflows into Thailand have always been welcome and there were specific restrictions on the movement of incoming foreign capital.[1] Unlike inflows, Thailand had always placed a great emphasis on controls over the outflow of funds, which normally required prior approval from the Bank of Thailand (BOT) before they could be taken out of the country.[2] As a result of its financial liberalisation policy, Thai government gradually removed controls on both incoming and outgoing capital during the process of financial liberalisation (1990–1994), as they believed free flow of capital plays a major role in economic growth and development of any country. First, the BOT allowed the commercial sector to process purchases of foreign currency without prior approval and the limit of outflows for a loan repayment was also raised on 21 May 1990. Second, on 1 April 1991, the BOT announced that the public could freely purchase and sell foreign exchange from commercial banks without prior approval. Third, on 1 May 1992, Thai exporters were allowed to transfer funds out of Thailand

---

[1] See Siksamat (1998) for a discussion of this view.
[2] Warr and Nidhiprabha (1989) argue that Thailand pursued this policy because it enabled the authorities to prevent the outward flows of capital, which would otherwise deprive them of the capital to expand the domestic money supply when desired.

to pay for exports or foreign loans without prior approval and the commercial banks were allowed to manage their funds more freely.[3] Finally, the limit on both Thai and foreign funds to be taken out of Thailand was increased on 10 January 1994 (see Table 5.1).

Table 5.1. Chronology of capital controls reform in Thailand

Date	Capital control reforms
17 July 1989	*First Round*: The public was allowed to borrow from foreign countries and were also permitted to make outflows for dividend, interest and principle payments.
21 May 1990	The BOT allowed commercial banks to process purchases of foreign currency without prior approval. The BOT also raised the limit on capital outflows for loans repayment.
1 April 1991	*Second Round*: The BOT allowed public purchasing and selling of foreign exchange without further approval.
1 May 1992	The government allowed the public to receive payments and investments in foreign currency and transfer them overseas. The commercial banks were permitted to withdraw funds from their account from the BOT and use it more freely.
10 January 1994	*Third Round*: The BOT increased the limit of Thai bahts to be taken out of Thailand from 250,000 baht to 500,000 baht. The amount permitted for overseas investments also increased from US$5 million to US$10 million.

As shown in Table 5.2, the net cross-border inflows of Thailand fluctuated from early 1980s to the end of 1987. The net inflows began to increase dramatically from 1988 onward with the majority being FDI flows. However, the pattern of flows changed early during the financial liberalisation process of 1990–1994, when most inflows switched from FDI to loans and net cross-border flows increased dramatically. In addition, the establishment of the BIBF played a major role in attracting cross-border funds to Thailand and to the banking sector, in particular. The BIBF scored the highest inflows from any single source in the very first year of its operation with total net flows of US$7,655 million which represents 73% share of total net flows in 1993. Most importantly, the BIBF had a significant role in increasing inflows to the banking sector. Prior to its establishment, net cross-border flows were mainly invested in the non-bank sector, but this trend changed when the BIBF came into operation in 1993. Large amount of capital began to flow into the BIBF, resulting in a rapid increase of net flows to the banking sector. Accordingly, the BIBF dominated the total net cross-border flows of Thailand during 1994 and 1995.

---

[3] See also Chap. 3 of this book.

Table 5.2. Net private capital inflows (US$ millions)

	1980	1981	1982	1983	1984	1985	1986	1987	1988	1989
Bank	108	112	463	672	67	−533	−835	239	850	−296
Commercial banks	108	112	463	672	67	−533	−835	239	850	−296
BIBFs	0	0	0	0	0	0	0	0	0	0
Non-bank	607	772	859	786	1,784	738	602	646	2,600	6,144
Direct investment	341	392	266	356	412	160	262	354	1,106	1,780
Loans	83	182	370	183	1,029	63	−125	−619	188	1,842
Portfolio investment	9	8	11	15	−6	141	97	499	447	1,429
Non-resident account	174	190	212	232	349	374	368	412	859	1,093
Total	715	884	1,322	1,458	1,851	205	−233	885	3,450	5,848

	1990	1991	1992	1993	1994	1995	1996	1997
Bank	1,603	−253	1,934	3,604	13,894	11,239	5,003	−5,717
Commercial banks	1,603	−253	1,934	−4,051	3,807	3,097	419	−5,212
BIBFs	0	0	0	7,655	10,087	8,142	4,584	−505
Non-bank	8,870	9,899	7,265	6,837	−1,343	10,349	14,134	−1,323
Direct investment	2,542	2,033	2,151	1,732	1,326	2,004	2,271	3,627
Loans	4,535	5,661	2,846	−2,432	−5,845	1,518	5,451	−3,688
Portfolio investment	457	163	561	4,852	1,110	3,420	3,488	4,550
Non-resident account	1,336	2,042	1,707	2,685	2,066	3,407	2,924	−5,812
Total	10,473	9,646	9,199	10,441	12,551	21,588	19,137	−7,040

Source: The Bank of Thailand Yearly Report (2000).

There was a small increase of net inflows in 1994, but a significant increase did not occur until 1995, when net inflows rose by 71%, reaching US$21,588 million (see Fig. 5.1). Wiboonchutikula et al. (1999) argue that the net capital flows of Thailand increased rapidly after the capital controls reform was completed. They found that net cross-border flows rose by more than 100% during the first and the second quarter of 1994. From then on, inflows continued to grow dramatically reaching a peak of US$7,605 million in the second quarter of 1995. This suggests that the financial reforms had a direct impact in increasing capital inflows. Overall, Thailand chalked up a net inflow totalling US$93,035 million within just seven years during 1990 to 1996, a considerably large increase compared to an inflow of US$16,385 million in the previous decade (see Table 5.2).

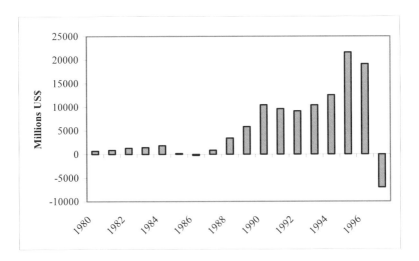

Fig. 5.1. Pattern of net cross border capital inflows (US$ millions)

Source: The Bank of Thailand Yearly Report (2000).

Thailand experienced a slowdown of capital flows with a decline in 1996. According to Table 5.3, the BOT's data shows that a serious decline of inflows occurred in the second half of 1996 with a drop from US$2,485 million in the second quarter to US$1,802 million and US$1,286 million in the third and fourth quarters, respectively. Finally, inflows turned negative for the first time in the second quarter of 1997 with US$-717 million and further declined dramatically throughout the year. In 1997, Thailand recorded net outflows as high as US$-7,040 million (see Table 5.2).

Such a decline of inflows was due to significant losses of capital inflows to both the bank and non-bank sectors. Data from Table 5.2 exhibits that there was a huge decline of net inflows to banking institutions in 1996 with a sudden drop of more that 50%. A year later, the net inflows declined more rapidly ending 1997 with a record of US$-5717 million (see Table 5.2). On the other hand, inflows to the non-bank sector increased from 1995 to peak in 1996. However, the situation became worse when inflows suddenly dropped from US$14,134 million in 1996 to US$–1,323 million in 1997.

Table 5.3. Net cross-border inflows (quarterly)

		Bank	Non-bank
1995	Q1	4,463	–1,029
	Q2	3,478	4,126
	Q3	1,570	3,593
	Q4	1,728	3,659
1996	Q1	–573	6,560
	Q2	2,485	3,328
	Q3	1,805	1,765
	Q4	1,286	2,481
1997	Q1	2,425	–671
	Q2	–717	–630
	Q3	–4,155	–1,176
	Q4	–3,270	1,100

Source: The Bank of Thailand Yearly Report (2000).

In sum, the pattern of net capital flows to both the bank and non-bank sector fluctuated since the beginning of financial liberalisation and capital controls deregulation until 1997 when the financial crisis struck. For the banking sector, capital inflows to commercial banks also fluctuated throughout the period. The BIBF experienced high capital flows, which rose markedly from its establishment in 1993 and it remained the highest capital flow generator for Thailand until 1995. From 1995 onward, the banking sector experienced a decline of capital flows in both commercial banks and the BIBF.

Like the banking sector, most capital flows to the non-bank sector also fluctuated throughout the period. Capital flows as loans, portfolio investment and non-resident account varied during 1990–1994. During 1995 and 1996, capital flows for these three purposes increased significantly after capital controls deregulation was completed. Unlike others, capital flows for FDI was very consistent throughout the period. As a result, FDI was the only sector that experienced stable capital flows while others fluctuated.

5.3 Characteristics of Thailand's Capital Flows

In the previous section, we analysed overall net private capital flows to Thailand from the early stages of financial liberalisation and capital controls deregulation in 1990 up to the financial crisis in 1997. This section explores the behaviour of capital flows to Thailand in greater detail by dividing the analysis into two major sections, the bank and non-bank sectors.

5.3.1 Capital Flows to the Banking Sector

For the banking sector, there are only two main recipients of foreign capital, commercial banks and the BIBF. As a result of capital control reforms, large amount of capital flows poured into the banking sector with a total of US$37,024 million from 1990 to 1996. This was a great increase compared to only US$2,286 million during 1980–1989 (see Table 5.2). Here, we explore the pattern of inflows to both commercial banks and the BIBF in order to understand the impact of capital controls reforms.

5.3.1.1 Capital Flows of Commercial Banks

In the light of financial liberalisation, the Thai government lifted several controls on its financial market, especially controls on the operation of the commercial banks during 1990–1994. First, on 21 May 1990, commercial banks were allowed to purchase foreign currency without prior approval. At the same time, the government also allowed commercial banks to make more outflows for loan repayments. Second, on 1 May 1991, the commercial banks were allowed to manage and withdraw from their accounts more freely. Finally, on 10 January 1994, the limit of international investment in Thailand, including investment via commercial banks was raised from US$5 million to US$10 million. As a result, the commercial banks experienced significant inflows after capital controls reform commenced in 1990. The total net inflows of commercial banks amounted to US$6,556 million within seven years from 1990 to 1997. This was a very large increase, compared to US$2,286 million for the earlier decade (see Table 5.2). Indeed, capital controls reform helped generate foreign capital flows to commercial banks, which saw a huge increase of inflows following the reform.

According to Table 5.2, net inflows to commercial banks were low and unstable during the process of financial reform from 1990 to 1993. For instance, inflows amounted to US$1,603 million for the first year of the reform in 1990. From then on, they fluctuated through to the end of the reform period in 1993, which had a high negative inflow of US$–4,051 million. A study by Hataiseree (1998) argues that the decline of inflows in 1991 and 1992 was a result of an increase of outflows, while inflows remained constant. We suggest there is another reason why the net foreign inflows of the commercial banks declined in 1991 and 1993: the decline was due to significant negative changes in both assets and liabilities of the commercial banks. Because the net capital flows account of the commercial banks includes assets and liabilities transactions, it declines when there is a negative change on one or both transactions. We found that there were negative changes in both assets and liabilities of the commercial banks in both years, especially in 1993 with a record high of US$–3,065 million for assets and US$–986 million for liabilities. This led to a negative net capital flow of US$–4,051 million for the commercial banks in 1993.

As soon as most capital controls were lifted, net inflows began to come into the commercial banks amounting to US$3,807 million in 1994 and US$3,097 million in 1995. According to Table 5.2, inflows to commercial banks declined sharply with US$419 million in 1996 and further declined to negative inflows of US$–5,212 million in 1997. This data suggests that capital control deregulation did not help generate capital flows to the commercial banks, which continued to fluctuate throughout 1990–1997. In 1997 alone, Thai commercial bank experienced a major drop of net inflows from US$1,158 million in the first quarter to US$–581 million in the second quarter. The situation was even worse in the last two quarters of the year as net inflows further declined to US$–3,327 million and US$–2,462 million in the third and fourth quarter respectively (see Table 5.4).

Furthermore, the data from our study provided interesting results with respect to the decline in capital flows to the commercial bank sector. Figure 5.2 shows that capital flows to commercial banks declined considerably while net inflows of the BIBF rose markedly after the BIBF was established in 1993. This suggests that foreign inflows to the banking sector were substitutable. Data from Table 5.2 revealed that the net capital flows of commercial banks fluctuated during 1990–1993, however, they recovered in 1994, as a result of the commercial banks raising interest rates. Figure 5.3 exhibits that commercial banks interest rates increased dramatically from 5.4% in January 1994 to 9% in December and continued to increase toward the end of 1995, reaching a peak of 10.5% in December. Thus, foreign capital began to flow into the commercial banks to take advantage of the benefits of rising interest rates, resulting in a marked increase of net capital flows (see Figs. 5.2 and 5.3).

Table 5.4. Net inflows: commercial banks (quarterly)

1993	Q1	610
	Q2	−426
	Q3	−1,981
	Q4	−2,254
1994	Q1	2,360
	Q2	1,872
	Q3	−1,007
	Q4	582
1995	Q1	2,667
	Q2	562
	Q3	−804
	Q4	672
1996	Q1	−2,325
	Q2	590
	Q3	1,660
	Q4	494
1997	Q1	1,158
	Q2	−581
	Q3	−3,327
	Q4	−2,462

Source: The Bank of Thailand Yearly Report (2000).

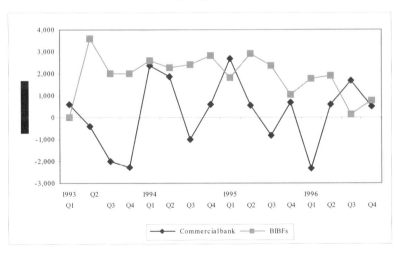

Fig. 5.2. Pattern of net cross-border inflows to banking sector (quarterly)

Source: The Bank of Thailand Yearly Report (2000).

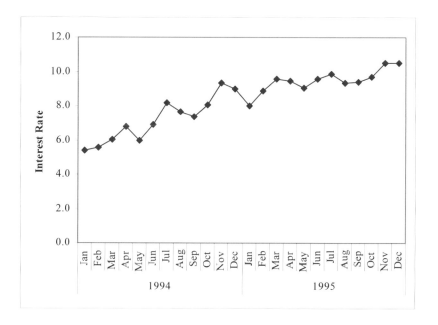

Fig. 5.3. Commercial banks' interest rate (monthly)

Source: The Bank of Thailand Yearly Report (2000).

Hataiseree (1998) argues that although the opening of the BIBF increased net capital flows of the banking sector, there was a decline in capital flows to commercial banks. We argue that a possible reason for this change lies in the tax privileges of the BIBF over commercial banks. Because the BIBF was established specifically to attract foreign funds, the government exempted it from most taxes on investment, and any remaining taxes were set at a lower rate than other financial institutions. For instance, the income tax for the BIBF was only 10% while it was 30% for other institutions. Additionally, there was no business tax, interest income tax and stamp duties for the BIBF, while these were 3.3%, 10% and 2% for others institutions, respectively. Accordingly, large amount of foreign capital flows shifted from the commercial banks to the BIBF, since investment via the BIBF provided distinct tax advantages. In all, the BIBF became the prime intermediary in mobilising funds to the banking sector and helped increase the share of the banking sector to the total net capital flows from 11% in 1990 to 1992 to 53% in 1993–1996.

5.3.1.2 Capital Flows of the BIBF

As discussed in Chap. 3, the BIBF was established as part of a financial liberalisation framework; with the aim to increase capital inflows into the country. If we consider the BIBF as a funds seeker, its performance would be regarded as successful in helping to boost inflows rapidly in just a very short period of time. For instance, the BIBF generated large amount of inflows of US$30,468 million since beginning operation in 1993 to the end of 1996. Furthermore, the BIBF's inflow was extremely high when compared to the inflows of commercial banks (US$3,277 million for the same period of time, see Table 5.2).

Despite being newly established in March 1993, the BIBF began to reap large amounts of inflows immediately after starting operation. BOT data revealed that the BIBF brought in the astonishing amount of US$7,585 million within just the first three quarters in 1993. As a result of financial liberalisation, the BIBF managed to raise inflows by 32% to a peak of US$10,087 million in 1994. However, inflows began to decline from 1995 onward. Table 5.5 shows that the BIBF's inflows started to drop from the second quarter of 1995 onward and continued to decline dramatically from then on.

The greatest decline of inflows occurred in 1996, when they there was almost a 50% decline of inflows from US$8,147 in 1995 to US$4,089 million in 1996. Most importantly, 1996 was a year that highlighted the beginning of the decline of inflows, particularly during the third quarter, when inflows dropped by −92% to US$145 million and continued to decline through to the end of the year (see Table 5.5). However, the situation got worse a year later in 1997 when inflows declined significantly to a record low, turning to a negative of US$−136 million in the second quarter of 1997 for the first time in the history of the bank (see Table 5.5). Inflows continued to drop by the end of the year, the BIBF had suffered a great loss in inflows, declining from US$4,584 million in 1996 to US$−505 million in 1997 (see Table 5.5).

In order to understand the importance of the BIBF flows, we further analyse the share of banking capital flows to total net capital flows to Thailand during 1990–1996. According to Fig. 5.4, we see that prior to the establishment of the BIBF, foreign capital flows to banking sectors were relatively low with a percentage share of less than 20% of total net capital flows. When the BIBF first operated in 1993, capital flows to the banking sector began to increase rapidly. Consequently, banking share of total net capital flows increased dramatically from 35% in 1993 to 53% in 1995. However, capital to the BIBF declined of almost 50% in 1996, this in turn resulted in a drop of net inflows to the banking sector by 50% (from 53%

Table 5.5. BIBF's gross flows (quarterly)

		Inflows (US$ million)
1993	Q2	3,596
	Q3	2,077
	Q4	1, 982
1994	Q1	2,598
	Q2	2,252
	Q3	2,401
	Q4	2,836
1995	Q1	1,796
	Q2	2,916
	Q3	2,374
	Q4	1,056
1996	Q1	1,752
	Q2	1,895
	Q3	145
	Q4	792
1997	Q1	1,267
	Q2	−136
	Q3	−828
	Q4	−808

Source: The Bank of Thailand Yearly Report (2000).

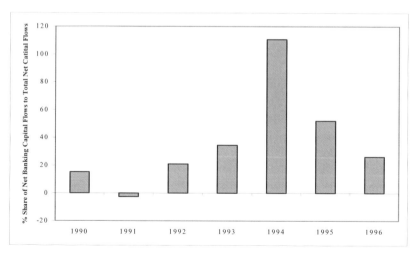

Fig. 5.4. Share of net banking capital inflows to total net capital inflows

Source: Authors' calculation from the Bank of Thailand Yearly Report (2000).

in 1995 to 26% in 1996). Clearly, the data indicates that the BIBF was an important factor in the increase of banking capital flows. The establishment of the BIBF together with capital controls deregulation encouraged foreign funds to shift from the non-bank sector (for instance FDI), to the banking sector.

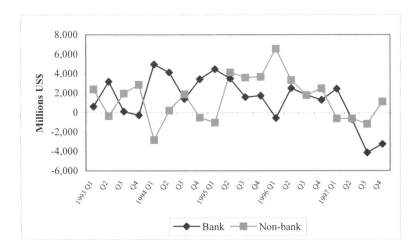

Fig. 5.5. Pattern of Thailand's net cross-border inflows (quarterly)

Source: The Bank of Thailand Yearly Report (2000).

In addition, we also found a crucial relationship between the net capital inflows to the bank and non-bank sector. That is, when capital flows to the banking sector (especially the BIBF) rose, those of investment as loan, portfolio investment and non-resident accounts in the non-bank sector declined and vice versa (see Fig. 5.5). In order to generate more understanding of this relationship, we develop a regression model to test whether inflows to the bank and non-bank sector share similar behaviour patterns, using net private capital inflows quarterly data from first quarter of 1993 to first quarter of 1997, the results exhibited in Table 5.6. According to the results, inflows to the banking sector measured by inflows to the non-bank sector explain 51%, where the R^2 value is 0.51 and is regarded as significant. The estimated equation of this model is shown below.

$$B = 3005.1 - 0.51\,NB \qquad\qquad (5.1)$$

where: B   =   inflows to banking sector
                NB   =   inflows to non-bank sector

Table 5.6. Summary output of regression model

Regression statistics			
Multiple R	0.72		
R square	0.51		
Adjusted R square	0.48		
Standard error	1187.7		
Observations	17		
	Coefficients	*Standard error*	*t Stat*
Intercept	3005.1	362.6	8.29
X variable 1	−0.51	0.13	−3.98

Source: Authors' calculation from the Bank of Thailand Yearly Report (2000).

Our statistical test shows that patterns of inflows to the bank and non-bank sector are significant and relationship of the two inflows are inversed to each other. As explained by the estimated model that given inflows to the non-bank sector equal to zero, inflows to the banking sector could be as high as US$3005.1 millions. On the other hand, if inflows to the non-bank sectors equal then the banking inflows will drop by 0.51 and could decline further when inflows to the non-bank sector continue to rise. In principle, this confirms that before 1997, net capital inflows to Thailand were biased toward one sector at a time either in the bank and non-bank sector which implied that inflows were indeed substitutable.

In terms of lending, the BIBF rolled out most of its funds within the domestic market for various investment purposes. It loaned funds for investment in agriculture, mining, public utilities, services, and personal consumption, with a majority of loans going to manufacturing, trade, banking and finance, and construction and real estate sector. For the BIBF's lending, further details are provided in the following chapter of this book.

5.3.2 Capital Flows to Non-bank Sector

Generally, capital flows to the non-bank sector can be classified into four major categories: FDI, loans, portfolio investment and non-resident account. Prior to financial liberalisation from 1980 to the early 1990s, net capital flows to the non-bank sector were high (see Table 5.2). From 1992 onward, these flows began to fluctuate and foreign capital flowed more to the banking sector, especially after the establishment of BIBF.

The aim of this section is to study in detail various aspects of capital flows to the non-bank sector: particularly the impact of capital control deregulation. The analysis includes capital flows of FDI, loans, portfolio investment and non-resident accounts.

5.3.2.1 Capital Flows as Foreign Direct Investment (FDI)

As reviewed in Chap. 3, FDI inflows had indeed helped to generate Thailand's economic growth in the late 1980s when the country was regarded as the fastest growing economy in the world with double-digit GDP growth during 1988–1990. With hope of duplicating the success, the government then liberalised its financial system and lifted various aspects of capital control, aiming to promote foreign investment into the country. From 1990, when the capital controls deregulation commenced, until 1997, Thailand had received FDI inflows totalling US$14,425 million.

Table 5.7. Gross FDI flows of Thailand, 1990–1997 (US$ millions)

	1990	1991	1992	1993	1994	1995	1996	1997
Inflows	3,030	3,700	5,340	2,638	2,455	3,051	3,941	5,141
Outflows	−488	−1,667	−3,189	−906	−1,129	−1,047	−1,670	−1,514
Net	2,542	2,033	2,151	1,732	1,326	2,004	2,271	3,627

Source: The Bank of Thailand Yearly Report (2000).

Table 5.7 demonstrates that FDI inflows grew rapidly from US$3,030 million in 1990 to a peak of US$5,340 million in 1992. Unfortunately, inflows declined by approximately 50% in 1993 and dropped further to a low of US$2,455 million 1994. However, more capital started to flow in again from 1995 onward, rising dramatically by 25%, 29% and 31% during 1995–1997.

Additionally, capital controls reform did not only lead to higher FDI inflows, but also increased capital outflows as well. Our study shows that large amount of capital flowed out of Thailand from the beginning of capital controls deregulation. Table 5.7 shows that FDI outflows rose rapidly in just a very short period of time, rising more than 240% from US$488 million in 1990 to US$1,667 million in 1991. A year later, they further increased by 90% to a peak of US$3,189 million in 1992. In 1993, capital outflows did slow down and dropped to US$906 million but then began increasing significantly again during 1994–1996. In order to understand how those FDI flows were used, we further analyse the pattern of foreign investment funds by sectors, during the period of 1990–1997. In general, foreign capital was distributed and invested for various purposes and in different sectors, namely, industry, financial institutions, trade, mining and quarrying, agriculture, services, investment in holding companies, and real estate and constructions. However, the majority of capital was invested in four sectors; industry, financial institutions, trade, and real estate and constructions.

Table 5.8. FDI investment by sector (US$ millions)

	1990	1991	1992	1993	1994	1995	1996	1997	Total
Industry	1,217	935	369	452	513	567	709	1,820	6,582
Financial institutions	180	286	281	65	7	26	72	110	1,027
Trade	508	303	281	219	341	446	545	1,033	3,676
Real estate & constructions	460	271	959	847	543	910	823	273	5,086

Source: Authors' calculation from the Bank of Thailand Yearly Report (2000).

According to Table 5.8, FDI flows had been varied and fluctuated in all sectors throughout the period. The industry sector experienced a massive decline in capital flows during the process of financial reform with a drop of –23% in 1991 to US$935 million and declined –61% to a low of US$369 million in 1992. From 1993 onward, FDI to the industry sector accelerated year after year and peaked at US$1,820 million in 1997. Inflows to the trade sector also declined in the early stages of the reform, dropping from US$508 million in 1990 to 303 million in 1991, 281 million in 1992 and 219 million in 1993. The inflows began to grow again from 1994 onward moving from US$341 million to 446 million in 1995, 545 million in 1996 and increasing sharply in 1997 to US$1,033 million. Similarly, the financial sector also experienced relatively low inflows during the financial reform process. The inflows declined from US$286 million in 1991 to 281 million in 1992, 65 million in 1993 and reached a low of 7 million in 1994. However, from 1995 onward the inflow grew consistently to US$26 million, 72 million and 110 million from 1995 to 1997, respectively.

Perhaps, the real estate and construction sector was a showcase for the impact of capital control reform. Inflows to the sector rose rapidly from the beginning of the reform in 1990. This sector marked the highest FDI flows between the period of 1990–1996 with a record total US$4,831million. This compares with US$4,762 million for industry, US$2,643 million for trade and US$997 million for financial institutions for the same period of time. Additionally, the inflows to the sector grew more significantly than the other sectors; especially in some years it reached the highest inflows from 1992 to 1996 (see Table 5.8). The inflows declined from US$460 million in 1990 to US$271 million in 1991, rose to a peak of US$959 million in 1992, slightly declined in 1993 and 1994. In 1995, capital flows to the sector rose significantly again by almost 70%, reaching US$910 million, declining slightly to US$823 million in 1996 and reaching a low US$273 million in 1997.

Most importantly, we observed that the pattern of FDI inflows changed rapidly, following the reform of capital controls. FDI flows to the real estate and construction sector increased tremendously in 1992 when it held the biggest share of net FDI inflows from then on. According to Fig. 5.6, the share of real estate and construction sector in net FDI flows rose rapidly from 18% in 1990 to 45% in 1992, peaking at 49% in 1993 and continued to dominate net FDI flows to the end of 1996. Vichyanond (1994, 2000a,b) argues that the significant change in FDI investment from 1992 onward was a result of the capital controls reform, which reduced operational guidelines to direct FDI investment. We argue that the rapid increase of FDI inflows in real estate and constructions was a direct impact of the second round of capital controls reform. The Thai government allowed the public to receive investment in foreign currency and they were free to invest for the first time on 1 May 1992. Consequently, the pattern of FDI inflows changed rapidly from investment in industry to investment in the real estate and construction sector.

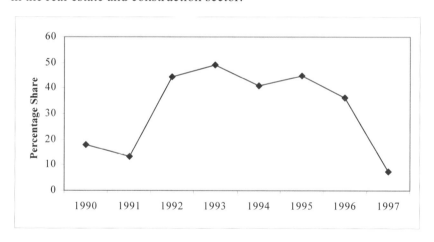

Fig. 5.6. Real estate and constructions' shares of net FDI inflows (yearly)

Source: Author's calculation from the Bank of Thailand Yearly Report (2000).

A study of Thailand's capital flows by Siksamat (1998) concluded that foreign capital in the form of FDI has been flowing to the industry and services sectors. She argues that there are at least two reasons for this.[4]

---

[4] Siksamat (1998) refers to service sector inflows as an investment mainly for transportation and travelling purposes.

First, these sectors are more profitable and have a higher rate of returns. Second, the government policy has encouraged foreign capital into these sectors. Finally, she concluded that the surge of inflows to the industry and services sectors has been associated with very strong growth in these sectors. However, evidence from our study suggests several differences with Siksamat (1998).

First, we found that most FDI inflows were not invested in industry and services; instead, the majority of them were invested in real estate from 1992 to 1996. Although, it is true that most of FDI inflows were invested in industry during the period of 1980–1990, based on the BOT's data we argue that inflows to services were not crucial, compared to other sectors such as trade. Furthermore, we argue that FDI inflows were more likely to be invested in the real estate and construction sector after capital controls deregulation commenced.

Second, if higher FDI inflows suggested a higher rate of profit, which encouraged more capital inflows, then we argue that the real estate and constructions sector definitely provided higher returns as it has greater FDI inflows, especially from 1992 to 1996.

Third, we disagree that the Thai government would aim to boost funds to only one sector, the industry and services sector; it would aim to increase funds to every sector, and particularly to the financial system as a whole. If the aim of capital controls deregulation was to encourage FDI inflows to the industry and services sector, then we regard this policy as a failure because the majority of funds were invested in the real estate sector. The real estate sector scored the highest FDI inflows during 1990–1996 with a total of US$4,813 million, compared to US$4,762 million for industry, US$2,643 million for trade and US$917 million for financial institutions.

Fourth, we argue that the surge of net FDI inflows was not associated with strong trade growth because most of the capital was invested in the real estate sector and produced no foreign income, which would be reflected in the country's trade growth.

Finally, we found that FDI inflows were not increasing as Siksamat (1998) suggested, but were stable when compared to other types of capital flows. A study by Alba et al. (1999) argues that the amendment of the Investment Promotion Act, to promote more foreign investment, was a crucial factor that kept FDI inflows stable, because, it allowed 100% foreign ownership of firms that exported all their products. Therefore, foreign capital kept coming in consistently to claim such benefit, making net FDI inflows stable throughout the 1990s. On the other hand, Hataiseree (1998) argues that net FDI inflows barely fluctuated because investor concerns were long-term oriented. In other words, this suggested that FDI inflows were the only long-term investment in the non-bank sector. And investments of this kind are not normally subjected to any liquidity or other short-term disturbances. Lastly, we argue that financial liberalisation by lifting controls of capital and allowing FDI inflows to be invested more freely, resulted in a change of pattern of FDI inflows from the real sector (industry and trade) to real estate and construction investments.

In terms of FDI outflows, we found that capital flowed out of the country immediately from the early stages of capital control deregulation. Similar to inflows, Thailand also found its FDI outflows fluctuated throughout the period. Despite the fluctuations in FDI outflows, overall capital controls deregulation resulted in significant increase in outflows, especially in the early stages of capital reforms.

5.3.2.2 The Loan Component of Capital Flows

In the light of the financial reform, the Thai government gradually removed capital controls on loans for the private sector from 1989 to early 1994. On 17 July 1989, the government allowed private agents to borrow from foreign countries as well as transfer capital outflows as dividend, interest and principle payments with no prior approval from the BOT. On 21 May 1990, the limit on loan inflows and outflows had been increased. On 1 April 1991, the private agents were permitted to transfer inflows and outflows as loans up to the amount of US$5 million without prior approval. Lastly, on 10 January 1994, the limit on international investments, including loans, increased again from US$5 million to US$10 million. Consequently, foreign loans to Thai private sector rose rapidly after the commencement of capital controls reform.

Table 5.9. Cross-border capital flows, loans (US$ millions)

	1988	1989	1990	1991	1992	1993	1994	1995	1996	1997
Inflows	1,792	4,021	7,282	13,618	14,547	18,225	17,507	21,418	24,920	17,980
Outflows	−1,604	−2,179	−2,747	−7,957	−11,701	−20,657	−23,352	−19,900	−19,469	−21,668
Net	188	1,842	4,535	5,661	2,846	−2,432	−5,845	1,518	5,451	−3,688

Source: The Bank of Thailand Yearly Report (2000).

Table 5.9 demonstrates capital flows as loans to Thailand from the beginning of capital controls reform in 1989 to the start of crisis in 1997. Foreign loans began to pour into Thailand once the capital controls started to ease. When financial agents were allowed to engage in foreign transactions for the first time in 1989, Thailand experienced a rapid increase of foreign loans from US$1,792 million in 1988 to US$4,021 million in 1989, an equivalent of a 124% increase. Loan inflows continued to increase rapidly, especially when the government further raised the limit on loan transactions in 1990 and 1991. This resulted in an immediate increase of loans by 81% from US$4,021 million in 1989 to US$7,282 million in 1990 and further increased by 87%, reaching US$13,618 million in 1991. Loans continued to flow into Thailand's private sector after capital control reforms were finalised in January 1994. From then on, loan inflows rose rapidly, reaching a peak of US$24,920 million in 1996. In 1997, the country experienced a drop of inflows by −29% from US$24,920 million in 1996 to US$17,860 million. Table 5.10 reveals that foreign funds started to slow down in the last quarter of 1996 and continued to decline dramatically afterward. Particularly in 1997, foreign loans dropped significantly from US$5,548 million in the first quarter to US$5,163 million, US$3,837 million and US$3,432 million in the second, third and last quarter, respectively.

On the outflows side, Thailand experienced a similar pattern of capital flows as those of inflows, that is, outflows of foreign loans rose rapidly after the capital controls reform took place. Outflows began from the beginning of the reforms, when financial agents were allowed to transfer additional capital without any prior approval. The immediate outcome was an increase in outflows by 189% from US$2,747 million in 1990 to US$7,957 million in 1991. Loan outflows continued to increase dramatically and finally outstripped inflows during 1993 and 1994 when outflows were as high as US$20,657 million and US$23,352 million, while inflows were only US$18,225 million and US$17,507 million, respectively (see Table 5.9). These significant increases in outflows led to negative net capital flows as loans in 1993 and 1994 (see Table 5.9). Despite slight decline in 1995 and 1996, loan outflows rose again by 11% with US$21,959 million in 1997. According to Table 5.10, outflows began to increase rapidly from the third quarter of 1996 and continued to increase dramatically till the early signs of financial crisis in mid 1997.

Table 5.10. Cross-border capital flows, loans (quarterly, US$ millions)

	1995				1996				1997			
	Q1	Q2	Q3	Q4	Q1	Q2	Q3	Q4	Q1	Q2	Q3	Q4
Inflows	5,307	4,584	5,545	6,019	5,288	6,434	6,651	6,547	5,548	5,163	3,837	3,432
Outflows	–5,655	–4,358	–5,241	–4,684	–4,334	–4,713	–4,970	–5,452	–5,614	–5,983	–4,742	–5,329
Net	–348	226	304	1,335	954	1,721	1,681	1,095	–66	–820	–905	–1,897

Source: The Bank of Thailand Yearly Report (2000).

Phongpaichit and Baker (2000) argue that a cause of high foreign loans to Thailand in the 1990s was economic success in the earlier decade, when the economy grew rapidly and a double digit GDP growth rate provided foreign lenders with a handsome profit. These impressive returns had indeed encouraged foreign lenders to lend more with the expectation that the Thai economy would continue expanding and generating more returns. However, results from our study show one important point, which indicates a close link between capital controls deregulation and foreign loans. We observed that loan inflows rose significantly in the early stages of deregulation in 1989. Additionally, we found that outflows also grew significantly, particularly in 1993 and 1994 when loan outflows were higher than inflows. Critically, loan outflows peaked at the final stage of the reform in 1994, when the limit of outflows was raised from US$5 million to US$10 millions. Indeed, the above highlights the fact that while capital controls deregulation increased loan inflows into Thailand it also increased outflows.

Siamwalla et al. (1999) reported that capital controls deregulation increased the country's external debt, because the reform gave the private sector the freedom to borrow from foreign sources. Foreign lenders were also permitted to lend more freely without interference from the BOT. Hence, they began to lend more to the Thai private sector, and most of those loans were short-term, as foreign lenders aimed at making quick returns. Unfortunately, a high level of loan inflows simply implied a high level of external debts that need to be repaid. We argue that the significant increase of foreign loans was due to control deregulation on loan outflows. The Thai government lifted most controls on capital outflows, particularly for loan repayment. These provided enough confidence for foreign investors that they would be able to transfer their returns from investments out of the country more easily, and were willing to lend as long as this confidence was maintained. Consequently, foreign loans began to come into the country as soon as the capital controls on outflows were first lifted in 1989 and rose more rapidly when the controls were further liberalised.

5.3.2.3 Capital Flows as Portfolio Investment

Capital controls reform provides new investment opportunities for foreign investors as never before. With the reform, investors were permitted to invest more freely and also allowed more freedom to engage in portfolio investment, which include buying and selling of equity, shares and related assets. Accordingly, portfolio investment in Thailand rose significantly. In our research, we focus on the movement of portfolio investment, which includes discussion of both capital inflows and outflows from 1990 to 1997. Capital controls deregulation helped boost portfolio investment in Thailand, with the country absorbing total inflows of US$77,464 million from 1990 to 1997. Results from Table 5.11 indicate that portfolio inflows started to increase significantly by 222% in 1993 from US$3,407 million in 1992 to US$10,959 million. Later, inflows slightly declined by 17% in 1994, however, they began to increase dramatically from 1995 onward. Particularly, large amount of inflows took place in the year the financial crisis occurred, when portfolio inflows increased nearly two folds to a peak of US$24,757 million (see Table 5.11). A study on the Thai financial crisis by the BOT (1998b) reported that a decline of inflows in 1994 was due to a rapid increase of outflows, particularly during the first and second quarter of the year. There is little doubt, this was a result of the full liberalisation of capital outflows, when the government raised the limit of outflow transactions in January 1994 (see Table 5.1). Furthermore, the BOT (1998b) found that portfolio inflows rose significantly, from the third quarter of 1997. In fact, portfolio inflows increased rapidly with the devaluation of baht in the second quarter which made portfolio investment relatively cheap, boosting inflows to a peak of US$24,757 million in 1997.

Table 5.11. Cross-border portfolio investment flows (US$ millions)

	1990	1991	1992	1993	1994	1995	1996	1997
Inflows	3,417	2,303	3,407	10,959	8,995	10,111	13,515	24,757
Outflows	−2,960	−2,140	−2,846	−6,107	−7,885	−6,691	−10,027	−20,207
Net	457	163	561	4,852	1,110	3,420	3,488	4,550

Source: The Bank of Thailand Yearly Report (2000).

Like inflows, portfolio outflows also increased rapidly after capital control reforms were completed. Outflows were varied and fluctuated during the early stage of capital controls reform from 1990 to 1991. However, portfolio outflows began to increase from 1991 onward, as a result of the BOT raising the limit of outflows in 1991 (see Table 5.11). In 1993, portfolio outflows increased more than two fold, reaching US$6,107 million. It continued to increase towards the end of the capital control reforms in 1994. However, outflows declined in 1995, which the BOT (1998b) reported was due to foreign investors reinvesting their returns back into portfolio projects. Hence, portfolio inflows increased while outflows declined. Soon afterward, portfolio outflows rose again by 50%, reaching US$10,027 million in 1996. A year later, Thailand experienced the highest outflows increasing by more than 100% to a record high of US$20,207 million (see Table 5.11).

In order to understand the pattern of portfolio investment, we further analyse the investment made to individual sectors during the period of 1990–1997. In general, portfolio investments were made for various purposes, with the majority of capital being invested in three sectors; industry, trade, and real estate and construction. Figure 5.7 shows that most portfolio inflows were relatively low during the early days of the reform. Investment to the industry sector declined significantly from US$812 million in 1990 to US$675 million and US$249 million in 1991 and 1992. After the reform was complete, investment to industry rose dramatically from US$299 million in 1993 to US$460 million, US$604 million, US$785 million and peaked at US$1,780 million, between 1994 to 1997 respectively. Likewise, investment to the trade sector also declined during the process of financial reform from US$397 million in 1990 to US$244 million, US$215 million and US$203 million during 1991 to 1993. From 1994 onwards, investment began to grow more consistently from US$280 million in 1994 to US$430 million in 1995 and US$575 million in 1996 and reached a high of US$943 million in 1997.

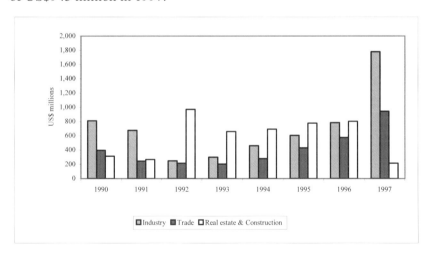

Fig. 5.7. Selected portfolio investment by sector (US$ millions)

Source: Reproduced based on data from the Bank of Thailand Yearly Report (2000).

Lastly, the real estate and construction sector was the biggest recipient of external investments. From the early years of reform in 1990 up to the pre-crisis year in 1996, portfolio investments to the real estate and construction sector accounted for a total of US$4,480 million, compared to US$3,884 million and US$2,344 million for industry and trade, respectively. In 1992, the sector received as high as US$970 million, which is a significant increase from US$314 million and US$264 million in 1990 and 1991. Towards the final stages of the capital controls reform in 1993, investment declined to US$657 million but began to increase steadily again from 1994 onward (see Table 5.11). In 1997, inflows to the real estate and construction sector dropped sharply from US$803 million in 1996 to US$215 million, equivalent to a decline by −73%. In essence, capital controls deregulation played a significant role in increasing portfolio investments, especially to the real estate and construction sector which scored the highest investment compared to other sectors during 1992–1996.

Alba et al. (1999) argued that an increase of portfolio investment in the 1990s was not a direct impact of financial liberalisation and capital controls deregulation. Instead, it was a consequence of the government policy to enhance portfolio investment via tax reductions for foreign investors who purchased Thai equity, shares and related assets in the mid 1980s. Our research found that portfolio investments were relatively low from the late 1980s to 1992 (see Table 5.2). As argued by Vajragupta and Vichyanond (1998), tax incentives were considered to be a major contributing factor in attracting portfolio investments because of the uncertainties of the Thai political and economic environment at that time. Furthermore, they found that portfolio investment rose rapidly after capital controls deregulation and soon dominated the non-bank sector as the biggest investment generator.

On the one hand, we agree that capital controls deregulation helped increase portfolio investments in Thailand, as the latter rose immediately after reforms took place. But on the other hand, we argue that portfolio investment did not hold the biggest share of net capital flows to the non-bank sector. We found that capital flows made by non-resident accounts in fact dominated the non-bank sector. Additionally, we observed that loan outflows also increased rapidly alongside the inflows. This could be due to the government's policy of raising the limit of outflows and allowing foreign investors to take funds out of the country more freely. In short, the evidence from our study demonstrates that capital control deregulation had a direct impact in increasing Thailand's portfolio investment.

Lastly, we argue that capital control deregulation resulted in a change of pattern in portfolio investments in Thailand when investments shifted from the tradeable to non-tradeable sectors. Our study revealed that portfolio investments moved from industry and trade sector to real estate and construction sector. Real estate and construction can be treated as non-tradeable sector, unlikely to generate foreign income, then capital control reforms had in fact helped direct more portfolio investment toward the non-tradeable rather than tradeable sector. Wiboonchutikula et al. (1999) suggest these kinds of investments to be short-term associated with high-risk, in turn making it easy to be manipulated by speculators. Thus, capital controls deregulation indeed exposed Thailand to speculative risk taken by foreign investors. Finally, we also found that over-investment in the non-tradeable sector (real estate and construction) became the norm, and foreign investors then shifted their investment back toward the tradeable sector (industry and trade) in 1997.

5.3.3.4 Capital Flows of the Non-resident Account

According to BOT (1998b), non-resident account measures the change in international transaction volumes invested into the Thai economy by both Thai resident abroad and foreign investors. Prior to the financial and capital reform of the 1990s, the non-resident account was strictly monitored by the government: capital outflows were especially subject to restrictions and always required pre-approval from the BOT before any transactions could be made. At the beginning of 1990s, the Thai government gradually removed controls on capital, allowing the non-resident account to bring more funds both in and out of the country. Consequently, capital flows made by this account escalated rapidly in a very short period of time.

Table 5.12. Gross flows of non-residential accounts (US$ millions, percentage)

	1990	1991	1992	1993	1994	1995	1996	1997
Inflows	1,571	11,961	22,627	76,963	231,264	416,410	810,397	710,349
(% change)	(33)	(661)	(89)	(240)	(200)	(80)	(95)	(−12)
Outflows	235	9,919	20,920	74,278	229,198	413,003	807,473	716,161
(% change)	(1,732)	(4,121)	(111)	(255)	(209)	(80)	(96)	(−11)
Net	1,336	2,042	1,707	2,685	2,066	3,407	2,924	−5,812

Source: Authors' calculation from the Bank of Thailand Yearly Report (2000).

In terms of inflows, the non-resident account was the highest generator with a total of US$2,228,542 million from 1990 to 1997. Inflows began to increase dramatically from the early part of the capital reform when they rose by 661% in 1991, increasing from US$1,571 million in 1990 to US$11,961 million. From 1992 onward, inflows made by non-residents continued to increase tremendously throughout the period. During the last stages of the reform in 1993, non-resident inflows grew by 240%, amounting to US$76,963 million. They grew by another 201% in 1994, 80% in

1995 and 95% with a record high of US$810,397 million in 1996 (see Table 5.12).

Although, the non-resident account outflows experienced the same pattern of growth as the inflows, we found that the growth rate of outflows rose more significantly as soon as the controls were lifted and continued to do so throughout the whole period. For instance, the non-resident outflows rose by 4,121% from US$235 million in 1990 to US$9,919 million in 1991. Afterward, outflows grew continuously at the rate of 111% in 1992 and by 255% by the end of 1993. The outflows growth rates were 255, 209, 82 and 96% during 1993–1996, compared to the growth of inflows by 240, 200, 80 and 95% for the same period of time (see Table 5.12). Despite a decline in 1997, the non-resident outflows were still considerably high at US$716,161 million, while inflows were US$710,349 million. As a result, the non-resident account deteriorated to a deficit for the first time of US$–5,812 million in 1997 (see Table 5.12).

Siamwalla et al. (1999) and Wiboonchutikula et al. (2000) pointed out that a pegged exchange rate regime is one of the reasons why non-resident account inflows rose so rapidly. Under the roof of financial liberalisation, the Thai government maintained the use of a basket of currencies, with the baht strictly tied to the US dollar. The aim was to attract more foreign capital by minimising exchange rate risk for investors. Accordingly, inflows poured into the non-resident account in a short period of time. We argue that the cause of high capital flows in the non-resident account was a result of capital control reform rather than the pegged exchange rate regime. If the currency regime was the cause, then inflows to the non-resident account should have been high long before financial liberalisation, as the baht had been pegged since World War II. According to our study, a significant increase in non-resident flows occurred only after financial liberalisation was implemented. This suggests that an increase in non-resident flows was not entirely due to pegged exchange rate regime, but due to capital controls deregulation.[5]

Limskul (2000) argues that financial reform and capital controls deregulation only encourage incoming and not out going funds and thus seem to have no impact on non-resident outflows. We argue that capital controls reform had a greater impact on increasing non-resident outflows. According to our findings, non-resident outflows rose dramatically from the early stage of capital controls reform. In most cases, non-resident outflows scored the highest outgoing capital from Thailand. Indeed, capital controls

---

[5] A detail discussion of impacts of Thailand's exchange rate will be carried out in the following chapter of this book.

deregulation not only increased non-resident inflows but also provided more opportunities for outflows.

Summing up, these high volumes of international transactions are signs of the impact of financial reform, which allowed Thailand to integrate with the global financial market. High level of non-resident flows could expose the country with potential risks of financial crisis if not managed properly.

5.4 Summary

This chapter presents a study on the issues of capital control and financial crises by focusing on the consequences of financial liberalisation. Some economists argue that control of both capital outflows and inflows is necessary for crisis prevention and resolution.[6] However, in the world of liberalising and emerging economies it is difficult for such controls to be put in practice effectively. In order to facilitate liberalisation, a country can abolish controls on both inflows and outflows just like Thailand which would affect the movement of capital.

In the banking sector, inflows to both commercial banks and particularly the BIBF escalated rapidly as a result of capital controls reform. In terms of commercial banks, we found that inflows increased rapidly in 1994, the year the reform was completed. However, we observed that a great deal of inflows came in via the BIBF as soon as it was established in 1993. Inflows to the BIBF were so great that it became the biggest inflow generator and dominated the banking sector (see Table 5.2, and Figs. 5.2 and 5.4). Moreover, we observed that capital flows to the banking sector were substitutable, that is, net flows to commercial banks declined dramatically when the BIBF came into operation. We argue that the reason behind a shift of foreign capital flows from the commercial banks was that investment through the BIBF provided significant tax advantages, thus, reducing the cost of foreign capital investment.

For the non-bank sector, we found that the control deregulation also encouraged more funds to this sector as soon as the controls were relaxed. Capital inflows for all four major types of investments (FDI, loans, portfolio investment and non-residential account) rose significantly from 1995 onward (see Table 5.2). In addition, we also found that the capital controls reform not only increased inflows but also provided opportunities for capital outflows to be made. Indeed, outflows from all four investment sectors rose immediately, following the capital controls reform (see Tables 5.7,

---

[6] See for example Krugman (1998b), Edwards (1999), Eichengreen (1999) and Chapter 2 of this book for discussion of this view.

5.9, 5.11 and 5.12). Additionally, we also found that the pattern of investment in Thailand changed after financial reform to the one where most net capital inflows were likely to be invested in the non-tradeable sector, especially short-term loan and portfolio investments. For instance, both FDI and portfolio inflows switched from industry and trade to real estate and construction investments. Our study shows that real estate and constructions projects received the highest proportion of inflows, compared to other investments such as FDI, trade and financial institutions (see Table 5.8, and Figs. 5.6 and 5.7). In other words, capital controls deregulation directed more foreign capital to be invested in a sector considered risky and unproductive.

In short, we conclude that financial liberalisation, by lifting capital controls, could cause economic disruption and instability in Thailand, as witnessed by a significant growth of net capital flows that occurred as soon as the liberalisation was implemented. This rapid increase of net capital flows could leave the country with numerous problems if they were not well managed. Evidence shows that majority of cross-border capital were invested in the unproductive sector, which indicate a lack of fund management and indeed prepared the ground for the crisis to occur.

6 Exchange Rate Policy and Its Consequences

6.1 Introduction

The choice of exchange rate policy is said to be inconclusive and there is no one particular policy that best suits one country (Hefeker 2000; Visser 2000). In most cases, the choice of exchange policy can be varied from one to another depending on the countries' economic policies and conditions (Collignon et al. 1999). In the case of Thailand, the fixed or pegged exchange rate had been in use since 1955. Later, this was replaced by a new system called a 'basket of currencies' to accommodate the financial liberalisation of the early 1990s. This chapter explores the consequences of Thailand's exchange policy in the light of financial liberalisation. It proceeds with a summary of the Purchasing Power Parity (PPP) concept which forms the core in explaining several theories of exchange rate determination. Section 6.3 provides brief background of Thailand's exchange rate policy. Section 6.4 studies the development of the basket of currencies and reviews the overall exchange rate of Thailand after this policy was implemented. Section 6.5 analyses the consequences of the basket of currencies on the Thai economy, focusing on trade growth and the increase in foreign funds to financial markets via the commercial banks and the BIBF. Additionally, in this section, we include a study of the lending behaviour of these two financial institutions by sector. Finally, Sect. 6.6 provides a summary of the chapter.

6.2 Exchange Rates and Their Determination

The exchange rate is the rate at which one currency can be exchanged for another in the exchange rate market. Now exchange rates regimes can be fixed or floating. Under floating exchange rates there is no government interference and the exchange rates are determined by the forces of demand and supply just like the price of any other commodity. Whereas under

fixed exchange rate regime, exchange rates are set by government decisions and maintained by government action as well.

In a free market, exchange rates are determined by the law of supply and
demand. The demand for a country's currency is derived from the demand
of foreigners for its export goods and services and for its assets, including
financial assets. The supply of a country's currency on the other hand
arises from its imports, and from foreign investment by its own citizens.
Now, to acquire some understanding of the reasons why some currencies
appreciate and some depreciate it is important to look into the factors
which move the demand and supply curves. Economists believe that the
determinants of the exchange rate movements are different in the long,
medium and the short run. One of the major theories of exchange rate determination in the long run is the PPP. In general terms PPP theory suggests that one should be able to buy the same bundle of commodities in
any country for the same amount of money. PPP theory is based on the law
of one price:

$$P^i = S\, P_f^i \tag{6.1}$$

where P^i is the price of good i in the home country, S is the exchange rate
defined as the amount of home currency required to buy one unit of foreign currency and P_f^i is the price of good i in the foreign country. Thus,
the price of good i in home country must equal its price in the foreign
country multiplied by the foreign exchange rate.

By rearranging (6.1) and summing all prices we get the absolute PPP
equation:

$$S = \frac{\sum_{i=0}^{n} \alpha^i P^i}{\sum_{i=0}^{n} \alpha^i P_f^i} \tag{6.2}$$

where α denotes the weights. It is assumed that same weights are used in
constructing each country's price level. The absolute PPP relates to the absolute price level of all goods traded in the two countries. When prices are
relatively stable, exchange rates will not fluctuate much, in times of rapidly
rising prices the exchange rates would vary with the relative prices. In such
a situation the concept of relative PPP becomes important. Taking natural
logarithms of (6.1) and considering just the overall price level we get:

$$S = \ln P - \ln P_f \tag{6.3}$$

The relative version of PPP simply states that, if relative prices double in the home country between a base period and any later period, the exchange rate will change by an equal proportion. Most economists believe that other factors besides relative price levels are important factors for exchange rate determination in the short run. However, purchasing power parity plays an important role. But in the medium run a country whose aggregate demand is growing faster than its trading partners will find its currency depreciating, as its imports are likely to be higher than its exports. While, economic activity is important in the medium run, interest rate differentials seem to be an important factor in determining the exchange rate in the short run. Thus, countries with high interest rates attract more capital than countries with low interest rates.

6.3 Overview of Thailand's Exchange Policy

Generally, the design and implementation of the exchange rate policy in Thailand rests in the hands of the BOT. Thailand adopted the fixed exchange rate regime by pegging the baht to the US dollar during 1955 to 1980.[1] The main objective of the BOT in pegging the currency was to maintain its stability, and thus attract foreign funds by minimising the risk for foreign investors. Also, this policy was aimed at ensuring confidence in the currency by providing a favourable environment for international trade and investment. During that period, the exchange rate stayed at the value of 20–21.50 baht to US$1 dollar.

Toward the end of 1978, the Thai government amended the *Currency Act B.E. 2501 (1958)* to allow Thailand to choose any exchange regime, which was consistent with the IMF's Agreement on Trade Openness forum. The new exchange system provided the BOT with more flexibility in adjusting the exchange rates to suit both domestic and international monetary conditions.

To accommodate the new exchange policy, the BOT established the Exchange Equalisation Fund (EEF) which was responsible for the exchange policy and also offered exchange rates to deal with commercial banks. The new system allowed Thai commercial Banks to participate in determining

---

[1] Ariff and Khalid (2000) argue that although the exchange rate policy depended on the Bank of Thailand (BOT), major decisions such as devaluation were subject to prior approval from the Ministry of Finance (MOF).

the exchange rates on a daily basis, called the 'daily fixing' system. It became effective on 1 November 1978.

Unfortunately, as argued by Christensen et al. (1997), the new policy caused widespread currency speculation in 1981 as the public lost confidence in the value of the baht and the rapid appreciation of the US dollar led to the deterioration of the balance of payments. Consequently, the EEF devalued the baht to the US dollar by 8.7%, from 21 baht per US dollar to 23 baht to the US dollar on 12 May 1981. Finally, the EEF also discontinued the 'daily fixing' and replaced it with a system which determined the exchange rates independently, without participation from the commercial banks, on 15 July 1981. In addition, during 1981–1984, the baht began to appreciate as a result of the appreciation of the US dollar against the yen.

In order to sustain the competitiveness of the country, the Thai government devalued the baht by approximately 15% in November 1984.[2] Moreover, the BOT officially declared a modification of the exchange system by replacing the pegging of the baht to the US dollar with a basket of currencies. The currencies in the basket included the US dollar, the yen, the mark, the pound sterling, the Hong Kong dollar, the Singapore dollar and the Malaysian ringgit. A study by Chaiyasoot (1995) revealed that the US dollar had the largest weight in the basket, although the authorities had never disclosed the official weightings. However, according to Ariff and Khalid (2000), the US dollar dominated the basket with a weight as high as 85%.

The objective of introducing such a basket consisted of two main aspects. First, the value of the baht determined by the EEF could be varied on a daily basis depending on the fluctuation of the value of major currencies in the basket of the currency. Second, the US dollar had to have the largest weight in the basket to ensure future economic expansion and development. Additionally, in conducting the new system the EEF set three main objectives, short term, medium term and long term. For the short term, the EEF needed to adjust the exchange rate according to the basket of currencies and day-to-day developments in the foreign exchange market abroad. For the medium term, the EEF needed to take into account the amount of foreign currency trading by commercial banks. For the long term, the EEF had to try to avoid any exchange rates disturbances that would impact on the export sector.

---

[2] See also Chaiyasoot (1995) for further discussion.

6.4 Development of Thailand's Basket of Currencies

Current account deficits in Thailand have been a major issue for a number of years. Particularly between 1981 and 1984, Thailand experienced an economic downturn as a result of the world oil shock.[3] In response, the Thai government implemented a stabilisation program aimed at reducing deficits, encouraging economic growth via an export-led growth policy and attracting foreign funds to service the economic growth. The main feature of the program was the establishment of the basket of currencies system in 1984. The Thai government clearly declared that the basket must provide the highest weight to the US dollar. In other words, the authorities believed that a closely tying the value of the baht to the US dollar would lead to a successful transition of the economy.

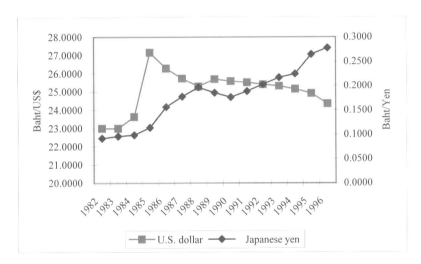

Fig. 6.1. Thailand's exchange rate compared to the US dollar and Yen

Source: Adapted from the Bank of Thailand Yearly, various issues.

According to Fig. 6.1, the baht stayed at approximately 23.20–23.60 to a dollar during 1981–1984. The use of the basket of currencies coupled with the depreciation of the US dollar against the yen led to the devaluation of the baht by 15% in 1985. This equated to a change from 23.60 to 27.20 baht to the US$1 dollar in 1985. From then, the US dollar continued to depreciate against the yen until the end of 1994, when the baht stayed around 25.20–25.30. In 1995, the US dollar appreciated sharply by 10% against

---

[3] See also Chap. 4 of this book for a detailed discussion of this view.

the Yen, which in turn caused the value of the baht to rise from 25.30 in 1994 to 24.90 to the US$1 dollar. At the same time, the yen depreciated sharply by almost 13% from 0.23 baht to 1 yen in 1994 to 0.26 in 1995. The value of the baht further appreciated against the yen in 1996.

Strictly tying the baht to the US dollar proved beneficial to the overall economy of Thailand during the many years it was implemented. However, the Thai economy grew dramatically after the use of the basket of currencies and a major devaluation of the baht by 15% in 1984. These contributed to Thailand's real economic growth in the late 1980s when the baht continued to devalue against the yen as a result of the depreciation of the US dollar (see Fig. 6.1). Consequently, these events made export products and investment in Thailand extremely attractive to the country's major trading partners, Japan in particular. Between 1987 and 1989, FDI from Japan alone reached a high of 45% share of total FDI compared to only 12% for the US.[4] More importantly, during this period the Thai economy escalated to double-digit growth rates, considered the highest in the world. Additionally, foreign reserves were increased and a long history of fiscal deficits was finally turned to surplus.[5]

With such an impressive economic performance, Thai authorities continued to tie the baht to the US dollar during the liberalisation of the 1990s, aiming for further development of the country's financial market and maintenance of its competitiveness.

6.5 Consequences of the Basket of Currencies

In the previous section, we analysed the features of the exchange rate in Thailand. In this section, we study the implications of the 'basket of currencies' exchange rate policy adopted to enhance trade growth, and generate economic growth and development by attracting funds from foreign sources. We first explore the impact of the exchange rate on international trade in Thailand. Then, we further study its effect on Thailand's financial sector.

6.5.1 Impacts of a Pegged Exchange Rate to Trade Growth

The Thai economy experienced economic slowdown with a major decline in exports and an increase in current account deficits, resulting from the oil

---

[4] A study by Suphachalasai (1995) asserts that during these periods FDI from Japan grew significantly while there was a huge decline for the US.

[5] See also Chap. 4 of the book for a more detailed discussion of this view.

shock and recession of the world economy in the early 1980s. For instance, Thai exports fluctuated from 1980 to 1983 and current account deficits grew almost threefold between 1982 and 1983. In order to solve these problems, the Thai government pegged the baht to a US dollar dominated basket of currencies in late 1984. Incidentally, the US dollar was depreciated against the yen in 1984, which also caused the bath to depreciate (see Fig. 6.1). This event had a direct impact in enhancing the competitiveness of Thailand's exports and investment from foreign countries.

Table 6.1. Current account summary (million baht)

	1980	1981	1982	1983	1984	1985	1986	1987	1988	1989
Exports	133,197	153,001	159,728	146,472	175,237	193,366	233,383	299,853	403,570	516,315
(% change)	23.5	14.9	4.4	−8.3	19.6	10.3	20.7	28.5	34.6	27.9
Imports	−188,686	−216,746	−196,616	−236,609	−245,155	−251,169	−241,358	−334,209	−513,113	−662,679
(% change)	23.4	14.9	−9.3	20.3	3.6	2.5	−3.9	38.5	53.5	29.1
Trade balance	−55,489	−63,745	−36,888	−90,137	−69,918	−57,803	−7,975	−34,356	−109,543	−146,364
Net income & transfers	15,576	9,733	12,999	22,952	19,328	19,751	20,883	34,472	60,252	75,220
Receipts	48,355	55,405	63,828	73,958	77,330	91,071	94,259	113,594	157,110	188,191
Payments	−32,779	−45,672	−50,829	−51,006	−58,002	−71,320	−73,376	−79,122	−96,858	−112,971
Current account balance	−39,913	−54,012	−23,889	−67,185	−50,590	−38,052	12,908	116	−49,291	−71,144

	1990	1991	1992	1993	1994	1995	1996	1997
Exports	589,813	725,630	824,644	921,433	1,118,049	1,381,660	1,378,902	1,789,833
(% change)	14.2	23.5	13.6	11.7	21.3	23.6	−0.2	29.8
Imports	−844,448	−958,831	−1,033,242	−1,166,595	−1,369,035	−1,763,587	−1,832,836	−1,924,281
(% change)	27.4	15.4	7.8	12.9	17.4	28.8	3.9	5.0
Trade balance	−254,635	−233,201	−208,598	−245,162	−250,986	−381,927	−453,934	−134,448
Net income & transfers	68,952	54,000	45,306	60,546	23,629	35,450	45,488	44,543
Receipts	223,830	252,557	300,201	365,195	404,982	494,355	573,456	641,347
Payments	−154,878	−198,557	−254,895	−304,649	−381,353	−458,905	−527,968	−596,804
Current account balance	−185,683	−179,201	−163,292	−184,616	−227,357	−346,477	−408,446	−89,905

Source: Adapted from the Bank of Thailand Yearly, various issues.

Table 6.1 presents a summary of Thailand's current account from 1980 to 1997. During 1980–1983, Thailand experienced economic instability when both imports and exports fluctuated and current account deficits rose almost threefold in 1983. From 1984 onward, Thai exports began to grow significantly, with export rising from 175,237 million baht in 1984 to

403,570 million baht in 1988. This highlighted the fact that Thailand benefited from the pegging of its currency to the US dollar, particularly when the dollar depreciated against the yen by 15% in 1984 and 1985 (see Fig. 6.1) that led to an immediate increase in exports. Table 6.2 shows that Thai exports to Japan grew significantly from 1984 onward, increasing almost threefold from 22,787 million baht in 1984 to 64,412 million in 1988. Interestingly, Thailand's exports to other regions also rose rapidly during the same period of time.

Table 6.2. Selected major destinations of Thailand's exports (million baht)

	1980	1981	1982	1983	1984	1985	1986	1987	1988	1989
Japan	20,098	21,704	21,947	22,087	22,787	25,828	33,134	44,590	64,412	87,996
US	16,834	19,794	20,257	21,895	30,102	38,016	42,219	55,727	80,865	111,938
EU	34,614	33,423	37,621	31,350	36,308	36,872	49,924	66,644	83,845	98,731
ASEAN	21,787	22,602	25,240	23,003	24,880	28,011	33,378	40,819	47,118	59,488

	1990	1991	1992	1993	1994	1995	1996
Japan	101,453	131,052	144,393	159,479	194,274	236,101	237,523
US	133,689	154,361	185,008	202,227	239,098	250,684	253,800
EU	126,963	150,121	161,350	155,979	169,385	212,202	225,979
ASEAN	67,068	85,921	104,826	145,209	200,570	268,192	264,397

Source: Adapted from the Bank of Thailand Yearly, various issues.

Falkus (1995) argues that the baht not only depreciated against the yen but also against other currencies that were not pegged to the US dollar, for example, the Swiss franc, German marc, British pound, and Singapore and Hong Kong dollar. Accordingly, Thailand's exports to the EU and ASEAN countries also grew after the depreciation in 1984. For instance, exports to the EU grew from 36,308 million baht in 1984 to 83,845 million baht in 1988, while exports to ASEAN countries rose from 24,880 million baht to 47,118 million baht during the same period of time (see Table 6.2). To our surprise, we observed that exports from Thailand to the US also rose significantly alongside with exports to others countries. In reality, this was unlikely to occur because the US dollar was depreciated at the time, leading to a decline in demand for imported products, including those from Thailand.

However, the reason why Thai exports to the US were still growing while the dollar depreciated seems to be a consequence of increased FDI from Japan.

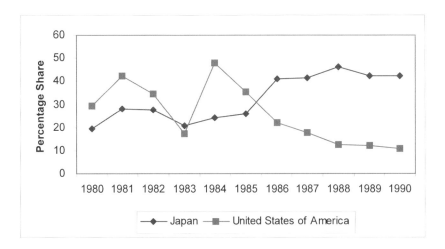

Fig. 6.2. Percentage share of FDI from the US and Japan

Source: Authors' calculations from the Bank of Thailand Yearly, various issues.

Figure 6.2 shows that the US was the major FDI investor in Thailand prior to the depreciation of the dollar in late 1984. When the dollar depreciated in value, FDI from the US began to decline sharply. Thus, the share of total FDI from the US to Thailand fell from 48% in 1984 to 35%, 28%, 18% and 13% between 1985 and 1988, respectively. In response to the baht depreciation, Japanese investors saw the benefit of relocating more of their production processes to Thailand in order to reduce production costs. Consequently, the percentage share of total FDI from Japan grew from 24% in 1984 to 26% in 1985. By 1986, FDI from Japan was as high as 41% of all FDI investment in Thailand. In fact, Japan became the biggest foreign investor in Thailand with a percentage share of total FDI of more that 40% to the end of the 1980s (see Fig. 6.2). This high level of investment from Japan highlights an important consequence of Japanese companies investing in the manufacturing sector in Thailand. This sector usually produced goods for the US export markets and thus, Thai exports to the US continued to grow in spite of the depreciation of the dollar (see Table 6.2).

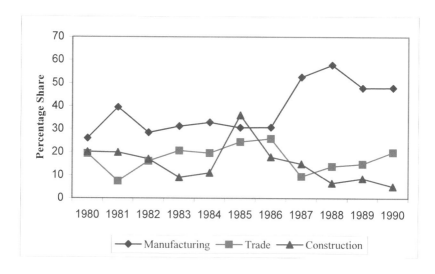

Fig. 6.3. Percentage share of FDI by sector

Source: Authors' calculations from the Bank of Thailand Yearly, various issues.

In general, foreign direct investment in Thailand was invested in various sectors, however, the bulk of the investments were made in the manufacturing, construction and trade sectors. According to Fig. 6.3, the pattern of FDI in Thailand was varied during the economic recession in the early 1980s. Investment in Thailand began to increase dramatically when the baht was depreciated against the yen in 1984. Furthermore, we observe that foreign investments trended toward the export-based sectors such as trade and particularly manufacturing rather than the constructions sector. FDI to constructions was relatively low and varied, and finally declined toward the end of the 1980s. On the other hand, investment in the trade sector rose steadily from 1984 until 1987, when its declined with a percentage share of total FDI dropped dramatically from 25% in 1986 to 9%. From 1987, it began to increase steadily again to a total FDI share of 20% in 1990.

A significant change of FDI occurred with investment in the manufacturing sector. Similar to the others, FDI to this sector also fluctuated during the early 1980s, but from 1982 to 1986, it enjoyed the largest proportion of total FDI investment in Thailand with an average of 30%, except in 1985 when the construction sector received the highest FDI investment with a total share of 35%. A study by Suphachalasai (1995) explained that this sudden increase of FDI in construction in 1985 was due to a rapid increase in construction projects required for producing exports, such as

infrastructure, processing plants and so on. FDI in the manufacturing sector rose rapidly in 1987 and continued to increase, reaching almost 60% of
total FDI in 1988. Our study suggests that the patterns of FDI from Japan
and investment in the manufacturing sector were more or less the same
(see Figs. 6.2 and 6.3). This seems to imply that the appreciation of the yen
against the baht (as a result of the basket of currency policy) attracted more
FDI from Japan in the manufacturing sector.

In the 1990s, the Thai economy had liberalised its financial system by
abolishing the interest rate ceiling, lifting controls on capital and establishing new offshore banking facilities (BIBF). However, the exchange rate
remained unchanged with the baht pegged to a US dollar dominated basket, which the government hope would duplicate the economic success and
high export growth of the 1980s. Our study earlier suggested that the success of Thai exports was a result of the depreciation of the baht relative to
the yen. Fortunately, the yen continued to appreciate against the US dollar
and the baht in the 1990s. The baht stayed at around 0.20–0.22 to 1 yen
during 1989–1994, while the baht to the US dollar varied from 25.30 to
25.60 for US$1 dollar (see Fig. 6.1). Consequently, Thailand's exports
continued to grow dramatically from 516,315 million baht in 1989 to a peak
of 1,381,660 million baht in 1995 (see Table 6.1). Moreover, in Chap. 5, we
found that FDI investments grew consistently throughout the same period
(see Table 5.2). The combination of these factors seemed to promise growth
for the Thai economy, particularly in the context of financial liberalisation,
which encourages trade and investment.

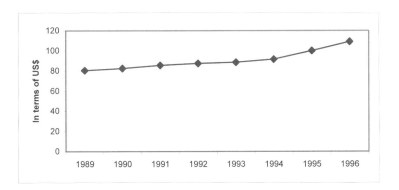

Fig. 6.4. Thailand's export price index (in terms of US$)

Source: Adapted from the Bank of Thailand Yearly, various issues.

Table 6.3. Thailand's exports by sector (million baht)

	1987	1988	1989	1990	1991	1992	1993	1994	1995	1996
Agriculture	83,259	106,432	118,508	100,003	109,279	123,809	101,472	120,606	159,398	159,843
Fisheries	18,163	20,826	28,538	32,507	43,704	48,795	55,643	67,490	71,804	63,511
Forestry	819	814	703	753	877	780	414	586	785	1,002
Mining	5,851	7,361	8,018	7,438	7,530	6,804	5,749	6,817	7,507	10,404
Manufacturing	188,031	264,007	354,154	440,396	553,186	634,387	747,395	912,608	1,128,216	1,125,444
Samples & unclassified goods	2,967	2,880	5,273	7,061	8,717	8,644	9,006	7,855	11,583	16,106
Re-Export	763	1,250	1,121	1,655	2,337	1,425	1,754	2,087	2,367	2,592
Total	299,853	403,570	516,315	589,813	725,630	824,644	921,433	1,118,049	1,381,660	1,378,902

Source: Adapted from the Bank of Thailand Yearly, various issues.

The story of Thailand's economic success finally came to an end in 1996 when the US dollar appreciated sharply against the yen in late 1995, which in turn caused the baht to appreciate because of its close peg to the US dollar. From Fig. 6.1, the value of baht rose 0.22 to 1 yen in 1994 to 0.26 and 0.28 in 1995 and 1996, respectively; while the baht to US dollar declined from 25.20 to 24.90 and 24.20 during the same period of time. The appreciation of the baht in this manner led to an increase in the prices of products and a decrease in the competitiveness of Thai exports. Figure 6.4 exhibits that Thai export price index rose significantly when the dollar appreciated in 1995 and 1996, from US$91.5 dollars in 1994 to US$100 dollars in 1995, and peaking at US$108.9 dollars in 1996. The immediate outcome of rising export prices was a decline in Thai exports. Table 6.3 shows that all three major exports of Thailand experienced a decline in growth in 1995. For instance, fisheries dropped from 71,804 million baht in 1995 to 63,511 million baht in 1996, manufacturing also declined from 1,128,216 million baht to 1,125,444 million baht, while agriculture exports experienced a 0% export growth during the same period time. A significant decline in growth of these three major exports contributed to a negative growth of by −2% for the first time in history with a drop from 1,381,660 million baht in 1995 to 1,378,902 million baht in 1996 (see Tables 6.1 and 6.3).

Furthermore, we found that the appreciation of the US dollar against the yen was responsible for a decline in Thai exports to Japan. Table 6.2 revealed that the growth of Thailand's exports to Japan came to a sudden stop when the yen began to depreciate. Exports to Japan experienced a slowdown of 0% growth with total exports of 236,101 million baht and 237,523 million baht in 1995 and 1996 respectively. Additionally, we observed that the appreciation of the baht did not only affect exports to the Japanese market but also to Asian export markets, with Thai exports declining by −1.5% from 268,192 million baht in 1995 to 264,197 million baht in 1996 (see Table 6.2).

A study by Warr (1997) concluded that the single most important factor contributing to the decline of the Thai economy in 1996 was the rise of real wages, averaging of 8% per year during 1994–1996. According to Warr, the constant increase of real wages in Thailand resulted in increasing costs of exports, thus reducing their competitiveness as a whole, which led to a sudden decline of exports in 1996. Falkus (1999) attacks this argument asserting that Warr's study does not clearly show how the increase in real wages contributed to a slowdown of Thai exports, eventually leading to the financial crisis. He argues that there are at least two initial reasons why he disagrees with Warr (1997). First, the data presented in Warr (1997) was not complete and only exhibits the change of Thailand's wages up to 1994 with the critical years of 1995 and 1996 omitted. Secondly, the data is based on average rather than actual wages, thus the trend of wages may not be accurate. He argues that the increase of real wages by 8% seems to imply that all Thai labourers who were paid the minimum wage would have received an 8% increase. But when compared to the consumer price index (CPI) at the time, the real wages were declining. Falkus found that the basic CPI at the time rose by at least 12%, while the price of food alone rose by 17.7%. Thus, a rise in wages of 8% with an accompanied increase in the CPI by 12% meant a decline of real wages by at least 4%. Accordingly, he concluded that the decline of Thai exports did not result from increasing real wages.

Our data of real wages and CPI shown in Fig. 6.5 are interesting to both arguments made by Warr (1997) and Falkus (1999). According to the figure, real wages in Thailand increased about 8% during 1994–1996 as suggested by Warr (1997). However, we query whether or not the increasing of real wages was the factor affecting Thai exports. The figure shows that wages in Thailand in the early 1990s rose more significantly at rates between 11 and 15% during 1990–1992, while there was an 8% increase from 1994–1996. As far as wages are concerned, we argue that a slowdown of Thai exports due to high wages is more likely to happen in the early 1990s rather than 1996. But exports continued to grow in the early 1990s in spite of high wage growth hence, the relative low growth of 8% is unlikely to be the major cause of the decline in Thai exports that weakened the economy in 1996. According to Falkus (1999), real wages in Thailand declined by 4% when compared to the CPI during 1994–1996. However, we found that the CPI of Thailand increased by only 5% during 1994–1996 rather than 12% as he reported (see Fig. 6.5). Our study shows that real wages increased even compared to the CPI, suggesting contradicting conclusions drawn by Falkus (1999).

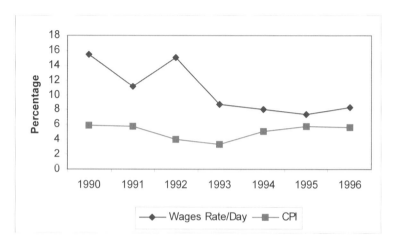

Fig. 6.5. Growth of money wages and CPI in Thailand (percentage)

Source: Authors' calculations from the Bank of Thailand Yearly, various issues.

In addition, other studies such as BOT (1998b) and Vajragupta and Vichyanond (1998) argue there was another factor that may have contributed to a decline in Thailand's exports, and that is the opening up of the Chinese financial market. According to Haihong (2000), China had undertaken a series of economic and financial reforms in the 1990s, including the devaluation of its currency by more than 50% from 5.7 yuan to 8.7 yuan in 1994. They argue that as a potential competitor of Thailand, the devaluation of the yuan made China's exports appear more attractive at a time when the baht was becoming more expensive with the appreciation of the US dollar. Therefore, Thailand lost much of its exports to China, which caused the recession in the Thai economy in 1996. Corsetti et al. (1998) argue the hypothesis that the devaluation of the Chinese currency pressurised Thailand is still a matter of debate, which needs to be explored in greater detail. Liu et al. (1998) and Fernald et al. (1998) argue that more than 80% of Chinese export transactions were already settled at the swap market rate before the devaluation commenced, so that the official exchange rate devaluation influenced only about 20% of the foreign exchange transactions. Furthermore, we argue that if the slowdown in Thai exports was due to the devaluation of the yuan, then the decline should have been witnessed from 1994 onward, but our study found that the slow-down in fact occurred in 1996. Thus, we argue that the devaluation of the yuan had little impact on the decline in Thai exports in 1996.

The arguments we make above do not intend to deny the importance of rising wages in slowing down Thai exports while causing weakness in the economy in 1996. Instead, we attempt to highlight the fact that the principle factor behind the slow down of Thai exports seems to lie with the depreciation of the yen in 1995, making Thai exports uncompetitive. The sudden decline in exports to Thailand's major trading partners, Japan, caused economic weakness and recession in 1996. In summary, we argue that Thailand's pegged exchange rate made Thai products very attractive as the price of Thai products were stable in relation to the US dollar. We found that Thailand's trade continued to grow from mid-1980s to early 1990s with the majority of exports from the manufacturing sector (see Figs. 6.2 and 6.3). The US dollar depreciating against the yen from 1984 enhanced the competitiveness of Thai exports, particularly to the Japanese market. Accordingly, Thai exports grew rapidly after the yen appreciated in 1984 and continued to grow until 1994 as the US dollar remained depreciated. Unfortunately, the golden years did not last long, when according to our study, the yen began to lose its value against the US dollar by almost 30% from mid-1995 onward. As a result, the Thai baht also appreciated falling from approximately 0.22 yen in 1995 to 0.28 yen to 1 baht by the end of 1996 (see Fig. 6.1) because the baht was pegged to a basket of currencies dominated by the US dollar. This event caused the exports indices in term of US dollar to rise significantly (see Fig. 6.4). Consequently, Thailand lost its competitiveness and exports suddenly dropped in 1996, which widened the current account deficit and led to the crisis in 1997 (see Table 6.1).

6.5.2 Surge in Funds to Thailand's Financial Market

Another main objective of Thailand's pegged exchange rate besides encouraging trade was to inject more foreign capital into the financial market. In previous chapters, we found that the Thai economy experienced an extraordinary surge in net capital flows as a result of financial and capital control reform. According to Hataiseree (1998) and the Bank of Thailand (BOT) (2001), the majority of inflows were located in the private rather than public sector, especially in the financial market via commercial banks and the BIBF. Thus, in this section, we analyse the origin of capital flows in relation to the basket of currencies, focusing on commercial banks and the BIBF. In addition, we also include the analysis of how these institutions distributed their funds to domestic users by sector.

6.5.2.1 Commercial Banks' Source of Funds

In the previous section, we found that the exchange rate pegged to a US dominated basket of currencies helped the Thai economy expand rapidly, especially when the baht depreciated against the yen. As a result, the Thai economy performed well with high levels of exports growth averaging almost 20% since the basket of currencies was first introduced in 1984 (see Table 6.1). With continuous economic expansion particularly from 1986 onward (when exports grew more at than 20%), there was an urgent need to mobilise more foreign funds for economic development, because domestic deposits had not expanded in the line with borrowing needs (Vichyanond 1994). Accordingly, the Bank of Thailand (BOT) decided to liberalise the interest rate by gradually lifting the ceiling on both long-term and short-term deposits during 1989–1992.

Table 6.4. Chronology of interest rate reform in Thailand

	Interest rate deregulation
02 June 1989	Interest rate ceiling on commercial banks' long-term deposits is abolished
16 March 1990	Interest rate ceiling on short-term deposits is lifted
26 June 1992	Interest ceilings on non-bank financial institutions' deposit and lending are removed
	Ceilings on commercial banks' lending are also removed

Source: Adapted from the Bank of Thailand Yearly, various issues.

Table 6.4 exhibits the major actions taken by the BOT in reforming interest rates during 1989–1992. On 2 June 1989, the BOT removed the ceiling on term deposits with maturity greater than one year so as to accelerate the process of savings mobilisation. On 16 March 1990, the ceiling on deposits with maturity less than one year was lifted. Two years later, the interest rate ceilings on finance companies' borrowings, deposits and, lending and on commercial banks' lending were terminated on 26 June 1992. This effectively completed the liberalisation of all types of interest rates.

Table 6.5 shows that an immediate impact of interest rate deregulation was to raise interest rates by almost 2%, from 8.66% in 1988 to 10.60% when the ceiling on long-term deposits was lifted in 1989. The market interest rate continued to rise by more that 2% when the ceiling on short-term deposits was abolished in 1990. The increase of Thailand's interest rate was so rapid after these ceilings were removed that it widened the gap between domestic and international rates. In 1990, the market rate of Thailand was

4.77% higher than the rate in the US market, and 5.63% higher than the Japanese rate. Thereafter, the gap between the domestic and international rate continue to widen by a minimum of 3% through to the end of 1996.

Table 6.5. Thailand and international market interest rates

	1988	1989	1990	1991	1992	1993	1994	1995	1996
Thailand	8.66	10.60	12.87	11.15	6.93	6.54	7.25	10.96	9.23
United States	7.57	9.22	8.10	5.69	3.52	3.02	4.20	5.84	5.3
Japan	6.46	8.87	7.24	7.46	4.58	3.06	2.20	1.21	0.47
Thai & US differentials	1.09	1.38	4.77	5.46	3.41	3.52	3.05	5.12	3.93
Thai & Japan differentials	2.2	1.73	5.63	3.69	2.35	3.48	5.05	9.75	8.76

Source: IMF Financial Statistics, CD-ROM.

Table 6.6. Commercial banks' sources of funds (million baht)

	1989	1990	1991	1992	1993	1994	1995	1996
Deposits	1,187	1,426.0	1,730.6	2,010.6	2,397.3	2,710.6	3,203.6	3,543.3
Borrowing from the BOT	41.2	42.4	37.6	36.3	21.2	24.9	36.2	53.3
Foreign borrowing	85.3	109.8	123.9	167.6	352.4	780.0	1,164.1	1,349.3
Bor. from other fin. inst.	14.9	15.4	10.4	14.9	20.0	55.9	86.3	85.7
Capital accounts	83.1	111.3	143.5	170.2	222.4	306.4	394.9	509.9
Other liabilities	63.3	84.7	101.6	128.5	158.3	158.2	150.1	113.9
Total	1,406.5	1,789.6	2,147.6	2,528.1	3,171.6	4,036.0	5,035.2	5,655.4

Source: Adapted from the Bank of Thailand Yearly, various issues.

The interest rate liberalisation had a significant role in encouraging foreign funds to the commercial banks. Table 6.6 shows that the total funds of commercial banks rose rapidly when the interest rate reform took place in 1989. For instance, the total funds from 1,406 million baht in 1989 to 2,528 million baht when the interest rate ceilings were completely lifted in 1992. They continued to grow after the ceilings were terminated, rising from 3,171 million baht in 1993 to a peak of 5,655 million baht in 1996.

In general, the funds to the commercial banks were derived from various sources, however, most of them came in as deposits and borrowing domestically (the BOT) and internationally (foreign banks and financial institutions). The deposits of the commercial banks grew steadily following the interest rate liberalisation in 1989 (see Table 6.6). In terms of foreign borrowing, the removal of long-term interest rates had little impact in attracting funds from foreign sources, which only increased from 85.3 million baht in 1989 to 109 million baht in 1990. Interestingly, foreign borrowing rose rapidly after the ceiling on short-term interest rates was removed in 1990 and grew even more significantly following the complete interest rate liberalisation in 1992. For instance, foreign borrowing of the commercial banks rose more than 100% for three consecutive years during 1992–1994. Foreign investors loaned more heavily to the commercial banks when the gap between domestic and international interest rates widened in 1995 and 1996. For example, the differential between the Thai and US rate was more than 5% in 1995, while the gap with Japan was even wider with a difference of almost 10% during the same year (see Table 6.5). Consequently, foreign borrowing of the commercial banks reached 1 billion baht in 1995 and peaked at 1.3 billion baht in 1996 (see Table 6.6). The pegged exchange rate provided foreign investors with confidence against any exchange rate risks that may have occurred. This coupled with a higher domestic interest rate made lending to the commercial banks look very attractive, and resulted in rapid increase in funds in form of deposits and particularly borrowing from foreign sources willing to lend as long as the commercial banks were willing to borrow.

In terms of lending, Thai commercial banks distributed most of their incoming funds as loans within the domestic market. Here, we analyse the commercial banks lending by sector for the period of 1989–1996 (see Table 6.7). According to the table, commercial banks' loans are classified into nine investment purposes with the majority of loans extended to only five of them; trade, manufacturing, construction and real estate, personal consumption, and banking and finance.

Table 6.7 shows that commercial banks' loans grew rapidly from the early stage of financial liberalisation. Within a 7-year period, total loans rose rapidly from 1.1 billion baht in 1989 to 2.7 billion baht in 1993 and a peak of 4.8 billion baht in 1996. The recipients of these loans can be delineated into two main sectors, namely, the tradeable and non-tradeable sector.

For the tradeable sector, commercial banks loaned heavily to investment for trade and manufacturing purposes, which accounted for more than 50% of total loans for the sector. High lending in such a manner seems to enhance economic growth, as most trade and manufacturing products are produced for export and generate foreign income. BOT (1998b) argued that high lending to trade and manufacturing did not guarantee foreign income in all cases. They further asserted that a large proportion of these loans to trade and manufacturing investments were used for basic requirements of the production process; such as infrastructure, production sites, machinery and so on. In fact, all these investments generally represent costs of production yet to generate income. Most importantly, the majority of Thailand's trade and manufacturing export products were produced by and for the Japanese market. Later, these investments suffered as Japanese demand for Thai products declined when the baht appreciated against the yen in 1995. Consequently, the manufacturers and traders found it difficult to repay loans, and many defaulted causing a problem of loan losses to the commercial banks. This highlights the fact that high lending in the tradeable sector does not always produce economic growth, particularly in the case of Thailand.

Table 6.7. Lending by commercial banks by sector (million baht)

	1989	1990	1991	1992	1993	1994	1995	1996
Tradeable	710,061	905,793	1,07,3,607	1,240,649	1,514,697	1,914,088	2,360,747	2,714,731
Agriculture	73,558	99,358	126,098	135,494	148,959	152,280	158,939	164,019
Mining	5,203	8,205	8,248	12,054	16,665	15,692	24,985	24,476
Manufacturing	290,519	375,108	457,617	517,914	647,286	836,234	1,097,337	1,313,546
Trade	340,781	423,122	481,644	575,187	701,787	909,882	1,079,486	1,212,690
Non-tradeable	415,973	588,274	733,952	941,711	1,180,254	1,543,620	1,890,078	2,140,956
Construction & real estate	143,615	237,021	279,235	339,497	407,521	506,199	586,035	662,441
Financial institutions	66,012	76,171	99,267	132,835	163,010	245,151	339,204	345,330
Public utilities	20,443	25,084	30,097	40,882	61,322	86,345	108,106	142,751
Personal consumptions	121,736	158,617	202,136	269,394	339,675	437,475	523,437	612,595
Services	64,167	91,381	123,217	159,103	208,726	268,450	333,296	377,839
Total	1,126,034	1,494,067	1,807,559	2,182,360	2,694,951	3,457,708	4,250,825	4,855,687

Source: Adapted from the Bank of Thailand Yearly, various issues.

In terms of the non-tradeable sector, commercial banks loaned mostly for investment in real estate and construction, financial institutions and personal consumption. Real estate and consumption projects received the highest proportion of loans from the commercial banks (see Table 6.7). An investment of this kind is regarded as risky and unlikely to generate returns. Gab (2000) argues that commercial bank lending to real estate and construction was not significant enough to cause the loan losses that led to the banks collapse. We do not deny that loans for these investment projects were relatively low, compared to loans for trade and manufacturing. However, we argue that commercial bank loans to real estate and construction projects were extremely crucial. Figure 6.6 reveals that commercial banks held the highest share of total loans to real estate and construction, which amounted to more than 60% throughout the period of 1991 and 1996. Thus, we argue that commercial bank loans to these investments involved high-risk investment and created excessive lending.

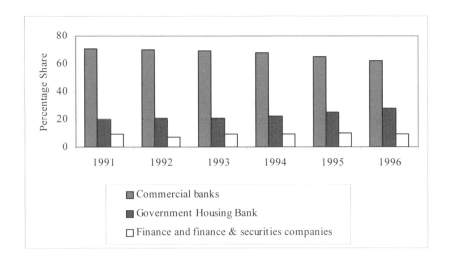

Fig. 6.6. Percentage share of major lending for real estate and construction

Source: Authors' calculations from the Bank of Thailand Yearly, various issues.

Commercial banks not only lend to private businesses, but also extended loans to other domestic financial institutions. In reality, this seems unlikely to occur under the financial liberalisation umbrella, particularly at a time when domestic interest rates were high and the exchange rate was pegged. One could think that financial institutions would have been better off borrowing directly from foreign sources and lending out to the domestic market. However, before liberalisation this was not the case for Thai financial institutions due to creditability constraints on borrowing. According to the BOT (1998b), financial liberalisation provided opportunities for financial institutions to be established more easily as entry requirements were gradually relaxed during the process of liberalisation in 1990 to 1993. Thus, the number of private financial institutions grew as high as 93 institutions by the end of 1993. As new entrants, these institutions found it hard to borrow in the overseas market, relying on the commercial banks in the domestic market. Additionally, Alba et al. (1999) argue that high commercial bank lending to financial institutions occurred because most of these institutions were under the commercial banks' control. They believed that there were at least two reasons why the operation of financial institutions was control led by the commercial banks. First, Thai financial laws do not allow any single shareholder to hold more than a 10% share in a financial institution. Secondly, the commercial banks were urged to have control over financial institutions because these institutions were permitted to provide specialised services (such as securities business) or loans to high-risk finance consumers (such as personal and car loans).

Commercial bank loans for personal consumption was usually rolled out for private housing and traveling purposes. Personal loans grew dramatically from the early 1990s as a result of the capital control deregulation in May 1991, which allowed commercial banks to provide loans to the public more freely (as we discussed in Chap. 5). However, we observed that personal consumption loans rose more significantly from 1994 onward. For instance, they grew from 269,394 million baht in 1992 to 437,475 million baht in 1994, peaking at 612,595 million baht in 1996. The reason for such an increase seems to lie with the increase on the limit of baht travelers could take out of Thailand from 250,000 to 500,000 million baht in July 1991 (see Chap. 5). Overall, commercial banks were enticed to lend at high interest rates as long as local consumers were willing to borrow for personal consumption purposes at the existing high rates. Again, this indicates a problem of excessive lending to high-risk consumers.

In all, we found that the basket of currencies helped enhance funds to the commercial banks. The pegged exchange rate together with a higher domestic interest rate made investment in Thailand's commercial banks very attractive. Accordingly, foreign investors poured more funds into the commercial banks usually in the form of a deposit or borrowing. Both deposits and foreign borrowing increased dramatically when the interest rate ceiling was first lifted in 1989. Foreign investments rose significantly after the ceiling on short-term rates was lifted in 1990 and grew even further following the completion of interest rate deregulation in 1992. In terms of lending, the commercial banks rolled out loans to both the tradeable and non-tradeable sector. For the tradeable sector, commercial banks loaned heavily to trading and manufacturing sectors. These kinds of investment seemed to promise high returns as long as Thai exports performed well. Unfortunately, the trade and manufacturing sectors experienced a major decline in exports, especially to the Japanese market, as a result of the US dollar appreciation. This affected the ability of these sectors to pay back already high loans, which led to huge loan losses for the commercial banks. On the non-tradeable front, our study shows that commercial banks lent mostly to investment in real estate and construction, financial institutions and personal consumption projects. These investments usually generate no foreign earnings and are associated with a high risk of loan loss. Thus, all these factors in one way or another contribute to the collapse of the commercial banks in 1996.

Apart from foreign borrowing, Thai commercial banks also borrowed domestically from the BOT, financial institutions and other sources. We observed that most borrowing grew significantly after financial liberalisation was completed in 1993. Although borrowings from the BOT and financial institutions were not significant, they increased at a rapid pace between 1990 and 1994, and from 1995 onward they began to increase more significantly. In short, a pegged exchange rate proved helpful in attracting funds to the commercial banks from a variety of sources, with total funds increasing rapidly. We argue that the majority of commercial bank funds were in the form of deposits from both domestic and international investors. Lastly, we found that most funds from foreign sources continued to increase while the baht was stable.

6.5.2.2 The BIBF's Sources of Funds

In the era of financial liberalisation, the Thai government had deregulated various rules and regulations once imposed on the financial sector. This was to ensure flexibility in mobilising funds in Thailand's banking sector. As we discussed earlier, the Thai government enhanced foreign funds to the commercial banks by lifting all interest rate ceilings on deposits, which increased the differential between domestic and international interest rates, making deposits and investment in these banks very attractive. However, the most important change undertaken was the establishment of the offshore bank, called the 'BIBF', aimed at attracting foreign funds to service the development of the economy and also to promote Thailand as the financial centre of the region. To do so, the government granted the BIBF several tax privileges.

Table 6.8. Tax privileges of the BIBF

	Normal	BIBF
Corporate income tax	30%	10%
Business turnover tax	3.3%	0%
Interest income withholding tax	10%	0%
Stamp duties	2%	0%
Short-term reserve requirement	7%	0%

Source: BOT (1996).

Table 6.8 shows the reduced taxes of the BIBF over other banking and the financial institutions. Among the most important are the reduction of corporate income tax from 30 to 10% and the exemption of several sales taxes, such as turnover and stamp duties. Importantly cross border borrowings were also not subject to withholding taxes. Finally, unlike others, short-term deposits via the BIBF were not subject to the 7% cash reserve requirements, thus favouring a short-term maturity structure. Clearly, this suggests that the government was encouraging short-term foreign funds via the BIBF. In Chap. 5, we found that most foreign capital flows shifted from other investments to the BIBF since it provided several tax benefits.

Accordingly, there was an immediate influx of capital flows to the BIBF when it began operation. In this section, we further analyse the sources of the BIBF's funds and how these foreign funds were distributed in the domestic market. In general, the BIBF's funds derived from three main sources, the BOT, branches of foreign banks operating in Thailand and direct funds from foreign banks abroad.

Table 6.9 demonstrates that most of the BIBF's funds in its first year of operation were derived from the BOT as major lender with 748,852 million baht. Thereafter, the BOT continued to raise more funds for the BIBF with a total of 1,021,923 and 1,309,426 million baht in 1995 and 1996, respectively. Apart from domestic funds, the BIBF also received funds from two other external sources: branches of foreign banks in Thailand and direct funds from foreign banks abroad. Funds from branches of foreign banks grew steadily from 297,412 million baht in 1994 to 470,372 million baht and 823,917 million baht in 1995 and 1996. However, direct funds from foreign banks rose much more rapidly within a short period of time. For instance, funds from foreign banks rose more that twofold within six months from 36,200 million baht in the March quarter to 257,822 million baht in December 1994. More importantly, total funds rose by almost fourfold from 535,815 million baht in 1994 to 2,288,896 million baht in 1995 and peaked at 2,913,082 million baht in 1996. Furthermore, this rapid increase of funds meant that offshore foreign banks became the BIBF's main source of funds overtaking the BOT, and other sources in 1995.

According to Fig. 6.7, the pattern of funds to the BIBF changed significantly within just a very short period time. In the first year, the BIBF received most of its funds domestically from the BOT with a proportion of 47% of total funds. Soon after, funds from the BOT relatively to other sources declined dramatically with a share of 27 and 25% in 1995 and 1996, respectively. Moreover, the evidence suggests that the BIBF came to rely heavily on funds coming directly from foreign sources. According to the figure, these foreign banks began with small contributions (compared to the BOT) in the first year of the BIBF's operation, which amounted to 34% of total funds in 1994. Funds from foreign banks operating in Thailand were considerably stable with a share of between 19 and 16% during 1994–1996. Lastly, since investment through the BIBF provide several tax benefits and was not subject to short-term reserve requirements, foreign investors poured huge amount of funds into the BIBF. Consequently, direct funds from foreign banks rose rapidly and soon became the BIBF's main source of funds with a percentage share of 59 and 54% in 1995 and 1996, respectively.

Table 6.9. BIBF's source of funds (million baht)

	BOT	Foreign banks in Thailand	Foreign banks
Mar 94	168,633	53,217	37,200
Jun 94	179,948	70,141	81,788
Sep 94	188,857	82,411	159,005
Dec 94	211,414	91,643	257,822
Total funds	748,852	297,412	535,815
Mar 95	224,293	87,401	353,811
Jun 95	247,694	114,816	445,578
Sep 95	274,424	131,446	687,490
Dec 95	275,512	136,709	802,017
Total funds	1,021,923	470,372	2,288,896
Mar 96	290,382	139,394	777,885
Jun 96	329,489	232,166	716,091
Sep 96	343,168	220,197	707,919
Dec 96	346,387	232,160	711,187
Total funds	1,309,426	823,917	2,913,082

Source: Adapted from the Bank of Thailand Yearly, various issues.

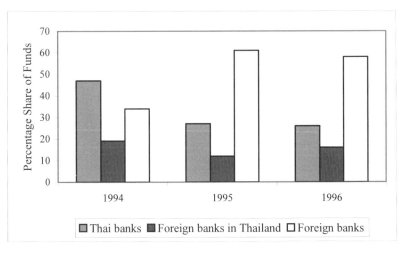

Fig. 6.7. Percentage share of BIBF's funds

Source: Authors' calculations from the Bank of Thailand Yearly, various issues.

The BIBF not only lends foreign funds but also lends them out domestically as well. Similar to commercial banks, the BIBF's loans were made for a total of nine investment purposes within the tradeable and non-tradeable sectors. Table 6.10 exhibits that the BIBF's loans to all nine investment sectors rose significantly throughout the period, growing more than threefold from 1,582,079 million baht to a high of 5,046,425 million baht within just three years from 1994 to 1996. In the tradeable sector, the BIBF loaned most of its funds to investments in trade and manufacturing projects. Loans to manufacturing were extremely high, with the BIBF lending more than one-third of its first year funds to domestic manufacturers with a total of 570,302 million baht. The BIBF continued to loan heavily to manufacturing businesses in 1995 and 1996 with loans as high as 1,083,859 and 1,717,510 million baht, respectively. Although loans to trade were not as high as manufacturing, our study shows that the BIBF's loans to trade also rose rapidly from 289,587 million baht in 1994 to 558,017 million baht in 1996.

Considering the non-tradeable sector, the data demonstrates that the BIBF loaned mostly to domestic financial institutions, and real estate and construction projects. We found that the BIBF's loans to real estate and construction projects rose more than threefold from 212,166 million baht in 1994 to 742,504 million baht in 1996. Perhaps, the most significant increase in the BIBF's loans was to financial institutions. Data from Table 6.10 reveals that total loans from the BIBF to financial institutions grew more than fourfold during the three year period from 298,420 million baht in 1994 to 1,465,065 million baht in 1996. Most importantly, we found the pattern of the BIBF's lending shifted from the tradeable to non-tradeable sector. During the first year, the BIBF loaned more than half of its funds to the tradeable sector with a high proportion to manufacturing and trade. However, the pattern began to change in 1995 when the BIBF extended massive amounts of loans to the non-tradeable sector, especially real estate and construction and financial institution (see Table 6.10). Evidence shows that loans to manufacturing were overshadowed by those to financial institutions and construction and real estate loans surpassed trade loans. Consequently, BIBF's loans to the non-tradeable sector rose from 41% in 1994 to 59 and 54% in 1995 and 1996, respectively (see Fig. 6.8).

Table 6.10. BIBF's total lending classified by sector (million baht)

	1994	1995	1996
Tradeable	877,496	1,579,190	2,335,849
Agriculture and forestry	12,827	17,666	23,689
Mining and quarrying	4,780	17,046	36,633
Manufacturing	570,302	1,083,859	1,717,510
Trade	289,587	460,619	558,017
Non-tradeable	704,583	2,202,001	2,710,576
Construction & real estate	212,166	592,055	742,504
Financial institutions	298,420	1,218,001	1,465,065
Public utilities	64,468	127,605	202,108
Services	124,678	258,250	293,782
Personal consumption	4,851	6,090	7,117
Total	1,582,079	3,781,191	5,046,425

Source: Adapted from the Bank of Thailand Yearly, various issues.

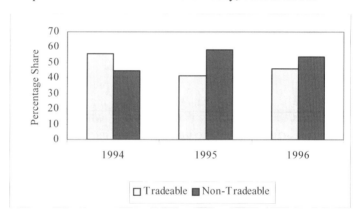

Fig. 6.8. Percentage share of the BIBF's major loans

Source: Authors' calculations from the Bank of Thailand Yearly, various issues.

In short, the basket of currencies coupled with major tax benefits (granted exclusively to the BIBF) indeed helped increase funds to the BIBF. With a pegged exchange rate, international lenders and investors were secured against exchange risks, and the tax privileges with no short-term reserve requirements made investments via the BIBF very attractive. As a result, foreign capital poured into the Bangkok International Banking Facilities (BIBF) from the first year of its operation (see Table 6.9). In terms of lending, we found that most of the BIBF's funds were extended to only four major investment areas; manufacturing, construction and real estate, financial institutions and trade. Our study indicates that the BIBF loaned heavily to the non-tradeable sector with a high proportion of loans to real estate and construction, and financial institutions. The nature of this kind of investment is regarded as risky and unproductive as it is unlikely to generate foreign income. Evidence of this kind suggests a problem in the management of the BIBF where the majority of its funds were misdirected and seemed to create little return and development of the economy as a whole.

6.6 Summary

This chapter explores the consequences of the exchange rate policy in Thailand in the era of liberalisation. The basket of currencies was introduced in 1984 as part of a stabilisation program implemented during the economic disruption of the early 1980s. Basically, the basket consisted of currencies of Thailand's seven major trading partners, with the highest weight given to the US dollar. The introduction of this system aimed at encouraging trade growth and generating development by attracting foreign funds to the financial market. Fortunately, the devaluation of US dollar against the yen made Thai exports and investment extremely attractive (see Fig. 6.1). Consequently, the Thai economy performed effectively with high levels of exports and foreign investment in the financial market. Undoubtedly, such impressive performance soon led Thailand to be regarded as 'the miracle of Asia' by the end of the 1980s.[6] The authorities believed that the Thai economy would enjoy enhanced growth and development by liberalising the financial system while keeping the basket of currencies in operation. Thus, the baht was kept closely tied to the US dollar. The Thai economy continued to growth as long as the US dollar was depreciated. Unfortunately, the growth lasted for just a very short period. Thailand's economy began to slow down and lose its competitiveness as the baht appreciated against the yen as a result of an appreciation of the US currency in 1995 (see Fig. 6.1 and Table 6.1).

From our study, Thailand experienced the following outcomes resulting from the basket of currencies policy. On the trade front, Thai exports grew rapidly as a result of the yen appreciation against the US dollar and the baht in 1984. They grew dramatically in the 1990s when the yen continued to appreciate against the US dollar. Unfortunately, the yen began to lose its

---

[6] See Chap. 3 for discussion of this view.

value against the US dollar, and hence the baht in the late 1995 (see Fig. 6.1). Consequently, Thailand began to lose its export competitiveness particularly with Japan, its main trading partner, thus a lengthy period of high export growth came to an end in 1996 with an export growth deficit of −2% (see Table 6.1). On the financial front, Thailand aimed to attract foreign funds into its financial market to service domestic economic growth and development and those funds mostly came through commercial banks and the BIBF. In order to attract foreign funds, the Thai government lifted all interest rate ceilings for commercial banks and provided several tax privileges for the BIBF (see Tables 6.4 and 6.8). These benefits together with the pegged exchange rate made investment in Thailand's financial market very attractive. Thus, the country experienced an enormous surge in foreign funds to both commercial banks and the BIBF in just a very short period of time (see Tables 6.6 and 6.9).

In terms of lending, the commercial banks and the BIBF extended most of their funds domestically to various sectors, however, our study shows that a high proportion of funds were provided to investment in the non-tradeable sector, for instance constructions and real estate, finance institutions (and personal consumption for the commercial banks). Although, the commercial banks rolled out much of their funds to the tradeable sector (represented chiefly by the manufacturing and trade sectors) (see Table 6.7), results from our study show that the commercial banks were the biggest lenders with for example, a more than 60% share of all loans to real estate and construction projects (see Fig. 6.6). Lastly, we found that the pattern of the BIBF's lending changed dramatically from the tradeable to non-tradeable sector, with most of its funds extended to construction and real estate and financial institutions (see Table 6.10 and Fig. 6.8). In principle, the lending of the commercial banks and the BIBF exhibited a problem of poor management foreign funds were extended to the non-tradeable sector. When the Thai economy began to shows sign of a slowdown in 1996, confidence in the economy among international investors slipped away. Foreign investments came to a sudden stop, causing the stagnation of the Thai economy, which finally precipitated the financial crisis.

The assessment part of this book is now complete, covering Chaps. 4–6. The next and last part of this book will be an analysis of possible causes of the crisis in Thailand in Chaps. 7–9 presents the conclusions of this book.

PART C: Welfare Economies, Economic Theory and Policy

7 Review of Financial Liberalisation Theory and the Thai Crisis

7.1 Introduction

This book has now fulfilled two prime tasks. The first task was to review the literature on international finance related to the issues of financial crises, the sequence of financial liberalisation, capital control, exchange rate policy and asymmetric information and examine the framework undertaken by Thailand in liberalising its financial system. This first task was undertaken in Chaps. 2 and 3, which is Part A of this book. The second task of this book was to make an assessment of Thailand's financial liberalisation taking into consideration the literature presented in Chap. 2. This was accomplished in Chaps. 4, 5 and 6, which is Part B of this book.

In this Part C which comprises Chaps. 7, 8 and 9, the aim is to provide an analysis of the contribution of Thailand's financial liberalisation as a cause of the crisis in relation to the literature reviewed in Chap. 2 and its social welfare analysis using a cost benefit analysis framework in Chap. 8. Chap. 9 is the conclusion of this book.

This current chapter analyses the role of financial liberalisation in Thailand's financial crisis in four major aspects. Section 7.2 studies the errors of sequence in Thailand's financial liberalisation. Section 7.3 examines the impact of capital control reform. Section 7.4 presents the problems of implementing an exchange rate policy. Section 7.5 investigates the issue of asymmetric information while focusing on problems caused by moral hazard.

But before we analyse the role of financial liberalisation in Thailand's financial crisis it is important to review some of the famous international crisis models. The main models discussed in this chapter are the first generation speculative attacks models and the second generation models.

The first-generation speculative attack model was developed by Krugman (1979), Flood and Garber (1984a) and Blanco and Garber (1986). The first generation model combines two main theoretical approaches, the monetary approach to the balance of payments and the flexible price monetary approach to the exchange rate. The models explain the currency crises in terms of overly expansive domestic macroeconomic activities.

The first-generation speculative attack model can be explained by a model which assumes perfect foresight, small country model with fixed output where both purchasing power parity and uncovered interest rate parity hold.

We can begin with a standard money demand equation:

$$m_t - p_t = \phi \; \gamma_t - \alpha i_t \qquad \varphi, \alpha > 0 \tag{7.1}$$

While money supply is given by:

$$m_t = \gamma D_t + (1 - \gamma) R_t \qquad 0 < \gamma < 1 \tag{7.2}$$

where:

m_t = nominal money supply,

p_t = the domestic price level,

D_t = credit created by the domestic central bank,

R_t = domestic currency value of foreign exchange reserves,

γ = share of domestic credit in the money supply.

The rate of domestic credit creation is considered to be constant at:

$$D_t = \mu \qquad \qquad \mu > 0 \tag{7.3}$$

The purchasing power parity is given as

$$p_t = s_t \tag{7.4}$$

Whereas the uncovered interest rate parity is given by:

$$i_t = i^* + E_t s_t \tag{7.5}$$

where:

i_t = home interest rates,

i^* = foreign interest rate,

E_t = expectation operator,

s_t = expected change in exchange rate.

Under perfect foresight assumption and holding at the standardised value of unity, substituting (7.4) in (7.5) the money demand equation can be written as:

$$m_t = s_t - \alpha s_t \tag{7.6}$$

The equation for foreign exchange reserves assuming a fixed exchange rate is given by:

$$R_t = (s - \gamma D_t)/(1 - \gamma) \tag{7.7}$$

Then substituting (7.3) into (7.7) gives us the rate as which foreign exchange reserves are running down:

$$R_t = - \mu / \Theta \qquad (7.8)$$

where:

$$\Theta = (1 - \gamma)/\gamma$$

Thus if foreign exchange reserves are constantly being run down because $\mu > 0$, agents expect the monetary authorities to abandon the peg. Now, assuming that, the new policy with regards to exchange rate is a clean float. The new floating rate can be shown as:

$$s_t = \gamma (D_o + \alpha\mu) + \gamma\mu t \qquad (7.9)$$

where:

$\gamma\mu t$ = the rate at which the new floating exchange rates depreciates.

As the pegged exchange rate collapses, the exact time of the collapse is given by:

$$t_0 = (\Theta R_0 / \mu) - \alpha \qquad (7.10)$$

The collapse will occur sooner the larger is the proportion of domestic credit in the money stock, the lower is the initial stock of reserves, the higher the rate of credit expansion and higher the interest elasticity of demand for money as with depreciation inflation is expected to increase leading to an increase in the nominal interest rates which in turn will reduce money demand.

Second-generation models emphasise the non linearities in the government behaviour and emphasises the fact that even with appropriate policies, attack conditional policy changes can pull the economy into an attack. Second-generation models are more concerned with speculative attacks. Speculative attacks are different from the crises studied by the first-generation models in two respects. Firstly, the state of the business cycle and the banking system feature prominently in the analysis. Moreover, countries experiencing a currency attack were unsuccessful in supporting exchange rate parities owing to tight borrowing constraints imposed by monetary policies in trading partners. Secondly, speculative attacks appear to be unrelated to economic fundamentals. More emphasis has been placed on other factors, particularly informational frictions and herding behaviour. Furthermore, volatility in foreign exchange markets is enhanced by the globalisation of financial markets. Changing expectations can induce or reverse capital flows instantaneously in these internationally integrated markets. In these circumstances herd behaviour could be encouraged when expectations are formed on the strength of imperfect and asymmetric information.

7.2 Inappropriate Sequence of Liberalisation

The design of a proper sequence of financial liberalisation is a widely debated issue among economists. The discussion centres on what sequence of financial liberalisation allows a country to maximise the benefits of liberalisation while minimising the associated risks. Currently, the conclusion of what constitutes a proper sequence has not yet been finalised. However, most economists believe that the sequence of liberalisation can be varied from one country to another, depending on the nature of the economy and the objective of such liberalisation. It is a preferred model that a proper sequence of liberalisation should be first to reduce the fiscal deficit and reform foreign trade, followed by domestic financial reform and foreign exchange and capital control reform (see Chap. 2). In the age of globalisation, Thailand adopted financial liberalisation in the early 1990s to enable the country to enjoy the opportunities and benefits a free flow of capital provides. The objective of liberalisation was to generate economic growth and development via export led growth and a capital led development policy. However, the sequence of Thailand's financial liberalisation was different than that suggested by most economists.

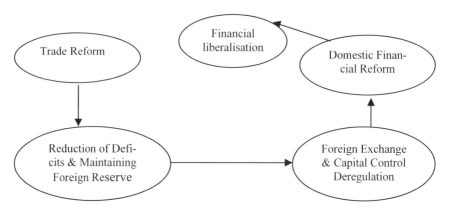

Fig. 7.1. Sequence of Thailand's financial liberalisation

From our study in Chap. 4, we found that the sequence of financial liberalisation in Thailand was the following: trade reform, reduction of deficits and maintaining foreign reserve, foreign exchange and capital control reform, and domestic financial reform (see Fig. 7.1).

Thailand's foreign trade had long been dominated by agriculture related products, which were also a major export of the country. During 1986 and 1987, the Thai government adopted the Sixth National Development Plan that included the transformation from an agriculture-oriented to manufacturing and industry export-led growth policy by reducing taxes and implementing a pegged exchange rate system. The aim of this policy was to promote economic growth and development, focusing on the industrial and manufacturing sector. In Chap. 4, we found that the pattern of Thailand's trade changed dramatically when the manufacturing and trade replaced the agriculture as the highest export for the first time in 1986. From then on, the foreign trade of Thailand has been dominated by industry and manufacturing exports. Shortly after this change of trade pattern, the Thai economy grew rapidly at a double-digit GDP growth rate and was said to be the fastest growing economy in the world during 1988–1990 (see Table 4.1).

Table 7.1. Thailand's fiscal and current account balance (percentage of GDP)

	Fiscal balance[1]	Current account balance
1990	4.7	−8.3
1991	4.9	−7.5
1992	3.0	−5.5
1993	2.2	−4.9
1994	1.9	−5.4
1995	2.8	−7.9
1996	2.3	−7.9
1997	−1.9	−2.0

Source: Adapted from the Bank of Thailand Yearly, various issues.

Theoretically, the country needed to maintain a high level of foreign reserves and fiscal surplus and a low current account deficit before other actions in financial liberalisation were commenced. The performance of Thai economy in the second half of the 1980s went extremely well with high exports and GDP growth. Such impressive growth led to a significant increase in foreign reserve and enables Thailand to achieve its first ever fiscal balance in 1988 (see Figs. 4.3 and 4.4). This provided enough confidence that a successful financial liberalisation was possible in Thailand. However, the current account balance of the country at the time cautioned against over-confidence in this idea. The account was in deficit as high as −8.3% when liberalisation took place in 1990 (see Fig. 4.5 and Table 7.1). The government seemed to ignore this fact and continued to liberalise the financial system until it was completed in early 1994. In most cases, undertaking financial liberalisation when the current account deficit is high results in widening the deficits even further. In Thailand, the situation showed no sign of improvement but further deteriorated. The country was

---

[1] Fiscal balance is surplus of government budgets.

losing its fiscal balance as well as increasing the current account deficit, especially during the export slowdown in 1995 and 1996. This indicates the error in liberalising financially at a when the current account deficit was high, which resulted in a widening problem of deficit and created economic instability.

Table 7.2. Sales of foreign exchange in Thailand

	Foreign banks trade of currency [% share]	Total sale of foreign exchange [millions of bath]
1990	35	1,176,432
1991	40	1,545,686
1992	49	2,102,824
1993	66	3,847,081
1994	79	8,227,287
1995	79	13,303,355
1996	76	23,856,678
1997	71	25,474,023

Source: Adapted from the Bank of Thailand Yearly, various issues.

The traditional view of sequencing financial liberalisation argues that the country should have completed its domestic financial reform with supervisory and monitoring system to assist financial institutions before foreign exchange and capital control reforms occur. This is to prevent misuse of funds and avoid the economic disruption that may be caused by high capital flows. However, Thailand reformed foreign exchange and capital controls first with a series of deregulations during 1989 to 1994 (see Chap. 4). The reform included allowing the public direct access to foreign capital for the first time and more freely than before, permitting commercial banks to processes freely any purchases or sales of foreign exchange and increasing the limit on capital outflows from Thailand. As a result, Thailand experienced a significant increase in foreign exchange trade and high level of outflows.

For foreign exchange rate, we observed there were significant increases in total foreign exchange trade, which was largely processed by foreign commercial banks (see Table 4.1 and Fig. 4.7). Data from Table 7.2 demonstrates that the foreign exchange sold in Thailand alone rose significantly since the early reform and continued to increase more dramatically after the reform was completed in 1994. More importantly, most of those sales of foreign exchange were made by foreign commercial banks. This indicated an error of the reform process where foreign exchange trade was under control by foreign investor, which provided more opportunity for the speculative behaviour to be implemented.

Table 7.3. Summary of balance of payments and foreign reserves (US$ billions)

	Balance of payments	Foreign reserves
1991	4.2	18.4
1992	3.0	21.1
1993	3.9	25.4
1994	4.2	32.2
1995	7.2	37.0
1996	2.1	34.2
1997	−10.1	26.9

Source: Adapted from the Bank of Thailand Yearly, various issues.

In terms of outflows, we discovered that Thailand experienced massive outflows of capital when the public was permitted to transfer funds out and the limit on capital outflows was raised. Our study in Chap. 4 indicated that there were extraordinary increases of capital outflows in all sectors following the reform, particularly outflows made from non-resident accounts and foreign loans. For instance, outflows made by foreign loans increased from 1,604 million baht in 1988 to 2,747 million baht by the end of the first capital control reform in 1991 and continued to rise dramatically through to the end of reform in 1994 (see Table 4.2). Perhaps, the showcase of the immediate effect of capital control reform was the non-resident outflows, which rose rapidly as soon as controls were lifted. For example non-resident outflows rose from 235 million baht in 1989 to 9,919 million baht by the beginning of the second stage of reforms in 1991 and outflows were as high as 229,198 million baht when the controls were completely lifted in 1994. These high levels of outflows have an impact in reducing foreign reserves and balance of payments of the country. We found that the problem became severe when Thailand was losing its foreign reserves, current account deficits widened and balance of payment was declining as a result of the rapid increase of outflows from the beginning of the reform (see Tables 6.1, 7.1, 7.2 and 7.3). Consequently, this generates panic over confidence of the Thai economy around foreign investors, resulting in further withdrawal of capital out of the country, in turn, weakening the macroeconomic fundamentals of the country and led to crisis in the end.

Clearly, the above mentioned elements exhibit the risks associated with an inappropriate sequence of liberalisation. Without proper reform of domestic market prior to foreign exchange and capital control reform exposes a greater risk of financial crisis to the country. For Thailand, we found that the reversal order between foreign exchange and capital control and domestic financial reform leads the country to financial crisis for two reasons. First, it resulted in high volume foreign currency trade that causes speculation on the currency. Second, it generated high level of outflows, which harm the country's macroeconomic fundamentals and finally led to serious fiscal deficits.

In the last stage of financial liberalisation, Thailand undertook domestic financial reform by establishing two institutions rather than providing the supervisory and monitoring system to assist and monitor the operation. The two new establishments were the Bangkok International Banking Facilities (BIBF) and the Export and Import Bank (EXIM Bank). Although, these institutions were newly established as part of the liberalisation framework, the objectives of the operation differed between the two financial institutions. The BIBF acted as a fund seeker, aiming to enhance economic development and promote Thailand as the region's financial centre via foreign inflows, while the EXIM bank was focusing on boosting the export sector by providing support and funds to exporters.

The BIBF was very successful in seeking funds mainly from foreign sources (see Fig. 6.8). It received a total of funds as high as US$7,655 million within the first three quarters of its operation in 1993 (see Table 6.2). Thailand also allowed the BIBF freedom to manage or operate itself, thus it loaned inflows out as quickly as they came in, mostly within Thailand itself in the form of out-in lending (see Table 4.3). High levels of lending within the domestic market had indeed fuelled the problem of over-investment with our study revealing that there was a significant growth of non-tradeable sector lending (see Table 6.10 and Fig. 6.8). This reveals the fact that the reform of capital control prior to domestic financial reform created a problem of over-lending in the domestic market, caused by a rapid increase of foreign inflows. Additionally, this also highlights the fact that the reform of domestic market without proper supervisory and monitoring system, resulting in mismanagement of funds that harmed the economy. Unlike the BIBF, the EXIM bank received most of its funds from domestic sources and mainly from the BOT. Although the bank was allowed to operate freely, the EXIM bank was considered to be ineffective because many of its investments after financial liberalisation were more in the financial sector, not the real sectors and definitely not the export sector. Therefore, the EXIM bank looked less attractive to foreign funds.

In essence, Thailand was a prime example of the inappropriate sequencing of financial liberalisation, which proved to harm the economy rather than generating sustained growth and development for three reasons. Firstly, financial liberalisation in Thailand while current account deficits were high exacerbated the problems arising form these deficits. Secondly, having reformed foreign exchange and capital markets before the domestic financial market was ready led to problems of speculative behaviour, reduce balance of payments and loss of foreign reserve. Finally, domestic financial reform without supervisory and monitoring system and left to the last caused problems of excessive lending to the domestic market.

7.3 Loosening Controls Over the Capital Account

The idea of capital controls as a means to reduce economic instability is not new. A study by Tobin (1978) first presented the idea of capital control by taxing foreign exchange transactions to avoid currency speculation and crisis. Subsequently, a number of economists (Dooley 1996; Edwards 1999; Neely 1999) have highlighted the importance of capital control as a core requirement in liberalising an economy. They believe that financial liberalisation allows capital to mobilise more freely and can create high instability in any financial system without the presence of proper capital control. As reviewed earlier in Chap. 2, the discussion on new international financial reform theories has focused on two types of controls on international capital mobility, namely, controls of capital outflows and inflows.[2] However, others economists such as Coy et al. (1998) and Cooper (1999) argue that capital controls on both inflows and outflows are difficult to manage in liberalising economies. As they believe that the controls would have negative impact on the movement of capital in the free economies.

Prior to financial liberalisation, the Thai government placed heavy controls on capital outflows where only a limited amount of outflows were allowed and also required authorisation from the BOT. In the light of financial liberalisation, the government gradually removed capital controls on foreign inflows and particularly outflows during July 1989 to January 1994 (see Table 5.1). The main feature of capital control deregulation is to allows both public and banking sectors with more freedom to borrow in and transfer out funds. As a result, Thailand experienced a massive influx of foreign capital, which poured into both the bank and non-bank sectors. For the banking sector, we found that foreign inflows poured into the sector as soon as the controls on capital were lifted. However, our study shows that foreign capital trended to invest more with the BIBF rather than in commercial banks. The total foreign capital inflows to the BIBF were extremely high from the first year of its operation and the single factor explaining this phenomenon was the tax privileges of the BIBF over other commercial banks and financial institutions. This significant increase of foreign capital flows to the BIBF resulted in an increase in total flows to

---

[2] See Chap. 2 of this book for a detailed discussion of controls on both capital outflows and inflows.

the banking sector, to the extent that the pattern of foreign capital flows changed from traditional investment, such as FDI, to the banking sector via the BIBF (see Fig. 5.5).

Table 7.4. Summary of non-bank flows (US$ millions)

		1990	1991	1992	1993	1994	1995	1996	1997
FDI	Inflows	3,030	3,700	5,340	2,638	2,455	3,051	3,941	5,141
	Outflows	−488	−1,667	−3,189	−906	−1,129	−1,047	−1,670	−1,514
Loans	Inflows	7,282	13,618	14,547	18,225	17,507	21,418	24,920	17,980
	Outflows	−2,747	−7,957	−11,701	−20,657	−23,352	−19,900	−19,469	−21,668
Portfolio	Inflows	3,417	2,303	3,407	10,959	8,995	10,111	13,515	24,757
	Outflows	−2,960	−2,140	−2,846	−6,107	−7,885	−6,691	−10,027	−20,207
Non-resident	Inflows	1,571	11,961	22,627	76,963	231,264	416,410	810,397	710,349
	Outflows	−235	−9,919	−20,920	−74,278	−229,198	−413,003	−807,473	−716,161
Net Flows		8,870	9,899	7,265	6,837	−1,343	10,349	14,134	−1,323

Source: Adapted from the Bank of Thailand Yearly, various issues.

In terms of the non-bank sector, foreign capital flows were invested mainly for four major purposes: FDI, loans, portfolio investment and non-resident account. Inflows to this sector were as high as those in the banking sector and rose dramatically after capital controls began to lift. Table 7.4 is a summary of capital flows to the non-bank sector, reproduced from our study in Chap. 5. The data shows that capital control reform changed the pattern of capital flows from the investment sector (FDI) to the non-tradeable sector (loans, portfolio investment and non-resident account). An influx of capital by itself was not a problem if managed wisely, however we found that most foreign capital flows were located in such risky sectors as real estate and construction. For instance, we found the percentage share of FDI and total portfolio investment in real estate and construction rose significantly following the capital controls reform (see Figs. 5.6 and 5.7). Moreover, we found that capital controls reform also provided opportunities for more outflows to be made. Table 7.4 exhibits that capital outflows from Thailand escalated quickly in a very short period of time, in particular outflows made by the non-residential account. Clearly, this was a result of the capital control relaxation, which allowed the outflows to move freely. Thus, funds rapidly left Thailand after the capital controls reform took place and grew even more when the reforms were completed from 1994 onwards with foreign investors as the biggest outflow makers.

It is well known that capital control deregulation is a basic requirement of financial liberalisation. Thailand gradually deregulated the control on capital flows as the country moved toward financial liberalisation. Consequently, massive capital flows poured into both the bank and non-bank sector as soon as controls were relaxed. In general, these inflows were supposed to help generate foreign income and enhance the economic growth and development of the country. Unfortunately, this was not the case in Thailand as most capital inflows were invested in risky sectors such as real estate and construction, which were unlikely to generate foreign income or lead to economic development. On the other hand, outflows also rose dramatically and in some cases increased even more significantly than capital inflows. Of course, such high and steady capital outflows led to a problem of macroeconomic imbalance and economic instability. The problem got worse when the Thai economy failed to perform in 1996, causing panic among foreign investors. As a result, they declined to invest in Thailand and began to pull their funds out of the country as confidence in the economy slipped away.

In essence, capital controls deregulation could harm the economy if it is not implemented properly. From the Thai point of view, the deregulation policy that allowed foreign capital to travel freely caused an influx of inflows to a risky or non-tradeable sector (real estate and construction). This demonstrated that capital controls deregulation in Thailand was indeed mismanaged, resulting in high level of unproductive investments and finally failed the economy. Indeed, capital control deregulation policy pursued by Thailand proved to be one of the causes of the crisis.

7.4 Problems of Stable Exchange Rates

The basket of currencies was designed to benefit Thailand in the liberalisation of its financial system and had two main objectives.[3] Firstly, it aimed to boost trade growth through an export-led growth policy. Secondly, the country also aimed to attract foreign funds in order to service economic growth and to promote Thailand as the financial centre of the region. Overall, Thailand's currencies basket was comprised of seven currencies; the US dollar, the yen, the mark, the pound sterling, the Hong Kong dollar, the Singapore dollar and the Malaysian ringgit. Although, the official weight of the basket was never made public, it is known that the US dollar had the highest weight of approximately 85% of the basket.[4] The basket of currencies proved its efficacy in generating export growth. Strictly pegging

---

[3] Ohno (1998) refers to the basket of currencies, which tie a currency to the US dollar, as the 'soft dollar zone', McKinnon (1999) refers to it as a 'dollar standard'.

[4] See Sect. 6.3 in Chap. 6 for a detailed discussion of Thailand's basket of currencies.

the baht to the US dollar made Thai exports look attractive when the US dollar depreciated relative to the yen during from 1984 to the early years of 1990s. In Chap. 6, we found Thai exports to the Japanese market rose rapidly after the depreciation (see Table 6.2). Additionally, we discovered that the depreciation of the baht increased direct investment in the manufacturing sector from Japan as well (see Figs. 6.2 and 6.3). Strong growth of exports to and investment from Japan lcd to impressive export growth with an average of 20 per cent per annum during 1984–1995 (see Table 6.1).

Table 7.5. Thailand's external account (US$ millions)

	1990	1991	1992	1993	1994	1995	1996	1997
Exports	22.9	28.3	32.2	36.6	44.7	55.7	54.7	56.7
Imports	32.7	37.8	40.1	45.1	53.4	70.4	70.8	61.3
Trade balance	−9.8	−9.5	−7.9	−8.5	−8.7	−14.7	−16.1	−4.6
Current account balance	−7.1	−7.4	−6.1	−6.1	−7.8	−13.2	−14.3	−3.1
Fiscal balance	103.3	123.7	85.9	68.9	65.8	112.5	104.3	−87.1

Source: Adapted from the Bank of Thailand Yearly, various issues.

Unfortunately, the story of Thailand's export success was limited. Thailand was faced with a major downturn of exports as a result of a sharply appreciating US dollar against the Japanese yen in 1995. This event had simply impacted in increasing Thailand's terms of exports as a result of the baht value rising along with the US dollar. Thailand began to lose its export competitiveness, due to a significant decline of exports to such a major market like Japan. As a result, the Thai economy experienced high level of trade imbalances and current account deficits in 1995 and 1996, while the fiscal balance also began to decline in the same period (see Table 7.5).

It is known that Thailand's trade was mostly dominated by the US dollar, despite the fact that the US was not its only major trading partner. In fact, Japan was Thailand's largest export market and a major investor, and the decision to strictly peg the baht to the US dollar alone was inappropriate, because the mismatch between the basket of currencies and real trade made Thailand vulnerable to fluctuations in the US dollar against the yen and other currencies. When the baht appreciated (as a result of the appreciation of the US dollar) against the yen, Thailand's trade to major markets like Japan suddenly declined, resulting in economic deterioration in the end. In principle, these relationships suggest that the yen was underweighted in Thailand's basket of currencies and strictly pegging to the US dollar did not ensure a healthy economy. Therefore, the weighting of the basket should have been adjusted according to the priority of the country's trading partners rather than the US dollar dominated market.[5]

Beside export growth, the basket of currencies also sought to generate more foreign flows to the financial market via the commercial banks and the BIBF. The aim was to enhance economic growth, development and promote Thailand as a financial centre. Together with the pegged exchange system, the Thai government had relaxed rules and regulations for the commercial banks and the BIBF to allow more freedom in mobilising funds. For example, the government lifted all interest ceilings for the commercial banks, while providing several tax privileges and removing short-term reserve requirements for the BIBF (see Tables 6.4 and 6.8). These benefits coupled with a pegged exchange rate resulted in a massive flood of foreign capital to both commercial banks and the BIBF in a very short period of time (see Tables 6.6 and 6.9). Moreover, we discovered that these high capital flows to the financial market had a direct impact in increasing external debts of the country in two instances. First, a stable exchange rate allows international investors to eliminate the risk of losses, which may occur with changes in the exchange rate. Second, the interest rate differential between domestic and international markets, and tax privileges offered investors more benefits in making returns. Accordingly, the international lenders were willing to lend without hedging as long as the borrowers were willing to borrow. In other words, the stable exchange rate ensured the price of the currency, so that, international lenders were willing to lend to Thailand without hedging.

High foreign capital flows to the financial sector simply meant high external debt because most inflows came in as borrowing to commercial banks and the BIBF. Table 7.6 and Fig. 7.2 show that Thailand experienced an increasing debt from the beginning of liberalisation. The external debt grew rapidly from 34 to 60% of GDP during 1990–1996. Obvious debt increases were witnessed in the commercial banks and the BIBF. We observed that a high proportion of these debts were short-term rather than long term. In 1994 alone, the commercial banks incurred short term debt amounting to US$6,414 million or 60% growth above the previous years total, while the BIBF accounted for a total of US$15,142 million or 138% growth. The accumulation of high short-term debt by commercial banks was largely due to the interest rate differential, resulting from interest rate deregulation. While the massive increase in debt of the BIBF was a result of tax privileges and particularly to the absence of short-term reserve

---

[5] A study by Rajan et al. (2000) suggested that to avoid the crisis, Thailand should have increased the weight of the yen by as much as 40 per cent in the basket before the crisis period.

requirements. All these factors led to a rapid increase in short-term debt to an unacceptable level, which led to a dramatic decline of international reserves (see Table 7.6 and Fig. 7.2). Furthermore, by itself a high level of short-term funds seems to cause no problems if they are extended wisely. According to our study in Chap. 6, we found that the commercial banks and the BIBF loaned out most of their funds, from short-term borrowing to long-term loans, in unproductive sectors such as real estate and construction. The problem began to appear when these sectors failed to service their loans to the commercial banks and the BIBF, this in turn caused the collapse of the financial sector.

Table 7.6. Thailand's private sector Foreign debt (US$ millions)

	1990	1991	1992	1993	1994	1995	1996	1997
Private sector	17,793	25,068	30,553	37,936	49,152	84,430	91,941	85,194
Long term	7,633	10,382	12,189	15,302	20,153	32,117	44,252	46,920
Short term	10,160	14,686	18,364	22,634	28,999	52,313	47,689	38,274
Commercial bank	4,233	4,477	6,263	5,279	9,865	14,436	10,682	9,141
Long term	286	338	731	1,263	3,451	4,443	2,314	3,923
Short term	3,947	4,139	5,532	4,016	6,414	9,993	8,368	5,218
BIBF	–	–	–	7,740	18,111	27,503	31,187	30,080
Long term	–	–	–	1,385	2,969	3,799	10,697	10,895
Short term	–	–	–	6,355	15,142	23,704	20,490	19,185
Non-bank	13,560	20,591	24,290	24,917	21,176	42,491	50,072	45,973
Long term	7,347	10,044	11,458	12,654	13,733	23,875	31,241	32,102
Short term	6,213	10,547	12,832	12,263	7,443	18,616	18,831	13,871
Debt / GDP (%)	34.3	38.5	39.1	41.6	44.9	60.0	59.7	70.0
International reserves/Short term debt (%)	137.0	119.7	112.0	112.4	103.8	70.7	81.1	70.4
Debt service ratio (%)	10.8	10.5	11.3	11.2	11.7	11.4	12.3	15.7

Source: Adapted from the Bank of Thailand Yearly, various issues.

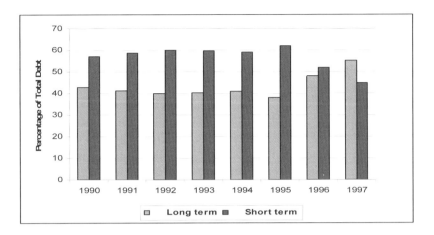

Fig. 7.2. Percentage share of total debt

Source: Authors' calculation from the Bank of Thailand Yearly, various issues.

In summary, we argue that there are two aspects of the pegged exchange rate which contributed to the crisis. First, Thailand's pegged exchange rate had generated an increase of Thai exports when the value of the baht fell, with the depreciation of the US dollar against the yen. If the US dollar had fallen further against the yen, Thai exports would have continued to expand. Unfortunately, the US dollar appreciated steeply against the yen in 1995, causing the prices of exports in US dollar terms to rise, resulting in a slowdown of exports to Japan and a sharp decline of total exports in 1996, causing trade imbalance which in turn created the country's largest current account deficit that led to the crisis in 1997. Second, Thailand incurred a high level of external debt partly as a result of a stable exchange rate in the context of financial liberalisation. On the one hand, the pegged exchange rate enabled investors or lenders to eliminate any risk, which may have occurred if the currency lost value. On the other hand, the interest rate differentials and tax privileges of the commercial banks and the BIBF offered major benefits for foreign investors. Thus, investors loaned short-term unhedged funds to commercial banks and the BIBF with an expectation of handsome profits.

7.5 Asymmetric Information: Problems of Moral Hazard

Asymmetric information problems have been a central issue when considering causes of the financial crisis. A number of studies have attempted to investigate the link between asymmetric information and the crisis.[6] However, our analysis extends other studies by focusing on the relationship between asymmetric information and the crisis in Thailand. The story begins with the pegged exchange rate regime that Thailand pursued rate in liberalising its financial system. As reviewed in Chap. 6, the pegged was introduced to enhance foreign capital into the economy, as the government believed that high level of capital flows could lead to further economic growth and developments. However, the hidden fact behind the pegged rate was that the government tended to provide the investors with confidence over any risks may be caused by the fluctuation of the currency, and encourage them to invest more into to the economy. As a result, international investors come to expect that the value of the Thai currency would hardly change and the pegged regime will last. Hence, foreign investors were willing to extend large amount of funds into the country. Furthermore, the pegged regime with various aspects of financial liberalisation has made it worse. Thailand experienced an extraordinary surge in foreign capital once the government removed most restrictions on the interest rate ceiling, capital controls, type of lending allowed and established the BIBF.

As we discovered in the earlier chapters, the country experienced a sharp increased of capital inflows as a result of financial liberalisation. In Chap. 5, we found that Thailand experienced a massive increase of capital flows following capital control deregulation. While in Chap. 6, we found that the deregulation of the interest rate did not enhance saving and investment, instead, it provided international investors with opportunities to benefit from the interest rate differential while the commercial banks were also advantaged by borrowing abroad at a cheaper interest rate. This lead to a massive influx of capital flows into commercial banks as soon as the ceiling was removed (see Table 6.6). These high capital inflows simply fuelled demand for spending and investing within the domestic market and we found that most investments in Thailand were made in the non-tradeable rather than the tradeable sector.

Our findings in Chap. 5 revealed that the majority of inflows were directed heavily toward the non-tradeable sector, particularly the real estate and construction sector. For instance, FDI and portfolio investment shifted from industry to the real estate and construction sector following financial reform (see Table 5.8, and Figs. 5.6 and 5.7). Moreover, the property indicators in Table 7.7 reveal that investments in this sector increased rapidly

---

[6] For a detailed discussion of asymmetric information see Chap. 2 of this book. See also Diaz-Alejandro (1985) for a study of Chile's crisis in 1982, Mishkin (1996) for a discussion of the Mexican crisis in 1994 and Kamin (1999) for a comparison study of the Chilean and Mexican crises.

during the period of financial liberalisation. The number of permits granted by the government for new housing and condominium projects rose from the early stages of liberalisation and continued to increase dramatically toward the end of 1996. Most importantly, the data also revealed that investments in this sector were definitely unproductive as it generated more and more outstanding debt over the period of 1989 to 1997. For instance, the debt rose almost fivefold between 1989 and 1993 and kept increasing to a peak in 1997 (see Table 7.7). In short, the pegged exchange regime provided foreign investors with positive expectation that value of currency would barely fluctuate, hence they were willing to extend their funds into the economy. The expectation coupled with financial liberalisation resulted in rapid increase of investment, which later leads to a problem of a bubble economy to Thailand with over-investment in non-tradeable sectors such as the real estate and construction sector.

Table 7.7. Thailand's property indicators

	Unit	1989	1990	1991	1992	1993	1994	1995	1996	1997
Land transactions nationwide	(million Baht)	238,240	367,089	270,105	279,008	344,783	404,747	396,150	441,291	338,946
Land development licences Nationwide	(units)	101,222	160,519	142,358	138,431	128,513	167,261	143,157	127,054	114,422
Construction Areas permitted in municipal zone	(1000 sq mts)	28,496.1	38,207.3	41,326.4	35,964.7	38,023.2	36,131.5	36,785.9	26,750.1	21,745.9
Condominium registration Granted nationwide	(units)	6,319	12,601	44,610	73,026	56,407	65,596	65,617	81,811	72,420
New housing in Bangkok metropolis and vicinity	(units)	80,031	102,335	129,688	108,001	134,086	171,254	172,419	166,785	145,355
Property credit outstanding	(million Baht)	134,882	264,985	323,809	408,421	519,954	651,772	773,468	862,641	937,326

Source: Adapted from the Bank of Thailand Yearly, various issues.

Another prime example of moral hazard was with the BIBF. As argued in Chap. 6 that the BIBF was established with an aim to enhance foreign funds into the country by providing several tax incentives over other financial institutions. On the one hand, international lenders always knew that the BIBF was in fact one of the government banks. On the other hand, they also benefit from the tax incentives if the investments were made via the BIBF. Thus, these elements sent over-optimistic signals to investors that their lending were guaranteed against any losses and the government would probably rescue or bailout the BIBF in the face of a financial crisis. As a result, massive foreign funds poured into the BIBF as soon as its was implemented (see Table 6.9). However, the key problem was the way these funds were used. Our study discovered that the BIBF channelled most of its funds toward risky investment with a high proportion to domestic financial institutions and real estate sector (see Table 6.10). For instance, we found that the BIBF's loans to the non-tradeable sector rose from 41% in 1994 to 59 and 54% in 1995 and 1996, respectively (see Fig. 6.8). In principle, the perception of guaranteed loans provided lenders with little incentive to monitor risks, which they were willing to take on in excessive amounts without hedging or monitoring of the BIBF's activities. This cavalier resulted in the onerous problem of an risky investment in the end.

In addition, the moral hazard problem in Thailand suggests one crucial error in regards to poor management of financial liberalisation. The problem lies with the government itself where they failed to provide an adequate regulatory system for the BIBF and guidance for investors to manage risk appropriately when new investing and lending opportunities were offered by financial liberalisation. In fact, this problem originated from inappropriate reform of the domestic market. As we discussed earlier that the government established the BIBF rather than reforming the domestic financial institutions with supervisory and monitoring systems. As our study confirmed that pattern of investment and lending in Thailand changed dramatically from the tradeable to non-tradeable sectors and the outcome of weak supervision and poor regulatory system allowed the moral hazard problem with high level of unproductive investments and lending.

In sum, from our study, we suggest the problem of moral hazard derived from two over-optimistic expectations of the Thai economy in the age of liberalisation. Firstly, the expectation that the country's economic growth would continue indefinitely, resulting in over investment in unproductive investments, such as real estate and construction projects. Secondly, the expectation of guaranteed loans to the BIBF, created problems of excessive lending in the non-tradeable sector. These expectations groomed the confidence over the economy among investors, who invested or lent funds without hedging against risks to Thailand. This resulted in growing numbers of non-performing loans and huge loan losses, which led to a collapse of the economy. Finally, the government was to blame for allowing moral hazard problem to ignite through the lack of government provision of the appropriate guidance and supervisory systems to assist investors and the BIBF.

8 A Cost and Benefit Analysis Model for Globalisation: Some Social Welfare Implications of Thailand's Globalisation Process

By Sardar M. N. Islam and Mathew Clarke

8.1 Introduction

Undoubtedly the most striking feature of the globalisation process has been financial liberalisation. In principle, financial liberalisation is the process whereby a country seeks to increase its competitiveness and growth by freeing up its financial system for international capital through reforming trade, foreign exchange policy, capital controls and the domestic financial market. The ultimate aim of globalisation and financial liberalisation is to foster economic growth. This chapter analyses the benefits of these two interdependent and intertwined processes from a social welfare perspective. Various inter and intra-dependent development issues, processes, innovations and public policies have intersected and accelerated social and economic change resulting in what is commonly referred to as globalisation over the past three decades (Bird and Rajan 2001; for a review of the welfare and political issues see Sen 1999; Gilpin 2001; Islam 2001a). Globalisation is widely considered to be a contributor to global prosperity.

This chapter proposes, develops and applies a welfare economic framework with a focus on a cost-benefit analysis of the intra-country sharing of the development impact of global prosperity from globalisation and states the resultant welfare economic, development strategic and public policy perspectives.

The process of globalisation produces a wide range of welfare economic outcomes, both costs and benefits, in terms of the economy, the environment and social relationships. The benefits may include higher incomes, improved health and greater political freedom. The costs can include greater inequality, environmental degradation and social dislocation. To determine the desirability of globalisation, it is important to move beyond listing the separate costs and benefits and to undertake a welfare economic analysis of globalisation based on cost-benefit analysis methods. This will facilitate the consideration of intertemporal preferences, intergenerational equity, etc. to determine the desirability of globalisation at the intra-country level.

A systematic consideration, quantification, and numerical estimations of the costs and benefits of globalisation has not yet been undertaken within the current literature. The objective of this chapter is to present a study of globalisation which can overcome this limitation. An illustrative, though realistic, estimation of the costs and benefits of globalisation is undertaken and analysed within a welfare economics framework.

The estimation of these costs and benefits of globalisation are based on operationalising social choice theory. Cost-benefit analysis is a technique that determines the desirability of globalisation in terms of its net benefits and the preferred or optimal levels of social welfare. It is possible to develop a cost-benefit analysis framework using normative social choice perspectives.

This framework explicitly considers society's values, choices and preferences on these issues. Cost-benefit analysis provides a more accurate measure of the social welfare effects of policies, projects or economic states compared to conventional measures of the net benefits of globalisation. By incorporating cost-benefit analysis into calculating and adjusting national income, a more accurate understanding of optimal levels of society's welfare provided by development processes can be reached. The use of cost-benefit analysis allows the new measure of net social welfare as both costs and benefits of globalisation are now included, rather than just the benefits.

Social choice theory makes explicit the societal value judgements upon which the definition and measure of social welfare are based. By applying cost-benefit analysis to the calculation of national income in order to measure society's welfare, national income is made to more closely resemble real social welfare corresponding income levels.

A new cost-benefit analysis of the development impact of globalisation's prosperity is presented in this chapter for a twenty-five year period for Thailand, 1975–1999, based on social choice theory. This adjusted measure shows stark differences exist between conventional measures of globalisation and cost-benefit adjusted measures of globalisation. The welfare economic, development strategic and public policy perspectives are also evident from the results. This approach has wider applications to other economies in the world.

This chapter is structured as follows: Section 8.2 presents a brief review of the Thai experience of globalisation and financial crises. Section 8.3 introduces the welfare economics framework. Section 8.4 introduces the illustrative cost benefit analysis. Section 8.5 presents welfare analysis of the results of this illustrative exercise. Finally Sect. 8.6 presents a summary conclusion.

8.2 Overview of Globalisation and the Thai Experience

Globalisation is commonly considered to be characterised by the increasing interdependence of national economies, trade, corporations, financial markets, production, distribution and consumer marketing (Henderson 1999; McNutt 2002).

The desirability of globalisation is dependent upon how its resultant prosperity is shared. A social welfare evaluation of globalisation at the intra-country level can be performed by adapting the framework of global welfare economics (Sen 1999; Islam 2001a). The prosperity from globalisation affects different sections of society in different ways. Globalisation results in both winners and losers and has both benefits and costs (Williamson 2002). As such, globalisation is an important issue for evaluating social welfare of a nation, especially for Thailand, for example, due to its experience within the 1997 Asian financial crisis which was mainly a result of rapid globalisation (Arunsmith 1998; Siamwalla 2000; Julian 2000; Ryan 2000).

Within the developed world and certain developing countries (such as Thailand), a number of factors have been important drivers in the process of globalisation: (i) the rise of the knowledge economy; (ii) financial liberalisation; (iii) accelerated transportation and communication systems; (iv) increased direct foreign investment; and (v) increased economic and political interdependence of countries.

Over the last three decades, most economies have moved towards international economic deregulation. This deregulation has resulted in the dismantling of trade barriers such as tariffs in goods and services, relaxation of control over capital markets (including floating currencies, and deregulation of financial markets and direct foreign investments), and the deregulation of internal markets for goods and services.

Within Thailand though, the major effects of globalisation have only been felt since the mid 1980s. As mentioned in the previous chapters between 1975 and the mid 1980s, the Thai economy was relatively closed and tightly controlled by government regulations. Regulations on foreign investment were tight and the value of the baht was fixed and later tied to the US dollar and later still a US dollar dominated basket of currencies. The Thai government sheltered the economy from the excesses of the volatility of the world economy (Dixon 1996, 1999). However, from the late 1980s, the effects of globalisation, the rise of the knowledge economy and liberalisation of finance and capital markets began to be implemented (Warr and Nidhiprabha 1996; Leightner 1999). Foreign investment escalated, particularly into the export-manufacturing sector, as a direct result of this process (Kittiprapas 1999, 2000; Pilbeam 2001).

On the other hand, globalisation was directly impacting on communities at all levels especially the rural community. Villages produced agricultural exports, supplied labour to domestic market in cities, had access to telecommunication networks especially television (and satellite television). This globalisation of the village is considered by many non-government organisations responsible for increased debt and its ensuing poverty and the inability to become self-reliant. However, less globalised villages suffered more during the financial crisis of 1997, as they had fewer coping mechanisms and options available to them (Kaosa-ard 2000).

8.3 Welfare Economics Framework for Globalisation

8.3.1 The Elements

The welfare economic framework proposed to evaluate the relative welfare economic implications of globalisation for sharing global prosperity at the intra-country has several components or perspectives. They are cost benefit analysis, social choice theory, and a systems approach. This approach has been called by Islam (2001b) a *(new)[3] welfare economics*, which is based on the social choice possibility perspective, measurability of social welfare and a multi-disciplinary system approach incorporating welfaristic and non-welfaristic elements of social welfare.

8.3.1.1 A General Welfare Economics Framework

In welfare economics, a useful framework to rank social states (or projects) when the forces of private profitability are unable to rank them according to social orderings is through cost-benefit analysis (Boadway and Bruce

1984). There are several conceptual and methodological issues related to the measurement of society's welfare and economic performance which are central to all studies of welfare (see Arrow et al. forthcoming; Bos et al. 1988; Broadway and Bruce 1984; Johnson 1996; Ravallion 1994; Lahiri and Moore 1991; Islam 2001a; Sen 1985a, 1985b). They include:

- a definition of well-being and welfare;
- criteria for evaluation of welfare and performance;
- the specification of an aggregate social welfare function such as possibility and impossibility theorems in social choice;
- the numeraire of welfare and performance such as utility, consumption, GDP, capabilities, entitlement, wealth, capital stock, clean environment, the level of human development or a combination of non-economics factors such as rights, freedom, opportunity, equity etc.;
- units of measurement, i.e. money or physical units, market prices, shadow prices, contingent valuation or willingness to pay;
- the level of measurement at the aggregative (macro) or disaggregative (micro) levels; and
- models for measurement and analysis such GDP or other aggregative performance indices, family budget analysis, economy wide macro-econometric models, econometric estimates of demand functions, game theory, constrained optimisation, cost-benefit analysis, micro and macro economic or growth models.

Within this new approach, welfare is defined as a function of the cost and benefit consequences of globalisation upon welfare outcomes. It is operationalised through a democratic social welfare function using social choice theory. The numeraire of this index will be Thai baht, in 1988 prices, based on standard national accounts. The measurement units are a mix of market and shadow prices and are calculated at the macro-level. By incorporating the above elements of social choice and welfare economics, a social welfare function of the following form can be developed:

$$SWF_t = W_t(NB_t\{P_{t)}\})$$ (8.1)

where:
W_t = welfare
t = time
NB_t = $[(B_t\{P_t\}) - (C_t\{P_t\})](1+r)^t$
B_t = benefits of program
C_t = costs of program
r = discount rate
P_t = the program

The time value of money needs to be addressed when undertaken a monetary based cost-benefit analysis. The future value is discounted to net present value (NPV) by a factor. The net discounted present value of a project is calculated as:

$$NPV = \frac{B_0 - C_0}{(1 + r)^0} + \frac{B_1 - C_1}{(1 + r)^1} + \ldots\ldots + \frac{B_n - C_n}{(1 + r)^n} \qquad (8.2)$$

$$= \sum_{t=0}^{n} \frac{B^t - C^t}{(1 + r)^t}$$

where NPV = net present value
       B   = benefits
       C   = costs
       r   = discount rate
       n   = number of years

The Cost-Benefit (C-B) ratio reveals the dollars gained on each dollar of cost:

$$\text{C-B ratio} = \frac{\sum_{t=0}^{N} \dfrac{B_t}{(1 + r)^t}}{\sum_{t=0}^{n} \dfrac{C_t}{(1 + r)^t}} \qquad (8.3)$$

a. If C-B ratio is greater than 1, the health program is of value.
b. If C-B ratio is equal to 1, the benefit equals the cost.
c. If C-B ratio is less than 1, the health program is not beneficial.

Debate on the appropriate discount rate is unresolved in the literature. For financial valuation, the market rate of interest is considered the appropriate social discount rate (Johansson 1987). However, within social welfare considerations, such a discount rate renders the rights of future generations to almost zero within only a few decades. Within this book, a pragmatic decision has been made to use a social discount rate equal to zero as the impacts of globalisation on social welfare is considered as equally important for both the present and future generations (Ramsey 1928; Harrod 1948). The consequence of a zero discount rate is that the needs of the present generation are explicitly made equal to the needs of the future generations.

8.3.1.2 Application to Globalisation

Cost-benefit analysis will be incorporated in this chapter to consider the benefits of globalisation. This will account for both economic and non-economic, direct and indirect effects and concerns of globalisation on social welfare through identifying and incorporating these effects, then assigning monetary values through the use of market prices and shadow prices, and using social time preferences for intertemporal welfare comparisons. This will make the cost-benefit analysis of globalisation an appropriate tool for ranking different social states. If we adapt the above social welfare function, the cost-benefit model can be stated as follows:

$$NSBGt = \Sigma(DBGt + IBGt) - (DCGt + ICGt) \qquad (8.4)$$

where NSBG = net social benefit of globalisation
   t = time
   DBG = direct benefits of globalisation
   IBG = indirect benefits of globalisation
   DCG = direct costs of globalisation
   ICG = indirect costs of globalisation

Cost-benefit analysis has several components or elements. The first component is to consider all the direct economic and non-economic inputs and outputs. Social states (or projects) considered within a cost-benefit analysis framework have economic inputs and outputs that would be considered in a financial analysis, but they also have non-economic inputs and outputs that also need to be fully captured. These may include time saved, risk taking or health improvements. The second component is to consider all the indirect costs and benefits. These indirect effects are primarily externalities that are not captured elsewhere in the economy. They include such things as pollution, which affects third parties, to the production-consumption relationship. Having identified all the direct and indirect, economic and non-economic costs and benefits, the third component of cost-benefit analysis is to assign monetary values to these effects. The monetary value of the direct, economic costs and benefits are found within the market. However, a variety of techniques have been developed (i.e. hedonic pricing, border prices, willingness to pay, etc.) to calculate the prices of indirect, non-economic costs and benefits. These are known as *shadow prices*. By assigning monetary values to these non-economic goods, they can be considered with the economic costs and benefits to determine the final ranking. The final component of cost-benefit analysis is to sum all these impacts for each period but to also convert all these current values into a present value. This is achieved through the use of time preferences and social discount rates (Boadway and Bruce 1984).

8.3.2 Social Choice Theory

Social choice theory is concerned with the study of issues surrounding social welfare on the basis of individual preferences but also considering the requirement for an optimal social outcome. Social choice theory is concerned with defining and measuring social welfare consistent with individual preferences for improving social welfare conditions, with the provision that society's preferences are paramount.

Social choice theory has a long history (see Sen 1999 for a survey). The difficulties in making a judgment on the state of social welfare have long been recognised (Borda 1780, reprinted 1953; de Condorcet 1785). Arrow (1951) formulated the difficulties and inconsistencies of social choices within his 'impossibility theorem'. He showed through using axiomatic set theory that it was not possible to make a non-dictatorial social choice that satisfied a set of axioms of reasonableness. An alternative theorem was developed by Sen (1966, 1970, 1973; and subsequently added to by others, see Hammond 1976) that argued that Arrow's set of axioms of reasonableness were not reasonable but based on restrictive assumptions, which are not necessary in operational social choice making in real life environments. Therefore, it was possible to make non-dictatorial social choice decisions.

8.3.3 A Systems Analysis

Society is made up of many sub-systems (or domains) that inter-relate in a dynamic manner (Dopfer 1979; Clayton and Radcliffe 1996; Bossel 1999; Islam and Clarke 2003). Each of these sub-systems has a direct impact on society's well-being and therefore, measures of social welfare must take into account each of these sub-systems for that measure to be legitimate. It is rare for national welfare measurement to include all sub-systems (see Islam 2001a, 2001b for a measure containing the social, environmental and economic factors).

Understanding society as systems-based can impact on policy-makers' planning paths of increased development or welfare.

8.3.4 Issues in the Application of the Framework

A large set of controversial issues has emerged in regard to the process of globalisation, its causes, consequences and welfare impacts. The set of issues relevant for social welfare analysis and measurement include (see also Islam 2001b):

1. How can social welfare be measured and assessed within a open economy?
2. Will globalisation increase social welfare via economic growth?
3. Is globalisation beneficial for society given its consequences?
4. How much importance should be given to the influence of foreign factors relative to national factors especially to evaluate the importance of welfaristic and non-welfaristc elements of social welfare in a global economy?

In this chapter, social welfare is estimated by various adjustments to GDP which represents the social and environmental benefits and costs of globalisation and its resultant prosperity. In the rest of the chapter, the above issues in the welfare economics of globalisation are investigated by adopting a quantitative and empirical framework (assuming the aforementioned principles and features) of social choice theory based cost-benefit analysis.

8.4 Costs and Benefits of Globalisation

8.4.1 Illustrative Numerical Estimation of the Costs and Benefits of Globalisation

Globalisation is not new to Thailand. Following the sacking of its previous capital city, Ayutthaya in 1767 by the Burmese, the strategically safer Bangkok was settled. By 1782 Bangkok had flourished and become a important regional trading centre. Bangkok become a regional centre for shipbuilding and was soon building the largest ships outside of Europe. Trade brought Thailand into contact with Europe, and various colonial powers such as the Dutch, French and English, began to show political interest in Thailand. Thailand was able to avoid colonisation through establishing various trade treaties, such as the *Burney Treaty* in 1826 and the *Bowring Treaty* in 1855, with these colonial powers that both ensured independence but also incorporation into the world economy. But throughout this period of globalisation, the majority of the population remained unaffected enjoying a high standard of living (Falkus 1995). Farmers supplemented their rice crops with hunting and gathering high value goods from the tropical forests (Phongpaichit and Baker 1995).

The more recent experience of globalisation however, has been financial liberalisation and deregulation that has occurred through much of the world (including the developing countries) over the past two to three decades (see Agenor and Montiel 1996). This liberalisation occurred within structural adjustment programs prepared for developing countries by the

IMF and World Bank. These packages of liberalisation closely reflect the policies adopted by developed countries in removing trade barriers, reducing barriers to capital movements and investments, privatisation of state-owned enterprises, reduction in government fiscal spending, deregulation of labour markets and a focus on global trade. The support for economic openness is now widespread (see Edwards 1992; Dollar 1992; Ben-David 1993; Sachs and Warner 1995; Frankel and Romer 1999; Alesina et al. 2000). However, opposing views have recently resurfaced (see Rodrik 1998; Harrison and Hanson 1999; Rodrik and Rodriguez 2000).

Although qualitative arguments for and against are common in mainstream economic discussion (see Stiglitz 2002), the costs and benefits of financial liberalisation are not easy to estimate or quantify (McKibben 1997, 1998). A preliminary effort for identifying and quantifying the costs and benefits is made here.

8.4.1.1 Benefits

The benefits of financial liberalisation within globalisation (Wacziarg 2001; Singh 1999) include (but are not limited to):

- transmission of knowledge;
- improved government fiscal and monetary policies;
- personal gains to currency traders which has grown to be valued at US$1.5 trillion per day;
- technological spillovers;
- productiveity increases; and
- gains in efficiency due to a wider scale of market interactions.

8.4.1.2 Costs

The major costs of financial liberalisation within globalisation (Borland et al. 2001b; Wacziarg 2001; Arunsmith 1998; Siamwalla 2000) have been identified as (but are not limited to):

- an increase in polarisation of households between those with access to well-paid employment and those in poorly paid casual employment;
- pressure to decrease government size and market presence and government interference in resource allocation;
- loss of manufacturing jobs to cheaper overseas locations;
- an increase in divergence of earnings in various employment classifications; and

- the floating of currencies and degradation of financial markets has left countries exposed to capital flight and unstable investments. The Asian financial crisis in 1997 was largely due to this financial deregulation and freedom from investment controls (Julian 2000; Ryan 2000).

Often though, these costs are not a result of the globalisation process but rather that of insufficient liberalisation and privatisation, coupled with rampant corruption, etc. (Aziz 1999).

Financial liberalisation did not occur until the late 1980s in Thailand (Dixon 1996, 1999). Previously, there were strict controls over the value of the baht and capital movement. During the 1990s, foreign capital flooded Thailand's financial markets. The result was speculative spending, lending and borrowing creating macroeconomic imbalances and aggravating the current account deficits and inflation. These poor outcomes occurred through poor management of both the domestic and the international financial systems (Kaosa-ard 2000; APEC 2000). However, despite these poor controls, the resultant financial crisis can be considered a consequence of globalisation. The Thai investment boom which occurred over the decade 1987–1996, was responsible for both the extraordinary growth rates experienced during that decade, and simultaneously responsible for the financial crisis in 1997 (Vines and Warr 2000). Following the July 1997 crisis, a massive capital flight occurred leaving Thailand in debt to the value of US$89 billion (APEC 2000).

Within this grossly over simplified illustrative cost-benefit analysis, the net benefits (prosperity) of globalisation are assumed to be fully reflected in economic growth. As stated this is an over simplification, but is acceptable for illustrative purposes (indeed, globalisation is considered to be a driving force of economic growth, see World Bank 1999, 2001). *No additional benefits of globalisation will be added as it is considered that all benefits (such as higher incomes, increased consumption, better health care, etc.) are represented within this figure.*

The Thai economy has had three distinct periods of economic growth over the last twenty-five years, 1975–1999. The first phase 1975–1985, was a period of steady growth; the second phase 1986–1995, was a period of accelerated growth, whilst the final phase, 1996–1999 was characterised by the financial crisis and apparent recovery (Clarke and Islam 2003).

Achieving economic growth in Thailand has been the major public policy priority for some time (NESDB 1996, 2000) – often to the exclusion of other goals (Parnwell 1996; Schmidt 1996). Indeed, all policies to plan or control the direction of economic growth in the early 1990s were abandoned in order to achieve high growth rates (Phongpaichit and Baker 1995). This pursuit was successful, yet in terms of other possible welfare outcomes, such as environmental damage and growing inequality, the costs have also been high.

8.4.2 Numerical Application: Methodology, Data and Results

8.4.2.1 GDP Index

When economists explicitly or implicitly accept the identification of economic welfare with the supply of goods and services, they effectively ignore the differences between economic and non-economic welfare and the fact that activities affecting economic welfare favourably may conceivably affect non-economic welfare unfavourably (Abramovitz 1961). Therefore whilst economic growth might increase economic welfare, it may reduce non-economic welfare. The cumulative effect on social welfare may be positive, negative or neutral, but this approach assumes it to be positive.

GDP is based on the calculation of prices and quantities:

$$GDP = q \cdot p$$

where: q is a vector of outputs (n x 1), $[q^1, q^2, \ldots, q^n]$
p is a vector of prices (1 x n), $[p^1, p^2, \ldots, p^n]$

An index is a statistical measure that shows changes in variables over time. Periods are compared to a base year. A simple index is the price index defined as p^n/p^0, where p is the price, n is the given year and 0 is the base year. The result is a base year of 100% and comparisons, in percent, are made.

Most indices, such as the GDP index, are computations of prices and quantities. The most common is the Laspeyre base-weighted model $(p^n.q^0)/(p^0.q^0)$. This results in the Laspeyres index being biased towards the base quantity purchased and thus can be made redundant if the index covers too lengthy a period. The GDP index for Thailand (used in this chapter) is calculated on the Laspeyres Index.

By observing how individuals allocate a certain sum of money over a specified period of time, data can be collected on people's preferences for particular consumption bundles (Hufschmidt et al. 1983).

At an aggregate level, GDP is the summation of all individuals' revealed preferences. Just as revealed preferences can indicate whether the welfare of an individual has increased or decreased, thus, so to can GDP indicate this for the entire economy. GDP as [1] is a consumption bundle for a given period. Changes in [1] are implicitly assumed to indicate changes in social welfare.

8.4.2.2 GDP Adjustment Data

The empirical application of this social welfare function relies on techniques developed by others (Adelman and Morris 1973; Atkinson 1970; Daly and Cobb 1990; Diefenbacher 1994; Hamilton 1998; Islam 1995, 1998; Jackson and Marks 1994; Lawn and Sanders 1997; Miringoff 1996; Nordhaus and Tobin 1973; United Nations Development Program (UNDP) 1990) that have been adapted to more closely fit the Thai experience. Whilst economic data is collected by the Thai government to assist in the calculations of the national accounts, many of the calculations required are not included in these accounts. Data gathered by tertiary institutions and local and international non-government organisations are therefore used (Table 8.1).

Table 8.1. Summary of calculations

Income Distribution (cost)		
	$I \quad = $	$1 - \sum\limits_{i=1}^{n} (y^i / \mu)^{1/1-\epsilon}$ $\epsilon \neq 1$
Commuting (cost)	C =	NRC(219.XR)
Urbanisation (cost)	U =	BY(0.08) + BY(0.1)
Air pollution (cost)	A =	cCO_2+cCO+cNOX+cSOX+cSPM
Water pollution (cost)	W =	[(7.5 x IP) + (7.5 x 4.6 x MP)] x 2
Noise pollution (cost)	N =	GDP(0.01)
Deforestation (cost)	D =	DF(886)
Long-term environmental Damage (cost)	L =	cCD_t + $cCWR_t$ + cCF_t

where:

I	=	measure of income inequality
y^i	=	income of individuals in the ith income range
μ	=	mean income
ϵ	=	society's perspective on equality
C	=	cost of commuting
NRC	=	number of registered cars in Bangkok
XR	=	exchange rate
U	=	cost of urbanisation
BY	=	average income for Bangkok residents
A	=	cost of air pollution
cCO2	=	cost of carbon dioxide (.03335 baht per kilogram)
cCO	=	cost of carbon monoxide (.03335 baht per kilogram)
cNOX	=	cost of nitrogen monoxide (2.84 baht per kilogram)
cSOX	=	cost of sulfur monoxide (7.4 baht per kilogram)
cSPM	=	cost of suspended particulate matters (4.15 baht per kilogram)
W	=	cost of water pollution
IP	=	industrial pollution =	FI + DI + PI + CI + TI
		FI	=	food industry BOD
		DI	=	drink industry BOD

	PI =	chapter industry BOD
	CI =	chemical industry BOD
	TI =	textile industry BOD
MP	=	municipal population BOD
BOD	=	biochemical oxygen demand
N	=	cost of noise pollution
GDP	=	gross domestic product
D	=	cost of deforestation
DF	=	hectares of deforestation
L	=	cost of long-term environmental damage
cCD_t	=	cost of carbon emissions of deforestation
	=	21.59 x tonne of carbon emission
$cCWR_t$	=	cost of carbon emissions of wet rice farming
	=	21.59 x tonne of carbon emission
cCF_t	=	cost of carbon emissions of fuel consumption
	=	21.59 x tonne of carbon emission

When these social and environmental consequences of globalisation are considered, the welfare implications of globalisation can be reconsidered (Islam and Clarke 2002; Clarke and Islam 2003). Within this illustrative exercise, eight adjustments will be made to Thailand's GDP over a twenty-five year period (1975–1999), to estimate the costs and benefits of globalisation. These adjustments are income inequality, commuting, urbanisation, water pollution, air pollution, noise pollution, deforestation and long-term environmental damage. The full calculation of these adjustments can be found in Clarke and Islam (2003) (Fig. 8.1).

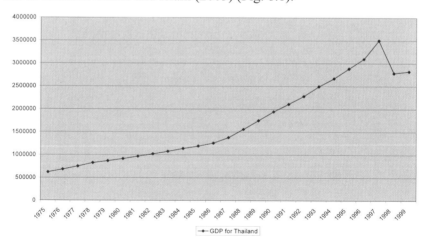

Fig. 8.1. GDP for Thailand, 1975–1999 (1988 prices, millions of baht)

Source: Authors' estimates.

Having considered these social and environmental costs of globalisation, another significant cost was the financial crisis. Sufficient evidence now exists that the crisis of July 1997 was caused by various factors attributed to financial deregulation (see Julian 2000; Ryan 2000). The most visible short-term cost of financial liberalisation within Thailand (and the region) occurred in 1997, and its impact has been high. The costs of this crisis were obvious and not simply contained to multi-national corporations. Within Southeast Asia, there was an immediate and large fall in the standard of living of all sectors of society (McKibben 1998; Aziz et al. 2001; Kakwani and Pothong 2000). The average reduction in real income across Thailand was over 21% in 1998 and up to 28% in rural Thailand (Kakwani and Pothong 2000; also see Kaosa-ard 2000). Those living under the poverty line increased by 1.5 million people, from 7.9 million to 9.4 million and nearly one million extra people were classified as ultra poor (Kakwani 1999). The fall in real income is not dissimilar to levels experienced in other countries (see Aziz et al. 2001). However, this initial fall has not continued in the long-term and the levels of real income have begun to recover (Kakwani and Pothong 2000) (Fig. 8.2).

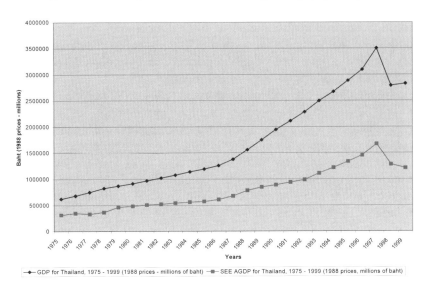

Fig. 8.2. Comparison of GDP and adjusted GDP for Thailand, 1975–1999 (1988 prices, millions of baht)

Source: Authors' estimates.

8.5 Welfare Implications of Globalisation

The process of globalisation can be effectively analysed from a welfare economic perspective by adopting a cost-benefit analysis model. A global welfare economic perspective is the relevant paradigm for this analysis (Sen 1999; Islam 2001a). As has been discussed, globalisation has both benefits and costs. By analysing these costs and benefits from such a per spective, new insights can be gained in whether social welfare has been enhanced or stunted by this process.

The welfare implication of these estimates of the costs and benefits of financial liberalisation include the intertemporal nature of the experience of the costs and benefits. The costs are short-term but give way to longer-term benefits. The needs of the present generation must be considered in light of the needs of future generations. (This is an unusual example of the costs being borne in the present.) How the separate costs and benefits are distributed must also be considered. The financial crisis appeared to hurt the poorest in Thailand more so than other income groups (Kakwani and Pothong 2000). Such an outcome raises issues of justice.

As part of the process of globalisation and financial liberalisation, developing countries will continue to further incorporate their domestic economies into the rising global economy. The impact on social welfare of the net benefits of the rise of globalisation must be considered when discussing the desirability of economic growth.

In terms of equity, like all other markets, the newly fashioned global market is efficiency based and equity-neutral. Considerations of equity are thus ignored (or more accurately, efficient outcomes are considered to Pareto optimal in an equity sense). For instance, in terms of changes within labour markets, a significant shift that has been evidenced in developing countries is the movement towards the casualisation of labour and the divergence of labour rates between well-paid employment and poorly paid casual labour (Borland et al. 2001a, 2001b). These new characteristics of the labour market in developed countries have increasingly come to more closely reflect the labour conditions (insecurity, high wage differentials, casual employment) typical of developing countries such as Thailand. Within developing countries, in which dualistic economies exist, these characteristics might be exacerbated by the increasing impact of globalisation. In this regard, the widening gap between high income and low income earners in Australia has increased (Borland 1998), possibly reflecting an increase in income inequality in Thailand (Clarke 2001).

Thailand is currently a dualistic economy with a significant proportion of its population wholly or partially reliant on agriculture for their main source of income. In addition, income distribution is already quite unequal in Thailand (Clarke 2001; Warr 2001) and the movements towards globalisation may exacerbate the inequality between those with "knowledge" and those without. However, the changing economy may also lead to changing patterns of consumption and resource use and may be better distributed across societies and nations (Chichilnisky 1997). This is a large assumption though and yet to be empirically tested.

Further, the process of globalisation will have lasting effects as it has reshaped the global economy and by implication the domestic Thai economy. Within Thailand therefore, future generations will have to operate within an economy that is less regulated, outwardly focussed and open to international events. The welfare impacts of this change in economic organisation may be profound but are difficult to assess. An open economy may bring improved opportunities whilst bringing higher levels of uncertainty. Most likely though, the benefits and costs will not be equally shared (Bird and Rajan 2001).

The results of this illustrative cost-benefit analysis appear intuitively correct and plausible. It is reasonable to assume that the benefits of globalisation were effective and significant in increasing the social welfare within Thailand. Likewise, the resultant financial crisis had serious negative implications for the Thai economy, particularly those on low incomes (Kakwani and Pothong 2000; Kaosa-ard 2000). It is expected that the results in this exercise would be replicated in other Asian countries.

Clearly, the rise of the global economy will affect the social welfare within Thailand. Thailand has recognised the importance of improving the performance, for example, of the knowledge economy in achieving "quality growth" in the future (Ministry of Finance 2001). An illustrative estimation and quantification of some of the selected costs and benefits of globalisation allows greater insight into the social welfare impact of globalisation of Thailand.

8.6 Conclusions

This chapter has recognised the lack of empirical studies on the social welfare consequences of globalisation and financial crises. Comparably little work has been undertaken on exploring the inter-country social welfare implications of globalisation and global prosperity, in terms of its costs and benefits. Analysis of globalisation and financial crisis within this framework is not well known. This chapter developed a cost-benefit analysis model based time series, 1975–1999, in which illustrative (although realistic) estimates of the costs and benefit of globalisation and financial crisis were made. The results show that while the financial crisis had a dramatic negative impact on average income levels, the processes of globalisation that preceded the crisis were highly beneficial. The results provide the information for various public policy initiatives, especially to determine optimal globalisation theory that can now be more fully considered than was possible in the past. The modeling and analytical framework and numerical calculation are based on the concepts and methods of welfare economics such as welfare criteria, cost-benefit analysis, welfare measurement and social choice theory. More extensive integration of the welfare economic issues in the analysis of globalisation and its impact of the intra-country sharing of the prosperity from globalisation and global growth is necessary in future work in this area (Table 8.2).

Table 8.2. Thai economic and environmental data

Year	GDP	Adjusted GDP for inequality	Air	Water	Noise	Deforestation	Long term Environmental damage	Urbanisation	Commuting	Adjusted GDP
1975	621,555	415,261	4,117	4067	6216	62,013	4,960	18,084	3,066	102,523
1976	680,778	451,934	4,509	4454	6808	58,844	5,965	20,164	3,466	104,210
1977	750,053	494,735	4,913	4956	7501	113,162	6,932	22,255	3,829	163,548
1978	824,706	540,471	5,515	5362	8247	113,162	13,575	24,634	3,939	174,434
1979	867,796	565,022	5,758	5,503	8,678	33,949	16,893	25,712	3,787	100,280
1980	913,768	591,071	6,046	6,143	9,138	33,949	20,087	27,382	3,560	106,305
1981	967,374	621,634	6,069	6,854	9,674	33,949	23,175	29,172	4,704	113,597
1982	1,020,084	642,775	6,301	7,151	10,201	33,949	26,170	31,258	5,441	120,471
1983	1,075,922	664,532	6,773	7,583	10,759	30,327	28,255	30,869	6,171	120,737
1984	1,138,329	688,871	7,382	8,336	11,383	30,327	30,344	32,420	7,192	127,384
1985	1,191,089	705,934	7,930	8,033	11,911	29,875	32,428	33,843	9,141	133,161
1986	1,256,538	729,043	8,030	8,364	12,565	11,316	34,498	35,177	9,710	119,660
1987	1,377,026	805,422	9,299	8,833	13,770	11,316	35,653	37,963	10,012	126,846
1988	1,559,804	919,660	10,508	10,213	15,598	11,316	37,762	41,374	10,164	136,935
1989	1,750,228	995,442	12,146	11,533	17,502	11,316	38,981	48,611	9,133	149,222
1990	1,946,119	1,066,278	14,243	12,145	19,461	25,348	41,914	53,538	10,218	176,867
1991	2,111,740	1,132,104	16,144	13,528	21,117	25,348	44,848	62,459	9,947	193,391
1992	2,282,995	1,196,974	17,520	14,443	22,830	24,896	47,047	70,775	10,647	208,159
1993	2,494,748	1,327,580	19,479	15,060	24,947	25,348	49,194	70,927	11,497	216,452
1994	2,669,573	1,441,569	21,880	16,733	26,696	24,896	51,269	70,560	12,107	224,141
1995	2,884,495	1,578,828	24,307	18,422	28,845	25,348	53,460	81,507	12,406	244,295
1996	3,095,336	1,716,983	27,104	19,493	30,953	24,896	56,206	90,561	13,289	262,502
1997	3,502,012	1,946,944	29,257	20,033	30,520	25,348	58,210	93,200	17,099	273,667
1998	2,787,395	1,553,137	31,657	18,296	27,874	24,896	60,469	87,740	22,264	273,196
1999	2,823,416	1,480,317	34,056	18,533	28,234	4,526	62,727	98,231	22,495	268,802

9 Conclusions and Policy Implications

9.1 Conclusions

The 1997 Asian Financial crisis has led to the generation of some debate on the degree and the pace with which the openness and reform in the financial system should be pursued. The financial crisis that has afflicted many emerging countries is a costly reminder of the disastrous consequences for development of weak financial markets and inappropriate reform. Historical evidence suggests that periods of financial liberalisation coincided with, or are soon followed by financial instability ending in financial crisis like the East Asian crisis in the late 1990's. Clearly, the transition has not been smooth; therefore some people believe that there is some form of causality between financial reform and the liberalisation and financial instability. The financial liberalisation process as well can undoubtedly be handled well if the existing inefficiencies and distortions in the financial markets are taken care of with appropriate policy by developing a strong regulatory and institutional framework prior to the liberalisation process. Also, research has shown that the sequence of the reforms process and the pace of liberalisation play a crucial role in avoiding financial instability of any emerging economy.

It is argued in this book, it is necessary to analyse the policy issues of financial reform including the issues of liberalisation, institution, building, exchange rate determination, capital control, etc. by adopting an explicit framework of welfare economies. Welfare economies can provide an appropriate framework for analysing these issues, investigating the ex post and ex ante impacts and suggesting the right form of reform of a country. In this study a general welfare economies framework of asymmetric information, market failures, moral hazard, and incomplete information is adopted to analyse financial reform issues. A social cost benefit analysis is undertaken to conceptualise, measure and compare the costs and benefits of financial reforms. The welfare economic framework adopted in this study is a derivative of new welfare economics developed is Islam (2001b) (see also Clarke and Islam 2004; Craven and Islam 2005, Islam and Mak 2006).

This book analyses these issues in relation to the Thai economy as a case study although the arguments and concerns are equally relevant for many developing and developed countries as given its relative openness, the Thai economy presents an example of a complex international financial system with emerging issues of significant public policy, economic development and social welfare. Like many developing countries, Thailand experienced a series of economic disruptions in the first half of the 1970s and the beginning of the 1980s, resulting from the oil shock and world economic slump. In response, the Thai government developed an economic stabilisation program to restore economic stability and encourage growth by pegging the baht to the US dollar and introducing manufacturing and industry led growth policy. Consequently, the economy began to pick up and performed well from mid 1980s onward. This was a critical period in Thailand's development, as the economy experienced strong economic growth led by high export growth with significant foreign direct investment. These factors contributed to the Thai success story between 1980 to 1990, especially during 1988 to 1990 when the economy expanded at a double-digit GDP growth rate and was hailed as the fastest growing economy in the world. Such an impressive economic performance led the IMF to suggest that Thailand liberalise its financial system, in part by accepting the Article VIII agreement (see Appendix A). The overall objective of financial liberalisation was to increase the flexibility of the financial system so that the Thai economy could compete successfully in the international economic community, and have assured economic growth rates. The main features of the agreement stated that Thailand needed to remove restrictions on foreign exchange transactions and ensure the convertibility of the currency by allowing more freedom in foreign currency trade, for instance, capital controls deregulation and foreign exchange reform.

Having accepted the IMF's Article VIII, Thailand gradually liberalised its financial system during 1989–1994. First, Thailand began with interest rate reform on long-term deposits in June 1989 and all other interest rate ceilings were completely removed by June 1992. Second, the government reformed its exchange rate and capital controls, which can be delineated in three episodes. The first change was announced at a time during 1989–1990, allowing the public direct access to foreign funds and permitting them to make outflows for the purpose of dividend, interest or principle repayments. Commercial banks were also allowed to get involved in foreign exchange trade without prior approval from the Bank of Thailand. The second change was implemented during 1991 and 1992 and allowed the public more freedom in buying and selling foreign exchange, receiving payments in foreign currencies and transferring them overseas. The third change was declared in 1994 when the Bank of Thailand raised the limit on the outflows in baht from 250,000 to 500,000 baht, while the amount permitted to transfer for overseas investment also increased from US$5 million to US$10 million. The final action that Thailand undertook in liberalising its financial system was the establishment of an offshore bank, called the 'BIBF' in 1993, aimed at reducing the cost of finance and enhancing capital flows into the country.

Since the commencement of financial reforms, the Thai economy continued to perform well with growing exports and sustained fiscal balance. However, things changed when the country experienced an extraordinary surge in foreign capital flows into the private sector, especially inflows through the banking sector via the BIBF. Strong economic fundamentals coupled with high capital inflows at the time led some economists (Chaiyasoot 1995; Suphachalasai 1995) to conclude that opening up financially by accepting Article VIII of the IMF was the right choice for Thailand and the IMF was also praised for its role in enforcing financial liberalisation. To many observers' surprise, the story of Thai economic success was short lived. One of the world's fastest growing economies came to a sudden stop in 1996, contracting with problems of a high level of foreign debt, a trade imbalance and a massive decline in exports. When these problems began to unfold, confidence in the Thai economy among international investors slipped away. Hence, they suspended reinvestment into the country and started to pull funds out, resulting in economic stagnation and serious fiscal imbalance, which soon precipitated the country into financial crisis in mid 1997.

The financial crisis that erupted in Thailand has raised questions among economists as to why the Thai crisis occurred, what were the roots of the crisis and why the crisis struck so deep (Falkus 1999). Furthermore, the financial crisis in Thailand is said to be a showcase of a new kind of crisis, which the two traditional theories, the first-generation model by Krugman (1979) and the second-generation model by Flood and Garber (1984b), fail to explain as the fundamental economic conditions in Thailand prior to the crisis were reasonably strong. Brustelo (1998) and Krugman (1998b) argued that Thailand was in fiscal balance, with low inflation, low unemployment and no signs of stock or asset prices crashing before the crisis. Some economists (Bullard et al. 1998; Buckley 1999) blamed some international institutions for its role in enforcing financial liberalisation in Thailand. They argued that, without the agreement of some international institutions financial liberalisation in Thailand would not have been implemented and the crisis would not have occurred. On the other hand, other economists (Krongkaew 1999; Pilbeam 2001) believed that the financial crisis in Thailand occurred because the rapid injection of capital by foreign investors causing instability to the financial system. In other words, the Thai financial crisis was a new kind of crisis that cast doubt on the benefits of the financial liberalisation, which was once said to promise economic growth and developments. This study attempted to identify, using an asymmetric information paradigm (market, policy and institutional failures) the contribution of Thailand's financial liberalisation process to the crisis, and found four policy errors in the implementation of liberalisation process due to the prevalence of asymmetric information in the Thai economy, contributing to the crisis.

The first error was an inappropriate sequencing of financial liberalisation. Thailand undertook the transformation of its foreign trade pattern as the first sequence in liberalising the financial system. A once agricultural export oriented economy was replaced by a manufacturing and industrial led growth policy. As a result, Thailand's economy grew rapidly during the second half of the 1980s prior to the liberalisation. However, the critical mistake of Thailand's sequence of financial liberalisation occurred while the current account was heavily in deficit when reform of the exchange rate and capital controls were undertaken. Theoretically, a country pursuing financial liberalisation should reduce its current account deficit before other steps towards liberalisation are taken. Although, Thailand was able to achieve its first ever current account surplus in 1986, this was short lived, and the current account deficit returned to over 7% of GDP in 1990 and 1991. Failure to initially reduce the deficits further worsened the situation, and the current account deficit rose dramatically, particularly during the slowdown of Thailand's exports between 1995 and 1996, which forced the country into deep deficits. Thailand implemented the controls on capital flows and foreign exchange prior to the reform of domestic financial market by allowing more freedom for private financial institutions to trade in foreign currency and larger outflows to be made without prior approval from the Bank of Thailand. Under this sequence of reform, the volume of foreign exchange trading by private financial institutions rose significantly, in particular, exchange traded by foreign banks, causing speculative trading of the currency.

After the exchange controls were lifted, Thailand then needed to reform its domestic financial market as the final step towards financial liberalisation. Instead of reforming the domestic institution with supervisory and monitoring system, Thailand founded the BIBF to seek and absorb funds from abroad to service economic growth. Soon afterward, the BIBF's inflows increased massively in just a short period of time, increasing almost seven times between 1994 and 1995. The problem was accentuated when the government allowed the BIBF to borrow and lend freely. The latter extended their funds heavily within domestic market creating problem of over-investment in non-tradeable sector. More importantly, over-invest-ment of the BIBF in the non-tradeable sector indicated poor economic guidance from the government. Perhaps, with government involvement, the BIBF would have operated more wisely and redirected investment and lending to sectors with better returns.

Liberalising the financial system in the sequence described above proved to be disastrous. In short, from the Thai experience, we discover that there are three problems of sequencing liberalisation implemented by the government. First, liberalising the financial system before the current account deficit was reduced further worsened the deficit. Second, having reformed foreign exchange and capital controls before the domestic finan-cial market was ready, implied instability caused by free trade of foreign exchange, creating a problem of bank fragility and left them vulnerable to speculative attacks. Lastly, leaving domestic reform with establishment of the BIBF to the last, resulted in a shift of massive capital inflows from productive to unproductive users, leading to problems of excessive lending.

The second error, capital account liberalisation, is a prominent compo-nent in any liberalisation programme. Premature capital account liberalisa-tion could have a destabilising affect on any economy and should only be undertaken after domestic market reforms have been initiated. Thailand relaxed most of its controls on capital during the process of liberalisation during 1989–1994. The government permitted inflows to travel more freely. Like never before, the limits on outflows were raised and both for-eigners and domestic nationals were allowed to carry funds out of Thailand without government interference. As a result, Thailand experienced a mas-sive influx of funds with the majority of them invested in the risky sectors such as real estate, construction and financial sectors. This revealed the fact that the inflows were not indeed managed wisely. On the outflows side, foreign investors pulled funds out of Thailand immediately, after lib-eralisation was complete, leading to macroeconomic imbalance. The weakness of the Thai economy became apparent when the economy failed to perform and investors realised there were a serious problem of risky in-vestments. This caused panic and fear among investors, which led to sud-den reversal of capital flows, resulting in a significant decline in inflows and sudden economic stagnation. The loss of confidence in the Thai econ-omy and poor regulation on outflows paved the way for the investors to pull massive sums out of the country. Such reversal of capital flows is normally associated with the problems of asymmetric information leading to market failure and the need for government intervention. These were the causes and consequences of asymmetric information problem existing in the Thai economy during the study period.

Allowing inflows and outflows to be made more freely did not promise economic growth and development but rather brought problems to Thailand's economy. Massive inflows invested in risky investments rather than the tradeable sector revealed inappropriate management of inflows. Letting outflows move freely did not improve and enhance investments but rather weakened the economy.

The third error was the adoption of an inappropriate type of fixed exchange policy leading to balance of payments constraints. The baht was pegged to a basket of currencies to enhance export competitiveness and attract foreign funds to service the growth of the economy. Although, there were seven currencies in the basket, the Thai government heavily weighted the baht to the US dollar with a 85% share of total weight.

This strategy was very helpful in generating inflows and improving exports as long as the value of the US dollar stayed devalued against other currencies, especially the Japanese yen. However, the problems associated with a stable exchange rate began to appear when Thailand was faced with the appreciation of the baht along with the US dollar in April 1995, which in turn made the value of the baht appreciate automatically against the yen. Also, massive capital inflows lead to the appreciation in the real exchange rate of the currency. Considering Japan was Thailand's biggest trading partner, the rising baht weakened exports and investments. As a result, Thai exports dropped dramatically weakening the trade balance. The problem of appreciation of currency was further aggravated by massive capital inflows, which leads to slowdown in exports and subsequently an increase in current account deficits.

Another effect of a pegged exchange rate on the Thai economy was to increase external debt, in particular short-term. This was made attractive by benefits provided by the commercial banks and BIBF, such as favourable interest rate differential and other tax privileges. While the pegged currency provided international investors and lenders with confidence in the value of the currency, capital controls deregulation removed virtually all restrictions on cross border transactions. Accordingly, these investors and lenders were willing to invest largely in short-term without hedging against any loss of the currency. Thus, Thailand began to borrow heavily from abroad and loan out to domestic users, with a potentially dangerous bias toward over-investment in the non-tradeable sector, as real estate and construction. The problem became worse when these sectors failed to make returns, and drove the country into a heavy burden of debt. Confidence in the Thai economy among international investors began to slip when the country failed to service the already high external debt while concurrently experiencing a significant decline of exports. Indeed, these factors soon drove Thailand into a financial crisis. Finally, we conclude that Thailand's pegged exchange regime proved to be inappropriate and harmful to the economy in two ways. First, it caused the decline of Thai exports, leading to trade imbalance. Second, it increased the country's external debt caused by high levels of capital flows.

The fourth error was that of moral hazard and is associated to various aspects of financial liberalisation, which led to over-optimistic expectations among foreign investors. The first expectation originated from the pegged exchange regime. Because the currency was pegged, foreign investors knew that the value of the currency could hardly fluctuate, thus the risks that may arise from the loss value of the currency was minimum. Consequently, they invested heavily in the economy, creating overinvestment in non-productive sectors. During the process of liberalisation, the Thai government lifted both the ceiling on interest rates; the type of lending allowed for financial institutions and established the BIBF. The objective of doing this was to increase savings, expand investments and widen the financial market. Unfortunately, interest rate deregulation did not increase savings; in fact, it allowed foreign investors to benefit from the interest rate differential while making it beneficial for Thai financial institutions to borrow abroad at a cheaper rate. Consequently, large amounts of inflows came in and investment in unproductive sectors increased dramatically.

The second was the expectation of guaranteed loans to the BIBF. Foreign investors always knew that the BIBF was a government institution with several tax privileges over other institutions. These led investors to perceive that the BIBF is unlikely to fail, if it does then the government would come in to rescue in the face of financial crisis. Moreover, the tax benefits made lending to the BIBF sound extremely attractive, as a result we found that large amount of inflows came in immediately after its establishment and also rose rapidly in just a short period of time. Without proper reform of domestic institutions, those funds were shifted to risky investments, such as, in real estate and construction projects, which created a problem of poor returns. Lending in such a manner soon led to excessive lending, which involve in excessive lending without incentive monitoring. This implies that the Thai government failed to provide a regulatory or supervisory framework to monitor the lending of financial institutions in Thailand. Essentially, the problem was partly a result from inappropriate sequence of financial liberalisation where the BIBF was implemented instead of reform of domestic market with supervisory and monitoring system. If there had been government supervision or monitoring, the funds could have been invested in the real sector (e.g. manufacturing, industrial and agricultural sectors) that are more likely to generate returns rather than the losses of investment in real estate and housing projects. In all, we conclude that over-optimistic expectations from inappropriate liberalisation policy concurrent with poor supervision and mismanagement of financial resources caused a problem of moral hazard resulting from loan losses in a sector that was not performing and thus aided the country's slide into crisis.

Summarising, the evidence from our study suggests that the Thai financial crisis originated from poor management and inappropriate choice of policy in financial liberalisation by the government. While, others could argue that the implementation of financial liberalisation in Thailand at the time was not a wise choice for Thailand because the domestic market was not ready for high capital flows, resulting in misallocation of funds leading the country into crisis. However, we argue that economic fundamentals of Thailand at the time were strong with fiscal balance, high GDP growth and high levels of foreign reserves. Our study shows that the fundamental problems of the crisis indeed emerged from poor management of financial liberalisation with wrong sequence of financial liberalisation process, inappropriate capital control deregulation, misalignment of the currency and inadequate regulatory framework. These problems could have been avoided if the government had implemented its financial liberalisation appropriately. Problems of high current account deficits, trading of foreign exchange by foreign commercial banks and misallocation of funds will not appear if financial liberalisation follows a proper sequence. If the government had maintained minimal controls on capital flows, particularly outflows, it could have avoided the rapid withdrawal of funds that incapacitated the financial system and weakened the macroeconomic fundamentals of the country. Concerning exchange rate policy, if Thailand had pursued a trade-weighted basket rather than fixing the baht to a US dollar dominated basket, Thai exports would not have declined with the appreciation of the US dollar against the yen and the competitiveness of Thai exports would have been maintained. Lastly, the problem of moral hazard is unlikely to occur if the government monitors the activities of financial institutions more closely and provides them with prudential guidance in borrowing and lending.

9.2 Policy Implications

This book provides evidence that there is a close link between financial liberalisation and the crisis in Thailand and that the severity of the crisis depended on the latter's fundamental economic policy, public policy, institutional and social conditions. The study recommends the following, policy implications as a guideline to avoid future crises derived from financial liberalisation programmes.

The first implication is in the sequence of financial liberalisation. For Thailand, undertaking financial liberalisation while current account deficits were high proved detrimental to the economy. Thus, it is recommended that a country should aim at reducing its deficits prior to financial liberalisation. Moreover, it is clear that the sequence that allows foreign exchange rate reforms to happen before the domestic financial market is strengthened increases vulnerability to the crisis. Therefore, it is suggested that the government should first bolster the domestic market prior to reforms related to exchange rate and capital control. The government can strengthen its domestic financial market by strengthening prudential regulation, bank supervision and transparency standards. The market regulation and bank supervision should aim at creating managerial competence, effective risk control, adequate capital requirements, well-trained staff to monitor banking activities and control of cross-border financial transactions. Furthermore, transparency of the financial system should include better information disclosure and data dissemination, which discourages banks' excessive risk taking and rent-seeking behaviour.

The second implication concerns the issue of capital controls. Loosening control of capital was a key factor leading to financial instability in Thailand. On the one hand, relaxation of controls on capital inflows led to excessive lending that resulted in moral hazard when those inflows were extended to unproductive users. On the other hand, letting go of control on capital outflows reduced financial stability and weakened the financial sector when investors were free to pull capital funds out of the country. To avoid further financial instability, it is recommended that the government should monitor and improve controls on capital by taxing foreign inflows and outflows, placing limits on foreign currency transactions and introducing a higher weight of risk in the capital requirement for foreign currency loans to domestic financial institutions.

The third implication is to make the exchange rate flexible enough to adjust the market exchange rate to the changes in the domestic and international economic and financial fundamentals. Some form of managed float is justified based on a similar approach developed in Rusdyi and Islam (2007). From the Thai experience, a pegged exchange rate not only promotes economic growth and investment but also has the effect of decreasing the natural volatility of currency fluctuations. This decreases the hedging risk premium of foreign lenders and cheapens the cost of borrowing abroad resulting in a high level of external debts and a rapid influx of capital. In order to prevent these problems, the government should implement a flexible exchange rate as it provides foreign investors or lenders with no guarantee against losses due to currency fluctuation. Foreign investors or lenders simply need to use caution when investing or lending in a foreign currency, and this slowdown both inflows and lending from foreign countries. Additionally, if a basket of currencies were to be adopted, the government should appropriately weight each country's currency according to the level of trade with that country, so stabilising international trade transactions. In other words, we suggest a trade weight of basket rather than a US dollar dominated basket, which Thailand adopted.

The final implication is to curtail the problems of asymmetric information and moral hazard for eliminating market, policy and institutional failures. The lessons from the Thai crisis suggest several solutions to solve moral hazard problems. The government and financial institutions need to provide monitoring programs that ensure funds are channelled to the most productive investment opportunities. The government has to be certain that balance sheets of both financial and non-financial firms are produced and disclosed on a true and fair basis. Lastly, the government should note that they need to build efficient institutions and socio-economic organisations, especially by establishing a strong regulatory and supervisory system, penalties for the managers of insolvent institutions that continue trading, implementing an improved accounting system, and finally carefully monitoring the risk management of each institution ensuring that they are complying with the regulations (see also Islam and Watanapalachaikul 2005). In other words Thailand needs to develop an efficient and social welfare maximising economic and financial organisation (mechanism design) that is incentive compatible, and does not other problems of market failures, asymmetric information, moral hazard and principal-agent relationships.

9.3 Areas for Further Research

There are a number of ways that this study can be extended. Firstly, since this book focuses on the contribution of the Thai financial liberalisation to the crisis, the next study can be expanded by applying the theory and analysis developed in this book to investigate the crises in South Korea, Malaysia or Indonesia. Secondly, since this book combines theory and issues to study the consequences of financial liberalisation on the Thai crisis, the next study could look at one specific theory and issue from this book and apply them in greater detail to study the crisis in Thailand or elsewhere.

For example, one could study the contribution of the sequence of financial liberalisation on the Thai or South Korea crisis, and explore the consequences of exchange rate policy on the crisis in Thailand and other East Asia countries. On the other hand, once data becomes available one may empirically test further the linkages between the liberalisation measures and the expected outcome. Lastly, attempts could be made to compare the role of financial liberalisation to the Thai crisis with those of the other countries, for instance, Thailand and Mexico, South Korea, Chile, Indonesia and so on.

9.4 Final Comments

We have conducted an empirical analysis of the contribution of financial liberalisation to the Thai financial crisis and an appropriate time series analysis was assembled to explore the consequences of liberalisation to the Thai economy. Additionally, we also used contemporary theories on financial crises; namely, the sequence of financial liberalisation, capital controls, exchange rate policy and asymmetric information, to explain the crisis. By doing this, we aim to provide an insight on the extent of the changes and the contribution of financial liberalisation process to the Thai economy. We found that lack of proper sequencing and the fast pace of financial liberalisation process led to the onset of the crisis in Thailand. The Thai experience reiterates the fact that financial liberalisation comes with a cost together with the benefits. Moreover, the Thai crisis did not emerge from a single factor but is derived from a combination of problems and aspects of liberalisation. The problems in Thailand were largely due to an inappropriate sequencing of financial liberalisation, hasty capital account liberalisation, inappropriately exchange rate and failures to tackle structural and institutional problems like that of moral hazard. The results and implications drawn from this book can help in developing strategies and policies to deal with future financial liberalisation thus preventing crisis. It is hoped that the analysis developed in this book will generate a better understanding of the role of financial liberalisation in any developing economy by providing an insight on an appropriate management of the financial reform process such as the extent and sequence of liberlisation, institution building for developing a robust financial system.

References

Abramovitz, M. (1961), The Welfare Interpretation of Secular Trends in National Income and Product, in Abramovitz, M. et al. (eds.) *The Allocation of Economic Resources*, Stanford University Press, Stanford.

Adelman, I. and Morris, C. (1973), *Economic Growth and Social Equity in Developing Countries*, Stanford University Press, Stanford.

Agenor, P. -R. and Montiel, P. (1996), *Development Macroeconomics*, Princeton University Press, Princeton.

Aghevli, B. (1981), Experiences of Asian Countries with Various Exchange Rate Policies, in Williamson, J. (ed.) *Exchange Rate Rules: The Theory, Performance and Prospect of the Crawling Peg*, MacMillan, London, pp. 298–318.

Aghevli, B., Khan, M. and Montiel, P. (1991), Exchange Rate Policy in Developing Countries: Some Analytical Issues, IMF Occasional Paper no. 78, International Monetary Fund, Washington.

Aglietta, M. (2000), *Financial Globalisation*, University of Texas Press, Texas.

Akerlof, G. (1970), The Market for Lemons: Quality Uncertainly and the Market Mechanism, *Quarterly Journal of Economics*, vol. 84, no. 3, August, pp. 488–500.

Alba, P., Hernandez, L. and Klingebiel, D. (1999), *Financial Liberalisation and the Capital Account: Thailand 1988–1997*, World bank, Washington.

Alesina, A., Grilli, V. and Milesi-Ferretti, G. M. (1994), The Political Economy of Capital Controls, in Leiderman, L. and Razin, A. (eds.) *Capital Mobility: The Impact on Consumption, Investment, and Growth*, Cambridge University press, Cambridge, pp. 289–321.

Alesina, A., Spolaore, E. and Wacziarg, R. (2000), Economic Integration and Political Disintegration, *The American Economic Review*, vol. 90, no. 5, pp. 1276–1296.

Allison, T. and Suwanraks, R. (1999), Financial Reforms in Thailand: Macroeconomic Policy Program, *TDRI Quarterly Review*, vol. 14, no. 4, December, pp. 6–18.

Aoki, M. (1997), Comment on 'Understanding Financial Crises: A Developing Country Perspective' by Frederic Mishkin, The International Bank for Reconstruction and Development, World Bank, Washington DC.

APEC (2000), *Towards Knowledge-Based Economies in APEC*, APEC Secretariat, Singapore.

Arestos, P. and Demetriades, P. (1999), Financial Liberalization: The Experience of Developing Countries, *Eastern Economic Journal*, vol. 25, no. 4, pp. 441–458.

Ariff, M. and Hill, H. (1985), *Export-Oriented Industrialization: The ASEAN Experiences*, Allen and Unwin, Sydney.

Ariff, M. and Khalid, A. M. (2000), *Liberalisation, Growth and the Asian Financial Crisis*, Edward Elgar, Cambridge.

Arnott, R. J. and Stiglitz, J. E. (1988), The Basic Analytics of Moral Hazard, *Scandinavian Journal of Economics*, vol. 99, no. 3, pp. 383–413.

Arrow, K. (1951), *Social Choice and Individual Value*, Wiley, New York

Arrow, K. J., Sen, A., and Suzumura, K, (2003), *Handbook of Social Choice and Welfare Economics*, North Holland, Amsterdam.

Arunsmith, K. (1998), Thailand in Economic Crisis: A Multisectoral Forecasting Simulation (1997–1999) Derived from a CGE Model (CAMGEM)', *Chulalongkorn Journal of Economics*, vol. 10, no. 1, pp. 15–41.

Atkinson, A. (1970), On the Measurement of Inequality, *The Journal of Economic Theory*, Vol. 2, pp. 244–263.

Aziz, I. (1999), 'Challenges for International Development Cooperation: Reforming the Global Financial Architecture', paper prepared for comments in a session on Reforming the Global Financial Architecture? at Responding to Financial Crisis: Challenges for Domestic Policy and International Cooperation conference, Taiwan Institute of Economic Research, Taipai, March 22–23.

Aziz, I., Aziz, E. and Thorbecke, E. (2001), *Modeling the Socio-economic Impact of the Financial Crisis: The Case of Indonesia*, mimeo, IFPRI, World Bank, Washington.

Bakker, A. F. P. (1996), *The Liberalization of Capital Movements in Europe*, Kluwer Publisher, Amsterdam.

Balassa, B. (1990), Financial Liberalization in Developing Countries, *Studies in Comparative International Development*, vol. 25, no. 4, Winter, pp. 56–71.

Bank of Thailand (BOT) (1996), Analysing Thailand's Short-Term Debt, *Bank of Thailand Economic Focus*, vol. 1, no. 3, July, Bank of Thailand, Bangkok.

Bank of Thailand (BOT) (1998a), Financial Institutions and Markets in Thailand, *Economic Research Department*, November, Bank of Thailand, Bangkok.

Bank of Thailand (BOT) (1998b), "Focus on the Thai Crisis", *A Quarterly Review of Thailand's Economic Issues*, vol. 2, no. 2, April/June.

Bank of Thailand (BOT) (2001), *Economic and Financial Statistics*, vol. 41, no. 9, September, Bangkok.

Bank of Thailand Monthly Report, (2000, and various issues), Bank of Thailand, Bangkok.

Bank of Thailand Yearly Report, (2000, and various issues), Bank of Thailand, Bangkok.

Barro, R. (1997), *Determinants of Economic Growth*, MIT, Cambridge.

Ben-David, D. (1993), Equalizing Exchange: Trade Liberalization and Income Convergence, *Quarterly Journal of Economics*, Vol. 108, pp. 653–679.

Bergson, A. (1938), A Reformulation of Certain Aspects of Welfare Economics, *Quarterly Journal of Economics*, vol. 52, no. 2, February, pp. 310–334.

Bhongmakapat, T. (1990a), Prospects and Strategies of the Thai Economy in The Next Decade, paper presented at the Symposium on Directs for Policy Reforms for the Thai Economy in The Next Decade, Faculty of Economics, Chulalongkorn University, Bangkok, January 23–24, (in Thai).

Bhongmakapat, T. (1990b), Structural Changes and Industrial Promotion Policy, in Chiasakul, S. and Yoshida, M. (eds) *Thai Economy in the Changing Decade and Industrial Promotion Policy*, Tokyo: Institute of Developing Economies, pp. 1–22.

Bhongmakapat, T. (1999), Managing the Thai Crisis: Asset Bubbles, Globalization and Macroeconomic Policy, *Chulalongkorn Journal of Economics,* vol. 11, no. 1, January, pp. 1–42.

Bird, G. (1998), Exchange Rate Policy in Developing Countries: What is Left of the Nominal Anchor Approach?, *Third World Quarterly*, vol. 19, no. 2, pp. 225–227.

Bird, G. and Rajan, R. (2001), *Economic Globalisation: How Far and How Much Further*, mimeo, School of Economics, Adelaide University, Adelaide.

Blanco, H. and Garber, P. (1986), Recurrent Devaluation and Speculative Attacks on the Mexican Peso, *Journal of Political Economy,* vol. 94, no. 1, March, pp. 148–166.

Boadway, R. and Bruce, N. (1984), *Welfare Economics*, Basil Blackwell, Oxford.

Borda, J. (1780 – reprinted in 1953), Memoire sur les Elections au Scrutin, Histoire de L'Academic Royale des Sciences, translated by A. de Grazia, 'Mathematical Derivation of an Election System', *Isis*, vol. 44, no. 1-2, pp. 42–51.

Bordo, M. D. and Schwartz, A. J. (1996), Why Clashes Between Internal and External Stability Goals End In Currency Crises, NBER, Working Paper No. 5710, National Bureau of Economic Research, Cambridge.

Borland, J. (1998), *Earnings Inequality in Australia: Changes, Causes and Consequences*, Centre for Economic and Policy Research Discussion Papers, No. 390, Australian National University, Canberra.

Borland, J., Gregory, B. and Sheehan, P. (2001a), *Work Rich, Work Poor: Inequality and Economic Change in Australia*, Centre for Strategic Economic Studies, Melbourne.

Borland, J., Gregory, B. and Sheehan, P. (2001b), Inequality and Economic Change, in Borland, J., Gregory, B. and Sheehan, P. (eds.) *Work Rich and Work Poor*, Centre for Strategic Economic Studies, Melbourne.

Bos, D., Rose, M. and Seidl, C. (eds) (1988), *Welfare and Efficiency in Public Economics*, Springer, Berlin Heidelberg New York.

Bossel, H. (1999) *Indicators for Sustainable Development: Theory, Method, Applications*, International Institute for Sustainable Development, Winnipeg.

Branson, W. H. and Papaefstratiou, K. (1981), Exchange Policy for Developing Countries, in Grassman, S. and Lundberg, E. (eds.) *The World Economic Order: Past and Prospects*, Macmillan, London, pp. 391–419.

Brooks, D. H. and Oh, S. M. (1999), Asia's Financial Crisis: Is Financial liberalisation the Villain?, in Brooks, D. H. and Queisser, M. (eds) (1999), *Financial Liberalisation in Asia: Analysis and Prospects*, OECD, Paris.

Brooks, D. H. and Queisser, M. (eds) (1999), *Financial Liberalisation in Asia: Analysis and Prospects*, OECD, Paris, pp. 85–100.

Brustelo, P. (1998), The East Asian Financial Crises: An Analytical Survey, ICEI Working Paper no. 10, University of Madrid, Madrid, Spain.

Buckley, R. (1999), *Asian's Financial Crisis: Causes, Effects and Aftershocks*, Buxton Press, London.

Buffie, E. F. (1990), Economic Policy and Foreign Debt in Mexico, in Sachs, J. D. (ed.) *Developing Country Debt and Economic Performance*, University of Chicago Press, Chicago, pp. 395–551.

Bullard, N., Bello, W. and Malhotra, K. (1998), *Taming the Tigers: The IMF and the Asian Crisis*, CAFOD Publication, London.

Bundnevich, C. and LeFort, G. (1997), Capital Account Regulations and Macroeconomic Policy: Two Latin American Experiences, Working Papers Series Central Bank of Chile no. 6, March, Central Bank of Chile.

Burkett, P. and Lotspeich, R. (1993), Financial Liberalization, Development, and Marketization: A Review of McKinnon's The Order of Economic Liberalization: Financial Control in the Transition to a Market Economy 1991, *Comparative Economic Studies*, vol. 35, no. 1, Spring, pp. 59–85.

Calomiris, C. W. (1998), The IMF's Imprudent Role as Lender to Last Resort, *Cato Journal*, vol. 13, no. 3, winter.

Calvo, G. (1988), Servicing the Public Debt: The Role of Expectations, *The American Economic Review*, vol. 78, no. 3, September, pp. 647–661.

Caprio, G. Jr., Atiyas, I. and Hanson, J. A. (1994), *Financial Reform: Theory and Experience*, Cambridge University Press, Cambridge.

Caprio, G. Jr., Wilson, B. and Saunders, A. (1997), Mexico's Banking Crisis: Devaluation and Asset Concentration Effects, Development Economics Department, World Bank, Washington.

Cardenas, M. and Barrera, F. (1997), On the Effectiveness of Capital Controls: The Experience of Colombia during the 1990s, *Journal of Development Economics*, vol. 54, no. 1, pp. 27–58.

Chai, J. (1997), *China: Transition to a Market Economy*, Clarendon press, Oxford.

Chaiyasoot, N. (1995), Industrialization, Financial Reform and Monetary Policy, in Krongkaew, M. (ed.) *Thailand's Industrialization and Its Consequences*, St. Martin's Press, London, pp. 160–182.

Chao, C. C. and Yu, E. (1995), The Shadow Price of Foreign Exchange in a Dual Economy, *Journal of Development Economics*, vol. 46, no. 1, February, pp. 195–202.

Chatterjee, S. (1999), Unequal Partners: Globalisation in Retrospect and Prospect, Discussion Paper no. 99/05, June, Massey University, New Zealand.

Chen, C. L. (1997), The Evolution and Main Features of China's Foreign Direct Investment Policies, Chinese Economics Research Centre Working Paper no. 15, The University of Adelaide, Adelaide.

Chirathivat, S. (1999), Crisis and Its Impact on ASEAN Economic Integration, *Chulalongkorn Journal of Economics*, vol. 11, no. 1, January, pp. 97–130.

Chichilnisky, G. (1997), *Markets with Privately Produced Public Goods; The Knowledge Revolution*, mimeo, Program on Information and Resources, Columbia University.

Cho, Y. J. and Khatkhate, D. (1989), Lessons of Financial Liberalisation in Asia: A Comparative Study, World Bank Discussion Papers no. 50, World Bank, Washington.

Chowdhury, A. (1999), Villain of the Asian Crisis, *ASEAN Economic Bulletin*, vol. 16, no. 2, August, pp. 166–175.

Christensen, S. R., Siamwalla, A. and Vichyanond, P. (1997), Institution and Political Bases of Growth-Inducing Policies in Thailand, in Siamwalla, A. (ed.) *Thailand's Boom and Bust*, Thailand Development Research Institute (TDRI), Bangkok.

Claessens, S. and Glaessner, T. (1998), Internationalization of Financial Services in Asia, Policy Research Working Paper no. 1911, World Bank, Washington.

Clarke, M. and Islam, S. (2003), Measuring Social Welfare: Application of Social Choice Theory, *Journal of Socio-economics*, vol. 32, pp. 1–15.

Clarke, M. and Islam, S. M. N. (2004), *Economic Growth and Social Welfare*, Series *Contributions to Economic Analysis*, North Holland Publishing, Amsterdam.

Clarke, M. (2001), Does Economic Growth Reduce Poverty? A Case Study of Thailand, poster prepared for UNU/WIDER Development Conference, *Growth and Poverty*, Helsinki, 25–26 May.

Clarke, M., Islam, S. and Sheehan, P. (2002), Achieving Simultaneous Economic Growth and Sustainability – The New Impossibility Theorem for Development Economics, paper presented at Regional Symposium on Environment and Natural Resources, Kuala Lumpur, 10–11 April, 2002.

Clayton, A. and Radcliffe, N. (1996), *Sustainability: A Systems Approach*, Earthscan Publications, London.

Collignon, S., Pisani-Ferry, J. and Yung, C. P. (1999), *Exchange Rate Policies in Emerging Asian Countries*, Routledge, London.

Condorcet de, M. (1785), *Essai sur l' Application de l'Analyse a la Probabilitie des Decisions Rendues a la Plualite des voix*, L'Imprimerie Royal, Paris.

Cooper, R. N. (1999), Should Capital Controls Be Banished?, *Brooking Papers on Economic Activity*, no. 1, pp. 89–142.

Corsetti, G., Pesenti, P. and Roubini, N. (1998), What Caused the Asian Currency and Financial Crisis? Part 1 A Macroeconomic Overview, NBER, Working Paper No 6833, National Bureau of Economic Research, Cambridge.

Corsetti, G., Pesenti, P. and Roubini, N. (1999), Paper Tigers? A Model of the Asian Crisis, *European Economic Review*, vol. 43, no. 7, June, pp. 1211–1236.

Coy, P., Kripalani, M. and Clifford, M. (1998), Capital Controls: Lifeline or Noose, *Business Week*, no. 3597, October, pp. 36–38.

Craven, B. and Islam, S. M. N. (2005), *Optimisation in Economics and Finance: Some Advances in Non-Linear, Dynamic, Multi-Criteria, and Stochastic Models*, Series: Dynamic Optimisation and Econometrics in Economics and Finance, Vol. 7, Springer, Heidelberg.

Crotty, J. and Epstein, G. (1999), A Defence of Capital Controls in Light of the Asian Financial Crisis, *Journal of Economic Issues*, vol. 33, no. 2, pp. 427–434.

Cuddington, J. (1986), Capital Flight: Estimates, Issues and Explanations, Princeton Essays in International Finance no. 58, Princeton University, New Jersey.

Cumby, R. E. and Van Wijnbergen, S. (1989), Financial Policy and Speculative Runs with a Crawling Peg: Argentina, 1979–-1980, *Journal of International Economics*, vol. 27, no. 1, March, pp. 111–127.

Daly, H. and Cobb, J. (1990), *For the Common Good*, Beacon Press, Boston.

DeGregorio, J. and Guidotti, P. B. (1992), Financial Development and Economic Growth, IMF Working Paper no. 92/101, International Monetary Fund, Washington.

DeGregorio, J., Edwards. S. and Valds, R. O. (2000), Controls on Capital Inflows: Do They Work?, NBER Working Paper No. 7645, National Bureau of Economic Research, Cambridge.

Demirguc-Kunt, A. and Detragiache, E. (1997a), The Determinants of Banking Crises: Evidence from Developed and Developing Countries, IMF Working Paper no. 97/106, International Monetary Fund, Washington.

Demirguc-Kunt, A. and Detragiache, E. (1997b), Banking Crises Around the World: Are There Any common Threads?, Development Economics Department, World Bank, Washington.

Demirguc-Kunt, A. and Detragiache, E. (1998), Financial Liberalization and Financial Fragility, Policy Research Working Paper no. 1917, World Bank, Washington.

Devaney, M. (2000), Regulation, Moral Hazard and Adverse Selection in Appraisal Practice, *The Appraisal Journal*, April, pp. 180–183.

Dhiratayakinant, K. (1995), Public-Private Sector Partnership, in Krongkaew, M. (ed.) *Thailand's Industrialization and Its Consequences*, St. Martin's Press, London, pp. 99–115.

Diefenbacher. H. (1994), The Index of Sustainable Economic Welfare, in J. Cobb and C. Cobb (eds.) *The Green National Product*, University Press of America, Lanham.

Diaz-Alejandro, C. (1985), Good-Bye Financial Repression, Hello Financial Crash, *Journal of Development Economics,* vol. 19, no. 1, pp. 1–24.

Dixon, C. (1996), Thailand's Rapid Economic Growth: Causes, Sustainability and Lessons, in Parnwell, M. (ed.) *Uneven Development in Thailand*, Avebury, Aldershot.

Dixon, C. (1999), *The Thai Economy. Uneven Development and Internationalism*, Routledge, London.

Dollar, D. (1992), Outward Orientated Developing Economies Really Do Grow More Rapidly: Evidence From 95 LDCs, 1976-1985, in *Economic Development and Cultural Change*, vol. 40, pp. 523–544.

Dollar, D. and Driemeier, M. H. (2000), Financial Structure and Financial Crisis, *The World Bank Research Observer*, vol. 15, no. 1, February, pp. 1–31.

Dooley, M. P. (1996), A Survey of Academic Literature on Controls over International Capital Transaction, *IMF Working Papers*, vol. 43, no. 4, December, pp. 639–687.

Dopfer, K. (1979), *The New Political Economy of Development: Integrated Theory and Asian Experiment*, The MacMillan Press Ltd, Melbourne.

Dornbusch, R., Goldfajn, I. and Valdes, R. O. (1995), Currency Crises and Collapses, *Brookings Papers on Economic Activity,* no. 2, pp. 219–293.

Edwards, S. (1984), The Order of Liberalization of the External Sector in Developing Countries, Princeton Essays in International Finance no. 154, December, Princeton University, New Jersey.

Edwards, S. (1986), The Order of Liberalization of the Current and Capital Account of the Balance of Payments, in Choksi, A. M. and Papageorgiou, D. (eds.) *Economic Liberalization in Developing Countries*, Basil Balckwell, New York, pp. 185–216.

Edwards, S. (1989a), On the Sequencing of Structural Reform, NBER Working Paper no. 3138, National Bureau of Economic Research, Cambridge.

Edwards, S. (1989b), *Real Exchange Rates, Devaluation and Adjustment*, MIT, Cambridge.

Edwards, S. (1992), Trade Orientation, Distortion and Growth in Developing Countries, *Journal of Development Economics*, vol. 39, no. 1, pp. 31–57.

Edwards, S. (1996), The Determinants of the Choice Between Fixed and Flexible Exchange Rate Regimes, NBER, Working Paper no. 5756, National Bureau of Economic Research, Cambridge.

Edwards, S. (1998), Capital Flows, Real Exchange Rates and Capital Controls: Some Latin American Experiences, NBER Working Paper no. 6800, National Bureau of Economic Research, Cambridge.

Edwards, S. (1999), How Effective are Capital Controls, *Journal of Economic Perspectives*, vol. 13, no. 4, pp. 64–84.

Edwards, S. and Edwards, A. J. (1987), *Monetarism and Liberalization: The Chilean Experiment*, Ballinger Publishing Co, Cambridge.

Edwards, S. and Santaella, J. (1993), Devaluation Controversies in the Developing Countries, in Bordo, M. and Eichengreen, B. (eds.) *A Retrospective on the Bretton Woods System: Lessons for International Monetary Reform*, University of Chicago Press, Chicago, pp. 405–460.

Edwards, S. and Savastano, M. (1999), Exchange Rates in Emerging Economies: What Do we Know? What Do We Need to Know?, NBER Working Paper no. 7228, National Bureau of Economic Research, Cambridge.

Eichengreen, B. (1999), *Toward a New International Financial Architecture: A Practical Post-Asia Agenda*, Institute for International Economic, Washington.

Eichengreen, B. and Hausmann, R. (1999), Exchange Rates and Financial Fragility, NBER Working Paper no. 7418, National Bureau of Economic Research, Cambridge.

Eichengreen, B., Rose, A. K. and Wyplosz, C. (1995), Exchange Market Mayhem: The Antecedents and Aftermath of Speculative Attacks, *Economic Policy*, vol. 21, no. 3, October, pp. 251–312.

Ely, B. (1999), Regulatory Moral Hazard, *Independent Review*, vol. 4, no. 2, pp. 241–255.

Falkus, M. (1995), Thai Industrialization: An Overview, in Krongkaew, M. (ed.) *Thailand's Industrialization and Its Consequences*, St. Martin's Press, London, pp. 13–32.

Falkus, M. (1999), Historical Perspective of the Thai Financial Crisis, *UNEAC Asia Papers*, vol. 1, no. 1, pp. 10–20.

Falvey, R. and Kim, C. D. (1992), Timing and Sequencing in Trade Liberalization, *The Economic Journal*, vol. 202, no. 413, pp. 908–924.

Fernald, J. G., Edison, H. J. and Loungani, P. (1998), Was China the First Domino? Assessing Links between China and the Rest of Emerging Asia, Discussion Paper no. 604, Federal Reserve Board International Finance, Washington.

Flood, R. and Garber, B. (1984a), Collapsing Exchange Rate Regimes: Some Linear Examples, *Journal of International Economics*, vol. 17, no. 1, March, pp. 1–13.

Flood, R. and Garber, B. (1984b), Gold Monetization and Gold Discipline, *Journal of Political Economy*, vol. 92, no. 1, March, pp. 90–107.

Frankel, J. and Romer, D. (1999), Does Trade Cause Growth?, *American Economic Review*, vol. 89, no. 3, pp. 379–399.

Frankel, J. A. (1995), Monetary Choice of a Semi-Open Country, in Edwards, S. (ed.) *Capital Controls, Exchange Rates and Monetary Policy in the Economy*, Cambridge University Press, Cambridge, pp. 35–70.

Frankel, J. A. and Schmukler, S. L. (1997), Country Funds and Asymmetric Information, Centre for International and Development Economic Research, Working Paper no. C97-087, California: University of California at Berkeley.

Frankel, J. A., Goldstein, M. and Masson, P. (1991), Characteristics of a Successful Exchange Rate System, IMF Occasional Paper no. 82, International Monetary Fund, Washington.

French, K. and Poterba, J. (1991), Investor Diversification and International Equity Markets, *American Economic Review*, vol. 81, no. 2, May, pp. 222–261.

Fry, M. (1988), *Money, Interest and Banking in Economic Development*, John Hopkins University Press, Baltimore.

Gab, J. J. (2000), *The Role of International Capital Flows and Financial Contagion in the Asian Financial Crises*, Phd Thesis, The Claremont Graduate University, California.

Garber, P. M. and Grilli, V. (1986), The Bel-Morgan Syndicate as an Optimal Investment Banking Contract, *European Economic Review*, vol. 30, pp. 649–677.

Gehrig, T. (1993), An Information Based Explanation of the Domestic Bias in International Equity Investment, *The Scandinavian Journal of Economics*, vol. 95, no. 1, pp. 97–109.

Genesove, D. (1993), Adverse Selection in the Wholesale Used Car Market, *Journal of Political Economy*, vol. 101, no. 4, August, pp. 644–665.

Gelb, A. H. (1989), Financial Policies, Growth, and Efficiency, World Bank Research Working Paper no. 202, World Bank, Washington D.C.

Gibbons, R. and Katz, L. (1991), Layoffs and Lemons, *Journal of Labor Economics*, vol. 9, no. 4, October, pp. 351–380.

Gilpin, R. (2001), *Global Political Economy: Understanding the International Economic Order*, Princeton University Press, Princeton.

Glick, R. (2000), Fixed or Floating: Is It Still Possible to Manage in the Middle?, Centre for Pacific Basin Monetary and Economic Studies Working Paper no. PB00-02, October, Federal Reserve Bank of San Francisco, San Francisco.

Glick, R. and Hutchison, M. (2000), Capital Controls and Exchange Rate Instability in Developing Economies, Centre for Pacific Basin Monetary and Economic Studies Working Paper no. PB00-05, December, Federal Reserve Bank of San Francisco, San Francisco.

Goldstien, M. (1998), The Asian Financial Crises: Causes, Curses and Systematic Implications, Policy Analyses in International Economics no. 55, Institute for International Economics, Washington.

Goldstien, M. and Turner, P. (1996), "Banking Crises in Emerging Economies: Origins and Policy Options", BIS Economic Papers no. 46, Bank of International Settlements, Basle.

Gourinchas, P., Valdes, R. and Landerretche, O. (1999), *Lending Booms: Some Stylized Facts*, mimeo, July, University of Princeton, New Jersey.

Greenwald, B. C. and Glasspiegel, R. R. (1983), Adverse Selection in the Market for Slaves: New Orleans 1830–1860, *Quarterly Journal of Economic*, vol. 98, no. 3, August, pp. 479–499.

Greenwald, B. C., Stiglitz, J. E. and Weiss, A. (1984), Information Imperfections in the Capital Market and Macroeconomic Fluctuations, *The American Economic Review*, vol. 74, no. 2, May, pp. 194–199.

Grilli, V. (1990), Managing Exchange Rate Crises: Evidence From the 1890s, *Journal of International Money and Finance*, pp. 258–275.

Grilli, V. and Milesi-Ferretti, G. M. (1995), Economic Effects and Structural Determinants of Capital Controls, *IMF Staff Papers*, September, pp. 517–551.

Grossman, S. J. and Stiglitz, J. E. (1980), On the Impossibility of Informationally Efficient Markets, *The American Economic Review*, vol. 70, pp. 393–408.

Haggard, S. and Kim, E. (1999), The Source of East Asia's Economic Growth, *Access Asia Review*, vol. 1, no. 1, pp. 1–38.

Haihong, G. (2000), Liberalising China's Capital Account: Lessons Drawn from Thailand's Experience, ISEAS Working Paper no. 6, Institute of Southeast Asian Studies, Singapore.

Hallwood, C. P. and MacDonald, R. (2000), *International Money and Finance*, 3rd edn., Blackwell Publishers, Cambridge.

Hamilton, C. (1998), Measuring Changes in Economic Welfare, in Eckersley, R. (ed.) *Measuring Progress*, CSIRO Publishing, Melbourne.

Hammond, P. (1976), Equity, Arrow's Conditions and Rawls' Difference Principles, *Econometrica*, vol. 44, no. 4, pp. 793–804.

Hansanti, S. (2005), Pegged Exchange Rate: Cure or Kill?, paper presented at 'The 2nd Academic Conference of Huachiew University', Thailand.

Hansanti, S. (2006), Pricing is A Piece of Pie, *Executive Journal*, vol. 25, no. 1, pp. 108–111.

Harrison, A. and Hanson, G. (1999), Who Gains from Trade Reform? Some Remaining Puzzles, *Journal of Developing Economics*, vol. 59, no. 1, pp. 125–154.

Harrod, R. (1948), *Towards a Dynamic Economics*, Macmillan, London.

Hataiseree, R. (1998), The Transmission of Monetary Policy: The Case of Thailand Under the Floating Exchange Regimes, paper presented at 'A Macroeconomic Core of Open Economy for Progressive Industralization and Development in Asian Economies in the New Millennium', Bangkok, 16–18 December.

Hausman, D. and McPherson, M. (1996), *Economic Analysis and Moral Philosophy*, Cambridge University Press, Cambridge.

Hefeker, C. (2000), Sense and Nonsense of Fixed Exchange Rates: On Theories and Crises, *Cato Journal*, vol. 20, no. 2, Fall, pp. 159–178.

Henderson, H. (1999), *Beyond Globalisation*, Kumarian Press, West Hartford.

Hipsher, A. S., Hansanti, S. and Pomsuwan, S. (2007), *The Nature of Asian Firms: An Evolutionary Perspective*, Chandos Publishing, Oxford.

Higgott, R. and Phillips, N. (1999), The Limits of Global Liberalisation: Lessons from Asia and Latin America, CSGR Working Paper no. 22/98, Centre for the Study of Globalisation and Regionalisation, The University of Warwick, UK.

Honohan, P. (1997), "Banking System Failures in Developing and Transitional Countries: Diagnosis and Prediction", BIS Working Papers no. 39, Basle: Bank of International Settlement.

Hossain, A. and Chowdhury, A. (1996), *Monetary and Financial Policies in Developing Countries: Growth and Stabilisation*, Routledge, London.

Hufschmidt, M., James, D., Meister, A., Bower, B. and Dixon, J. (1983), *Environment, Natural Systems, and Development*, The John Hopkins University Press, Baltimore.

Hutchison, M. and McDill, K. (1999), Are all Banking Crises Alike?: The Japanese Experience in International Perspective, NBER Working Paper no. 7253, National Bureau of Economic Research, Cambridge.

Islam, S. (1995), Australian Dynamic Integrated Model of Climate and the Economy (ADICE): Model Specification, Numerical Implementation and Policy Implications, Centre for Strategic Economic Studies, Victoria University, December.

Islam, S. (1998), Ecology and Optimal Economic Growth, Fifth Biennial Meeting of the International Society for Ecological Economists, Santiago, Chile, November 15–19.

Islam, S. (2001a), *Optimal Growth Economics*, North Holland Publishing Company, Amsterdam.

Islam, S. (2001b), *Applied Welfare Economics*, CSES, Victoria University, Melbourne.

Islam, S. and Clarke, M. (2002), Measurement of Sustainability – A New Approach Based on Social Choice Theory, paper presented 7th PRSCO and 4th IRSA International Conference on Decentralisation, Natural Resource and Regional Development in the Pacific Rim, 20–21 June.

Islam, S. and Clarke, M. (2003), Indicators for Social, Ethical and Environmental Performance: Using Systems Analysis Based Social Choice Theory for Social Welfare Measurement, in Batten, J. and Fetherston, T. (eds.) *Governance and Social Responsibility*, North Holland, Amsterdam.

Islam, S. and Oh, K (2003), *Applied Financial Econometrics in E-Commerce*, 2003, with K. B Oh, Series Contributions to Economic Analysis, North Holland Publishing, Amsterdam.

Islam, S. M. N. and Mak, C. (2006), *Normative Health Economics: A New Pragmatic Approach to Cost Benefit Analysis, Mathematical Models and Applications*, Palgrave Macmillan, UK.

Ito, T. (1998), *The Development of the Thailand Currency Crisis: A Chronological Review*, Hitotsubashi University, Japan.

Ivan, P. P. L. (1998), *Managerial Economics*, Blackwell Publishers, Cambridge.

Jackson, T. and Marks, N. (1994), *Measuring Sustainable Economic Welfare*, Stockholm Environment Institute in cooperation with The New Economics Foundation, Stockholm.

Johansson, P. (1987), *The Economic Theory and Measurement of Environmental Benefits*, Cambridge University Press, Cambridge.

Johnson, A. (1991), Thailand's Export-Led Growth: Retrospect and Prospects, *TDRI Quarterly Review*, vol. 6, no. 2, June, pp. 24–26.

Johnson, L. (1996), Choosing a Price Index Formula, ABS Working Paper 96/1, May, Canberra.

Johnson, R. B., Darbar, S. M. and Echeverria, C. (1997), Sequencing Capital Account Liberalization: Lessons from the Experiences in Chile, Indonesia, Korea and Thailand, IMF Working Paper no. 157, International Monetary Fund, Washington.

Johnson, S., Boone, P., Breach, A. and Friedman, E. (1998), *Corporate Governance in the Asian Financial Crisis*, 1997–1998, mimeo, MIT, Cambridge.

Jomo, K. S. (2001), *Malaysian Eclipse: Economic Crisis and Recovery*, Zed books, London.

Julian, C. (2000), The Impact of the Asian Economic Crisis in Thailand, *Managerial Finance*, vol. 6, no. 4, pp. 39–48.

Jung, W. (1986), Financial Development and Economic Growth: International Evidence, *Economic Development and Cultural Change*, vol. 34, January, pp. 333–346.

Kahkonen, J. (1987), Liberalization Policies and Welfare in a Financially Repressed Economy, *IMF Staff Papers*, vol. 34, no. 3, September, pp. 531–545.

Kakwani, N. (1999), Poverty and Inequality During the Economic Crisis in Thailand, *Indicators of Well-being and Policy Analysis*, Vol. 3, No. 1, January, NESDB, Bangkok.

Kakwani, N. and Pothong, J. (2000), *Impact of Economic Crisis on the Standard of Living in Thailand*, mimeo, NESDB, Bangkok.

Kamin, S. B. (1999), The Current International Financial Crisis: How Much is New, *Journal of International Money and Finance*, vol. 18, no. 4, pp. 724–755.

Kaminsky, G. L. and Reinhart, C. M. (1999), The Twin Crises: The Causes of Banking and Balance of Payments Problems, *The American Economic Review*, vol. 89, no. 3, August, pp. 473–500.

Kanbur, E. (1987), The Standard of Living: Uncertainty, Inequality and Opportunity, in Hawthorn, G. (ed.) *The Standard of Living*, Cambridge University Press, Cambridge.

Kaosa-ard, M. (2000), *Social Impact Assessment: Synthesis Report*, TDRI, Bangkok.

Kasa, K. (1999), Time for a Tobin Tax?, *FRBSF Economic Letter*, no. 99/12, April.

Kenen, P. (1994), Floating Exchange Rates Reconsidered: The Influence of New Ideas, Priorities and Problems, in Kenan, P., Papadia, F. and Saccomani, F. (eds.) *The International Monetary System*, Cambridge: Cambridge University Press, pp. 139–161.

Khor, M. (1998), Using Capital Controls to Deal with a Financial Crisis, *Third World Network*, October.

King, R. and Levine, R. (1993), Finance, Entrepreneurship, and Growth: Theory and Evidence, *Journal of Monetary Economic*, vol. 32, December, pp. 513–542.

Kittiprapas, S. (1999), *The Asian Financial Crisis and Social Changes in Thailand*, TDRI, Bangkok.

Kittiprapas, S. (2000), Causes of the Recent Asian Economic Crisis: The Case of Thailand, TDRI, Bangkok.

Krongkaew, M. (1995), Introduction: The Making of the Fifth Tiger – Thailand's Industrialization and Its Consequences, in Krongkaew, M. (ed.) *Thailand's Industrialization and Its Consequences,* St. Martin's Press, New York, pp. 1–12.

Krongkaew, M. (1999), Capital Flows and Economic Crisis in Thailand, *The Developing Economics*, vol. 52, no. 4, pp. 395–416.

Krugman, P. (1979), A Model of Balance-of-Payments Crises, *Journal of Money, Credit and Banking*, vol. 11, no. 3, August, pp. 311–325.

Krugman, P. (1991), International Aspects of Financial Crises, in Feldstein, M. (ed.) *The Risk of Economic Crisis*, University of Chicago Press, Chicago, pp. 85–108.

Krugman, P. (1998a), Saving Asia: It's Time to get Radical, *Fortune*, September 7, pp. 74–80.

Krugman, P. (1998b), *What Happened To Asia*, mimeo, MIT, Cambridge.

Kumar, R. and Debroy, B. (1999), The Asian Crisis: An Alternative View, Economic Staff Paper no. 59, Asian Development Bank, Manila.

Lahiri, K. and Moore, G. (1991), *Leading Economic Indicators*, Cambridge University Press, Melbourne.

Lane, T., Ghosh, A., Hamann, J., Phillips, S., Schulze-Ghattas, M. and Tsikata, T. (1999), IMF-Supported Programs in Indonesia, Korea and Thailand: A Preliminary Assessment, IMF Occasional Paper No. 178, International Monetary Fund, Washington.

Lang, L. H., Litzenberger, R. H. and Madrigal, V. (1992), Testing Financial Market Equilibrium Under Asymmetric Information, *Journal of Political Economy*, vol. 100, no. 21, pp. 317–348.

Lau, L. (1996), The Sources of Long-term Economic Growth: Observations from the Experiences of Developed and Developing Countries in Landau, R., Taylor, T., and Wright, G. (eds.) *The Mosaic of Economic Growth*, Standford University Press, Stanford.

Laurens, B. and Cardoso, J. (1998), Managing Capital Flows: Lessons from the Experience of Chile, IMF Working Paper no. 98/168, October, International Monetary Fund, Washington.

Lawn, P. and Sanders, R. (1997), A Sustainable Net Benefit Index for Australia, 1966–67 to 1994–95, Working Paper in Economics No. 16, Griffiths University, Brisbane.

Leightner, J. (1999), Globalisation and Thailand's Financial Crisis, *Journal of Economic Issues*, vol. 333, no. 2, June, pp. 367–373.

Levine, R. (1996), Foreign Banks, Financial Development and Economic Growth, in Barfield, C. E. (ed.) *International Financial Markets: Harmonization versus Competitions*, The American Enterprise Institute Press, Washington, pp. 131–142.

Levy-Livermore, A. (1998), *Handbook on the Globalization of the World Economy*, Edward Elgar, London.

Limskul, K. (2000), The Financial and Economic Crisis in Thailand: Dynamic of the Crisis-Root and Process, *Chulalongkorn Journal of Economics,* vol. 12, no. 1, January, pp. 1–30.

Lindgren, C. J., Gillian, G. and Saal, M. I. (1996), *Bank Soundness and Macroeconomic Policy*, International Monetary Fund, Washington.

Liu, L., Noland, M., Robinson, S. and Wang, Z. (1998), Asian Competitive De-valuations, Working Paper no. 2,Institute for International Economics, Washington.

Manarungsan, S. (1989), *Economic Development of Thailand: 1850-1950*, Chulalongkorn University, Bangkok.

Mankiw, G. N. (1986), The Allocation of Credit and Financial Collapse, *Quarterly Journal of Economics*, vol. 101, no. 3, August, pp. 455–470.

Makinen, G. E. and Woodward, T. G. (1989), A Monetary Interpretation of the Poincar Stabilisation of 1926, *Southern Economic Journal*, vol. 56, pp. 191–211.

Marston, R. C. (1995), *International Financial Integration: A Study of Interest Differentials Between the Major Industrial Countries*, Cambridge University Press, Cambridge.

Massad, C. (1998), The Liberalization of the Capital Account: Chile in the 1990s, Princeton Essays in International Finance no. 207, Princeton University, New Jersey.

Makinen, G. E. and Woodward, T. G. (1989), A Monetary Interpretation of the Poincar Stabilisation of 1926, *Southern Economic Journal*, vol. 56, no. 1, pp. 191–211.

McKibben, W. (1997), Regional and Multilateral Trade Liberalization: The Effects on Trade, Investment and Welfare, paper presented at the US International Trade Commission APEC Symposium, Washington, 11–12 September.

McKibben, W. (1998), The Crisis in Asia: An Empirical Assessment, Brookings Discussion Papers in International Economics No. 136, The Brookings Institute, Washington.

McKibbin, W. J. (2000), Globalization: What Does It Mean?, paper presented at the Australian Coal Conference, Gold Coast, 7–10 May.

McKinnon, R. I. (1963), Optimum Currency Areas, *American Economic Review*, vol. 53, no. 3, September, pp. 717–724.

McKinnon, R. I. (1973), *Money and Capital in Economic Development*, Brookings Institution, Washington.

McKinnon, R. I. (1982), The Order of Liberalization: Lossons from Chile and Argentina, in Burnner, K. and Meltzer, A. H. (eds.) *Economic Policy in a World of Change*, Carnegie-Rochester Conference Series on Public Policy no.17, North Holland, Amsterdam, pp. 159–186.

McKinnon, R. I. (1988), Financial Liberalisation in Retrospect: Interest Rate Policies in LDCs, in Ranis, G. and Schultz, T. P. (eds.), *The State of Development Economics*, Basil Blackwell, Oxford, pp. 386–415.

McKinnon, R. I. (1989), Financial Liberalization and Economic Development: A Reassessment of Interest-Rate Policies in Asia and Latin America, *Oxford Review of Economic Policy*, vol. 5, no. 4, pp. 29–54.

McKinnon, R. I. (1993), *The Order of Economic Liberalization: Financial Control in the Transition to a Market Economy*, 2nd edn., The Johns Hopkins University Press, Baltimore.

McKinnon, R. I. (1999), The East Asian Dollar Standard: Life After Death, Working Paper no. 99/017, Economic Department, Stanford University, New Jersey.

McKinnon, R. I. and Pill, H. (1997), Credible Economic Liberalizations and Overborrowing, *The American Economic Review,* vol. 65, no. 2, pp. 189–193.

McNutt, P. (2002), *The Economics of Public Choice*, 2nd edn., Edward Elgar, Cheltenham.

Meltzer, A. (1998), Asian Problems and the IMF, Testimony Prepared for the Joint Economic Committee, U.S. Congress, Washington D.C., 24 February.

Ministry of Finance (2001), Strategy Plan Framework Toward Quality and Sustainability of Thailand Economic Development, NESDB, Bangkok.

Mishkin, F. S. (1991), Asymmetric Information and Financial Crises: A Historical Perspective, in Hubbard, R. G. (ed.) *Financial Markets and Financial Crises*, University of Chicago Press, Chicago, pp. 69–108.

Mishkin, F. S. (1992a), Anatomy of Financial Crisis, *Journal of Evolutionary Economics*, vol. 2, pp. 115–130.

Mishkin, F. S. (1992b), *The Economics of Money, Banking, and Financial Markets*, Harper Collins Publishers, New York.

Mishkin, F. S. (1996), Understanding Financial Crises: A Developing Country Perspective, in Bruno, M. and Pleskovic, B. (eds.) *Annual World Bank Conference on Development Economics 1996*, World Bank, Washington D.C., pp. 29–62.

Mishkin, F. S. (1997), "The Causes and Propagation of Financial Instability: Lessons for Policymakers", in Hakkio, C. (ed.) *Maintaining Financial Stability in a Global Economy*, Federal Reserve Bank of Kansas City, Kansas City , pp. 55–96.

Mishkin, F. S. (1999), Lessons from The Asian Crisis, *Journal of International Money and Finance*, vol. 18, no. 4, pp. 709–723.

Mishkin, F. S. (2000), Prudential Supervision: Why Is It Important and What are the Issues, NBER Working Paper no. 7912, National Bureau of Economic Research, Cambridge.

Miringoff, M. (1996), *The 1996 Index of Social Health*, Fordham Institute for Innovation in Social Policy, New York.

Moreno, R. (2001), Policy Options for Managing Capital Flows: Capital Controls, Paper presented at the 'Capital Flows Seminar', Bangkok: Thailand, March 11–14.

Munasinghe, M. (ed.) (1996), *Environmental Impacts of Macroeconomic and Sectoral Policies*, The World Bank, Washington.

Mundell, R. (1961), The Theory of Optimal Currency Areas, *American Economic Review*, vol. 51, no. 4, November, pp. 657–665.

Musgrave, T. (1959), *The Theory of Public Finance*, MacGraw-Hill, New York.

Mussa, M. (2000), Factors Driving Global Economic Integration, Conference paper presented at the 'Global Opportunities and Challenges', Kansas City, 25 August.

Mussa, M., Masson, P., Swoboda, A., Jadresic, E., Mauro, J. and Berg, A. (2000), Exchange Rate Regimes in an Increasing Integrated World Economy, IMF Occasional Paper no. 193, International Monetary Fund, Washington D.C.

Myers, M. G. (1931), *The New York Money Market,* Columbia University Press, New York.

Myers, S. C. and Majluf, N. S. (1984), Corporate Financing and Investment Decisions: When Firms Have Information That Investors Do Not Have, *Journal of Financial Economics*, vol. 13, pp. 187–221.

Nava-Campos, G. (2000), The Politics of Financial Crises Management, paper presented at the Conference on The Political Economy of Reform in Latin America David Rockefeller Center for Latin American Studies, Harvard University, 30 November.

National Economic and Social Development Board (NESDB) (1996), *Eighth Five Year Plan*, NESDB, Bangkok.

National Economic and Social Development Board (NESDB) (2000), *Ninth Five Year Plan*, NESDB, Bangkok.

Neely, C. J. (1999), An Introduction to Capital Controls, *Federal Reserve Bank of St. Louis Review*, vol. 81, no. 6, November/December, pp. 13–30.

Nordhaus, W. and Tobin, J. (1973), Is Growth Obsolete?, in M. Moss (ed.) *The Measurement of Economic and Social Planning, Economic Growth*, NBER, Cambridge.

O'Brien, P. (1967), Government Revenue, 1793–1815: A Study in Fiscal and Financial Policy in the Wars Against France, Phd Thesis, Oxford University.

Obstfeld, M. (1986), Rational and Self-Fulfilling Balance of Payments Crises, *The American Economic Review,* vol. 76, no. 1, March, pp. 72–81.

Obstfeld, M. (1995), International Currency Experience: New Lessons and Lessons Relearned, *Brooking Papers on Economic Activity*, no. 1, pp. 119–220.

Obstfeld, M. and Rogoff, K. (1995), The Mirage of Fixed Exchange Rates, *Journal of Economic Perspectives,* vol. 9, no. 4, December, pp. 73–96.

OECD (1995), *Economic Surveys: Mexico*, Organisation for Economic Cooperation and Development, Paris.

Ohno, K. (1998), Exchange Rate Management in Developing Asia: Reassessment of the Pre-Crisis Soft Dollar Zone, November, Asian Development Bank Institute, Manila.

Ouattara, A. (1998), Globalization, Lessons from the Asian Crisis and Central Bank Policies, paper presented at Reunion des Gouverners des Banques Centrales des Pays Francophones, Ottawa, June.

Ozkan, G. F. and Sutherland, A. (1994), A Model of the EMR Crisis, CEPR Working Paper no. 879, Centre for Economic Policy Research, London.

Paavola, J. and Bromley, D. (2002), Contested Choices, in Bromley, D. and Paavola, J. (eds.) *Economics, Ethics and Environmental Policy*, Blackwell Publishing, Oxford.

Pakhasem, P. (1972), Thailand's North East Economic Development Planning: A Case Study in Regional Planning, Phd Thesis, The Graduate School of Public and International Affairs, University of Pittsburgh, Pennsylvania.

Pantusane, A. (1998), A Review of the Economic Crisis: Lessons for Sustainable Development in ASEAM, *Thammasat Economic Journal*, vol. 16, no. 3, September, pp. 5–25.

Parnwell, M. J. G. (1996), *Uneven Development in Thailand,* Avebury, Aldershot.

Park, D. (1998), Southeast Asia's Economic Crisis, *Contemporary Review*, vol. 272, no. 1584, pp. 6–14.

Patmasiriwat, D. (1995), Impact of Industrialization on Government Finance, in Krongkaew, M. (ed.) *Thailand's Industrialization and Its Consequences,* St. Martin's Press, London, pp. 143–160.

Peake, C. F. (2000), Information, Risk, and Uncertainty in Economics, *National Forum*, vol. 80, no. 1, pp. 4–5.

Pezzey, J. (2001), *Sustainability Policy and Environmental Policy*, mimeo, Centre for Resource and Environmental Studies, Australian National University, Canberra.

Pezzey, J. (2002), *Concern for Sustainable Development in a Sexual World*, mimeo, Centre for Resource and Environment Studies, Australian National University, Canberra.

Phongpaichit, P. and Baker, C. (1995), *Thailand: Economy and Politics*, Oxford University Press, Kuala Lumpur.

Phongpaichit, P. and Baker, C. (1998a), *Thailand's Boom and Bust,* Silkworm Books, Chiang Mai.

Phongpaichit, P. and Baker, C. (1998b), Thailand's Crisis: Neo-Liberal Agenda and Local Reaction, *Thammasat Economic Journal,* vol. 16, no. 3, September, pp. 26–50.

Phongpaichit, P. and Baker, C. (2000), *Thailand's Crisis,* Silkworm Books, Chiang Mai.

Pilbeam, K. (2001), The East Asian Financial Crisis: Getting to the Heart of the Issues, *Managerial Finance*, vol. 27, no. 1, pp. 111–133.

Pindyck, R. S. and Rubinfeld, D. L. (1998), *Microeconomics*,Prentice-Hall, New Jersey.

Queisser, M. (1999), Introduction, in Brooks, D. H. and Queisser, M. (eds.) *Financial Liberalisation in Asia: Analysis and Prospects,* OECD, Paris, pp. 19–23.

Radelet, S. and Sachs, J. (1998), The East Asian Financial Crisis: Diagnosis, Remedies, Prospects, *Brooking Papers,* vol. 28, no. 1, pp. 1–74.

Rajan, S. R. (2001a), Economic Globalization and Asia Trade, Finance, and Taxation, *ASEAN Economic Bulletin*, vol. 18, no. 1, pp. 1-11.

Rajan, S. R. (2001b), (Ir)Relevance of Currency Crisis Theory to the Devaluation and Collapse of the Thai Baht, Princeton Studies in International Economics, no. 88, Princeton University, New Jersey.

Rajan, S. R. and Bird, G. (2001), Banks, Financial Liberalisation and Financial Crises in Emerging Markets, *World Economy,* vol. 24, no. 7, pp. 889–910.

Rajan, S. R., Sen, R. and Siregar, R. (2000), Misalignment of the Baht, Trade Imbalances and the Crisis in Thailand, Discussion Paper no. 0045, November, University of Adelaide, Adelaide.

Ramsey, R. (1928), A Mathematical Theory of Saving, *Economic Journal*, vol. 38, pp. 543–559.

Rasmussen, B. S. (1997), International Tax Competition, Tax Cooperation and Capital Controls, Department of Economics Working Paper no. 1997/9, University of Aarhus, Denmark.

Ratanakomut, S., Chiasakul, S. and Itoga, S. (1995), Manufacturing Industry in Thailand: A Sectoral Analysis, Institute of Developing Economies, Tokyo.

Ratanakomut, S. (1999), Thailand's Economic Crisis: Some Unexpected Experiences", *Chulalongkorn Journal of Economics*, vol. 11, no. 1, January, pp. 43–55.

Ravallion, M. (1994), *Poverty Comparisons*, Harwood Economic Publishers, Switzerland.

Rebelo, S. (1997), What Happens When Countries Peg Their Exchange Rates? The Real Side of Monetary Reforms, NBER Working Paper no. 6168, National Bureau of Economic Research, Cambridge.

Reinhart, C. M. and Smith, R. T. (2001), Temporary Controls on Capital Inflows, NBER Working Paper no. 8422, National Bureau of Economic Research, Cambridge.

Rodrik, D. (1987), Trade and Capital Account Liberalisation in a Keynesian Economy, *Journal of International Economics*, vol. 23, August, pp. 113–129.

Rodrik, D. (1998), Globalisation, Social Conflict and Economic Growth, *World Economy*, vol. 21, no. 2, pp. 143–158.

Rodrik, D. and Rodriguez, F. (2000), Trade Policy and Economic Growth: A Skeptic's Guide to the Cross-National Evidence, in Bernanke, B. and Rogoff, K. (eds.) *NBER Macroeconomics Annual 2000*, MIT, Cambridge.

Rogoff, K. (1999), International Institutions for Reducing Global Financial Instability, NBER Working Paper no. 7265, National Bureau of Economic Research, Cambridge.

Rusydi, M. and Islam, S. M. N. (2007), *Exchange Rate Economics in Developing Countries: Issues, Models and Options*, with Palgrave Macmillan, UK.

Ryan, L. (2000), The "Asian Economic Miracle" Unmasked, *International Journal of Social Economics*, vol 27, no. 7, pp. 802–815.

Sachs, J. (1989), Conditionality, Debt Relief and the Developing Countries' Debt Crisis, in Sachs, J. (ed.) *Developing Country Debt and Economic Performance*, University of Chicago, Chicago, pp. 225–298.

Sachs, J. and Warner, A. (1995), Economic Reform and the Process of GlobalIntegration, Brookings Papers on Economic Activity, Brookings Institution, Washington.

Samuelson, P. (1956), Social Indifference Curves, *Quarterly Journal of Economics*, vol. 70, no. 1, pp. 1–22.

Sandmo, A. (1999), Asymmetric Information and Public Economics: The Mirrlees-Vickrey Noble Prize, *Journal of Economic Perspectives*, vol. 13, no. 1, Winter, pp. 165-180.

Sauve, P. (1999), The Benefits of Trade and Investment Liberalisation: Financial Services, in Brooks, D. H. and Queisser, M. (eds.) *Financial Liberalisation in Asia: Analysis and Prospects*, OECD, Paris, pp. 173–188.

Schmidt, J. (1996), Paternalism and Planning in Thailand: Facilitating Growth Without Social Benefits, in Parnwell, M. (ed.) *Uneven Development in Thailand*, Avebury, Aldershot.

Sen, A. (1966), A Possibility Theorem on Majority Decisions, *Econometrica*, no. 34.

Sen, A. (1970), *Collective Choice and Social Welfare*, North Holland Publishing Company, Amsterdam.

Sen, A. (1973), Behaviour and the Concept of Preference, in *Economica*, vol. 40, pp. 241–289.

Sen, A. (1982), *Choice, Welfare and Measurement*, Basil Blackwell, Oxford

Sen, A. (1985a), *Commodities and Capabilities*, North Holland, Amsterdam.

Sen, A. (1985b), Well-being Agency and Freedom, *The Journal of Philosophy*, Vol. 82, pp. 169–221.

Sen, A. (1999), *Development as Freedom*, Oxford University Press, Oxford.

Sen, A. 1999, The Possibility of Social Choice, *The American Economic Review*, vol. 89, no. 3, pp. 349–378.

Sheehan, P. (1998a), International Overview, in 'Crisis in East Asia: Global Watershed or Passing Storm?', conference Report presented by Centre for Strategic Economic Studies, Victoria University and Australian Centre for Innovation and International Competitiveness, The University of Sydney, March, pp. 99–110.

Sheehan, P. (1998b), The Global Context, in 'Crisis in East Asia: Global Watershed or Passing Storm?', conference Report presented by Centre for Strategic Economic Studies, Victoria University and Australian Centre for Innovation and International Competitiveness, The University of Sydney, March, pp. 3–20.

Sheehan, P. and Tikhomirova, (1998), The Rise of the Global Knowledge Economy, in Sheehan, P. and Tegart, G. (eds.) *Working for the Future*, CSES, Melbourne.

Shirai, S. (2001), Overview of Financial Market Structures in Asia: Cases of the Republic of Korea, Malaysia, Thailand and Indonesia, ADB Institute Research Paper no. 25, Asian Development Bank, Manila.

Siamwalla, A. (1997), *Thailand's Boom and Bust*, Thailand Development Research Institute, Bangkok.

Siamwalla, A. (2000), *Anatomy of the Thai Economic Crisis*, TDRI, Bangkok.

Siamwalla, A., Sethboonsarng, S. and Patamasiriwat, D. (1993), Agriculture, in Warr, P. G. (ed.) *The Thai Economy in Transition,* Cambridge University Press, Cambridge, pp. 81–117.

Siamwalla, A., Vajragupta, Y. and Vichyanond, P. (1999), *Foreign Capital Flows to Thailand: Determinants and Impacts,* Thailand Development Research Institute (TDRI), Bangkok.

Siksamat, S. (1998), A Multi-Regional Computable General Equilibrium Model of the Thai Economy, Phd Thesis, Centre of Policy Studies and the Department of Economics, Monash University, Melbourne.

Singh, K. (1999), *The Globalisation of Finance*, Zed Books, New York.

Slesnick, D. (2001), *Consumption and Social Welfare*, Cambridge University Press, Cambridge.

Stiglitz, J. (1999), Bleak Growth Prospects for the Developing World, *International Herald Tribune*, April 10–11, p. 6.

Stiglitz, J. (2002), *Globalization and its Discontents*, W.W. Norton and Company, Washington.

Stiglitz, J. (2003), 'Financial Market Stability, Monetary Policy and the IMF', in *Exchange Rate Regimes and Macroeconomic Stability*, eds Ho, L. S. and Yuen, C. W., Kluwer, Dordrecht.

Stiglitz, J. E. (1994), 'The Role of the State in Financial Markets', in *Proceedings of the World Bank Annual Conference on Development Economics*, Washington DC, pp. 19–52.

Stiglitz, J. and Weiss, A. (1981), Credit Rationing in Markets with Imperfect Information, *The American Economic Review*, vol. 73, no. 3, June, pp. 393–410.

Stoleru, L. (1975), *Economic Equilibrium and Growth*, North-Holland Publishing Company, Amsterdam.

Strunk, P. (1997), Thailand's Economic Structural Change, paper presented at The Thailand Business Conference, Berlin, 2 October.

Sundararajan, V. (1999), Getting It Right: Sequencing Financial Sector Reforms, International Monetary Fund, Washington, 15 July.

Sundararajan, V. and Balino, T. J. (1991), *Banking Crises: Cases and Issues,* International Monetary Fund, Washington.

Suphachalasai, S. (1995), Export-Led Industrialization", in Krongkaew, M. (ed.) *Thailand's Industrialization and Its Consequences,* St. Martin's Press, London, pp. 66–84.

Tobin, J. (1978), A Proposal for International Monetary Reform, *Eastern Economic Journal,* vol. 4, no. 4, pp. 153–159.

Tornell, A. and Velasco, A. (1995), Fixed Versus Flexible Exchange Rates: Which Provides More Fiscal Discipline?, NBER Working Paper no. 5108, National Bureau of Economic Research, Cambridge.

Tower, I. (1997), Mexico 1994 versus Thailand 1997, in Siamwalla, A. (eds.) *Thailand's Boom and Bust,* Thailand Development Research Institute (TDRI), Bangkok.

Tseng, W. and Corker, R. (1991), Financial Liberalisation, Money Demand, and Monetary Policy in Asian Countries, Occasional Paper no. 84, International Monetary Fund, Washington.

ul Haq, M., Kual, I. and Grunberg, I. (1996), *The Tobin Tax: Coping with Financial Volatility*, Oxford University Press, Cambridge.

United Nations Development Program (UNDP) (1990), *The Human Development Report*, UNDP, New York.

Vajragupta, Y. and Vichyanond, P. (1998), *Thailand's Financial Evolution and the 1997 Crisis,* Thailand Development Research Institute (TDRI), Bangkok.

Valdes-Prieto, S. and Soto, M. (1998), The Effectiveness of Capital Controls: Theory and Evidence from Chile, *Empirica*, vol. 25, no. 2, pp. 133–164.

Van-Ees, H. and Garretsen, H. (1993), Financial of Post Keynesian Economics, *Journal of Post Keynesian Economics*, vol. 16, no. 1, Fall, pp. 37–49.

Vasquez, I. (1999), Repairing the Lender-Borrower Relationship in International Finance, *Cato Foreign Policy Briefing Paper,* no. 54, 27 September, Cato Institute, Washington.

Vegh, C. (1992), Stop High Inflation: An Analytical Overview, *IMF Staff Papers*, no. 39, International Monetary Fund, Washington.

Velasco, A. (1987), Financial Crises and Balance of Payments Crises: A Simple Model of the Southern Cone Experience, *Journal of Development Economics*, vol. 27, no. 3, pp. 263–283.

Vichyanond, P. (1994), *Thailand's Financial System: Structure and Liberalization,* Thailand Development Research Institute (TDRI), Bangkok.

Vichyanond, P. (1995), The Evolution of Thailand's Financial System: Future Trends, *TDRI Quarterly Review,* vol. 10, no. 3, September, pp. 16–20.

Vichyanond, P. (2000a), *Financial Reforms in Thailand,* Thailand Development Research Institute (TDRI), Bangkok.

Vichyanond, P. (2000b), How to Prevent Another Crisis Country Report: Thailand, *TDRI Quarterly Review,* vol. 15, no. 2, September, pp. 18–28.

Villanueva, D. and Mirakhor, A. (1990a), "Interest Rate Policies, Stabilisation and Bank Supervisions in Developing Countries: Strategies for Financial Reform", International Monetary Fund Working Paper no. 90/8, Washington D.C.: International Monetary Fund.

Villanueva, D. and Mirakhor, A. (1990b), "Strategies for Financial Reforms", *IMF Staff Papers,* vol. 37, no. 3, pp. 509–539.

Vines, D. and Warr, P. (2000), *Thailand's Investment-driven Boom and Crisis,* Working Paper No. 00/11, Asia Pacific School of Economics and Management, Australian National University, Canberra.

Visser, H. (2000), *A Guide to International Monetary Economics: Exchange Rate Theories, Systems and Policies,* Cheltenham, UK: Edward Elgar.

Wacziarg, R. (2001), 'Measuring the Dynamic Gain from Trade', in *The World Bank Economic Review,* Vol. 15, No. 3, pp. 393–429.

Warr, P. (2001), "Poverty Reduction and Sectoral Growth: Evidence from Southeast Asia", paper presented for the WIDER Development Conference *Growth and Development,* Helsinki, 25 – 26 May 2001.

Warr, P. & Nidhiprabha, B. (1996), *Thailand's Macroeconomic Miracle: Stable Adjustment and Sustained Growth,* Oxford University Press, Kuala Lumpur.

Warr, P. G. (1993), "The Thai Economy", in Warr, P. G. (ed.), *The Thai Economy in Transition,* Cambridge: Cambridge University Press, pp. 1–80.

Warr, P. G. (1997), "The End of the Thai Miracle?', *Thailand Information Papers,* Working Paper no. 5, National Thai Studies Centre, Canberra: Australian National University.

Warr, P. G. and Nidhiprabha, B. (1989), *Macroeconomic Adjustment to External Shocks: Thailand,* Research School of Pacific Studies, Department of Economics and National Centre for Development Studies, Australian National University, Canberra.

Warr, P. G. and Nidhiprabha, B. (1996), *Thailand's Macroeconomic Miracle: Stable Adjustment and Sustained Growth,* Oxford University Press, Kuala Lumpur.

Whitt, J. (1999), The Role of External Shocks in the Asian Financial Crisis, *Reserve Bank of Atlanta's Economic Review,* vol. 84, no. 2, pp. 18–32.

Wiboonchutikula, P., Tubtimtong, B. and Chaivichayachat, B. (1999), An Analysis of Thailand's Capital Flows, *Chulalongkorn Journal of Economics,* vol. 11, no. 3, September, pp. 321–380.

Wibulswadi, C. (1995), *Strengthening the Domestic Financial System,* Bank of Thailand, Bangkok.

Wihlborg, C. and Willett, T. D. (1997), Capital Account Liberalization and Policy Incentives: An Endogenous Policy Approach, in Ries, C. P. and Sweeney, R. J. (eds.) *Capital Controls in Emerging Economies,* Westview Press, Boulder, Colorado, pp. 111–136.

Williamson, J. (1982), A Survey of the Literature on the Optimal Peg, *Journal of Development Economics*, vol. 11, August, pp. 39–61.

Williamson, J. (2002), Winners and Losers in Two Centuries of Globalization, paper presented at Wider Annual Lecture, Copenhagen, 5 September.

Williamson, J. and Mahar, M. (1998), A Survey of Financial Liberalization, Essays in International Finance no. 211, Princeton University, New Jersey.

Wolf, C. (1999), Financial Crises and the Challenge of Moral Hazard, *Society*, vol. 36, no. 5, July/August, pp. 60–63.

World Bank (1989a), *World Development Report*, Oxford University Press, Oxford.

World Bank (1989b), *Liberalizing Foreign Trade,* Basil Blackwell, Oxford.

World Bank (1993a), *Latin America a Decade After the Debt Crisis*, Basil Blackwell, Oxford.

World Bank (1993b), *The East Asian Miracle: Economic Growth and Public Policy,* Basil Blackwell, New York.

World Bank (1998), *Global Economic Prospects,* Basil Blackwell, Washington.

Yoon, J. C. (2000), The Financial Crisis in Korea: Causes and Challenges, Working Paper no. 79, Graduate School of International Studies, Sogang University, Seoul.

Yoshida, M. (1990), Foreign Direct Investment in Thailand, in Chiasakul, S. and Yoshida, M. (eds), *Thai Economy in the Changing Decade and Industrial Promotion,* Institute of Developing Economics, Tokyo, pp. 1–22.

Yoshitomi, M. (1999), The Asian Capital Account Crisis, in Brooks, D. H. and Queisser, M. (eds.), *Financial Liberalisation in Asia: Analysis and Prospects,* OECD, Paris, pp. 27–36.

Yoshitomi, M. and Shirai, S. (2000), *Policy Recommendations for Preventing Another Capital Account Crisis*, Asian Development Bank Institute, July, Asian Development Bank, Manila.

Young, S. (1999), Korea's Financial Crisis: Causes and Prospects, in Brooks, D. H. and Queisser, M. (eds.) *Financial Liberalisation in Asia: Analysis and Prospects,* OECD, Paris, pp. 55–60.

Appendix A

Regulatory Agency (Fig. A.1)

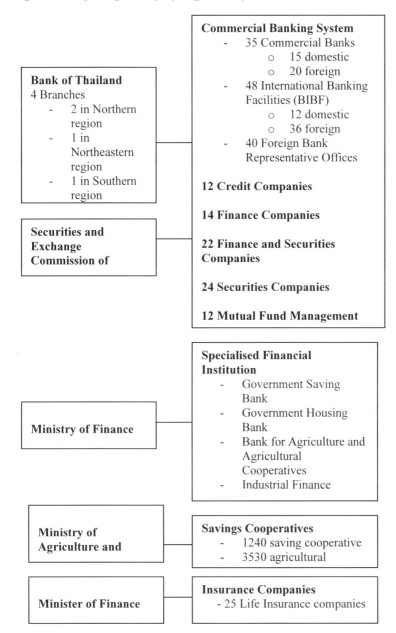

Fig. A.1. Structure of the Thai financial institutions

Source: Bank of Thailand 2002.

Appendix B

Articles of Agreement of the IMF

Article VIII: General Obligations of Members

Section 1: Introduction

In addition to the obligations assumed under other articles of this Agreement, each member undertakes the obligations set out in this Article.

Section 2: Avoidance of Restrictions on Current Payments

(*a*) Subject to the provisions of Article VII, Section 3(*b*) and Article XIV, Section 2, no member shall, without the approval of the Fund, impose restrictions on the making of payments and transfers for current international transactions.

(*b*) Exchange contracts which involve the currency of any member and which are contrary to the exchange control regulations of that member maintained or imposed consistently with this Agreement shall be unenforceable in the territories of any member. In addition, members may, by mutual accord, cooperate in measures for the purpose of making the exchange control regulations of either member more effective, provided that such measures and regulations are consistent with this Agreement.

Section 3: Avoidance of Discriminatory Currency Practices

No member shall engage in, or permit any of its fiscal agencies referred to in Article V, Section 1 to engage in, any discriminatory currency arrangements or multiple currency practices, whether within or outside margins under Article IV or prescribed by or under Schedule C, except as authorized under this Agreement or approved by the Fund. If such arrangements and practices are engaged in at the date when this Agreement enters into force, the member concerned shall consult with the Fund as to their progressive removal unless they are maintained or imposed under Article XIV, Section 2, in which case the provisions of Section 3 of that Article shall apply.

Section 4: Convertibility of Foreign-Held Balances

(*a*) Each member shall buy balances of its currency held by another member if the latter, in requesting the purchase, represents:

(i)   that the balances to be bought have been recently acquired as a result of current transactions; or

(ii)   that their conversion is needed for making payments for current transactions.

The buying member shall have the option to pay either in special drawing rights, subject to Article XIX, Section 4, or in the currency of the member making the request.

(*b*) The obligation in (*a*) above shall not apply when:

(i)   the convertibility of the balances has been restricted consistently with Section 2 of this Article or Article VI, Section 3;

(ii)   the balances have accumulated as a result of transactions effected before the removal by a member of restrictions maintained or imposed under Article XIV, Section 2;

(iii)   the balances have been acquired contrary to the exchange regulations of the member which is asked to buy them;

(iv)   the currency of the member requesting the purchase has been declared scarce under Article VII, Section 3(*a*); or

(v)   the member requested to make the purchase is for any reason not entitled to buy currencies of other members from the Fund for its own currency.

Section 5: Furnishing of Information

(*a*) The Fund may require members to furnish it with such information as it deems necessary for its activities, including, as the minimum necessary for the effective discharge of the Fund's duties, national data on the following matters:

(i)   official holdings at home and abroad of (1) gold, (2) foreign exchange;

(ii)   holdings at home and abroad by banking and financial agencies, other than official agencies, of (1) gold, (2) foreign exchange;

(iii)   production of gold;

(iv)   gold exports and imports according to countries of destination and origin;

(v)   total exports and imports of merchandise, in terms of local currency values, according to countries of destination and origin;

(vi)   international balance of payments, including (1) trade in goods and services, (2) gold transactions, (3) known capital transactions, and (4) other items;

(vii)   international investment position, i.e., investments within the territories of the member owned abroad and investments abroad owned by persons in its territories so far as it is possible to furnish this information;

(viii) national income;

(ix)   price indices, i.e., indices of commodity prices in wholesale and retail markets and of export and import prices;

(x)   buying and selling rates for foreign currencies;

(xi)   exchange controls, i.e., a comprehensive statement of exchange controls in effect at the time of assuming membership in the Fund and details of subsequent changes as they occur; and

(xii)   where official clearing arrangements exist, details of amounts awaiting clearance in respect of commercial and financial transactions, and of the length of time during which such arrears have been outstanding.

(*b*) In requesting information the Fund shall take into consideration the varying ability of members to furnish the data requested. Members shall be under no obligation to furnish information in such detail that the affairs of individuals or corporations are disclosed. Members undertake, however, to furnish the desired information in as detailed and accurate a manner as is practicable and, so far as possible, to avoid mere estimates.

(*c*) The Fund may arrange to obtain further information by agreement with members. It shall act as a centre for the collection and exchange of information on monetary and financial problems, thus facilitating the preparation of studies designed to assist members in developing policies, which further the purposes of the Fund.

Section 6: Consultation between Members Regarding Existing International Agreements

Where under this Agreement a member is authorized in the special or temporary circumstances specified in the Agreement to maintain or establish restrictions on exchange transactions, and there are other engagements between members entered into prior to this Agreement which conflict with the application of such restrictions, the parties to such engagements shall consult with one another with a view to making such mutually acceptable adjustments as may be necessary. The provisions of this Article shall be without prejudice to the operation of Article VII, Section 5.

Section 7: Obligation to Collaborate Regarding Policies on Reserve Assets

Each member undertakes to collaborate with the Fund and with other members in order to ensure that the policies of the member with respect to reserve assets shall be consistent with the objectives of promoting better international surveillance of international liquidity and making the special drawing right the principal reserve asset in the international monetary system.

Appendix C
Chronology of Financial Reforms in Thailand

	Trade Transformation and Interest Rate Deregulation
June 1989	Interest rate ceiling on commercial banks' long-term deposits is abolished
March 1990	Interest rate ceiling on short-term deposits is lifted
June 1992	Interest ceilings on non-bank financial institutions' deposit and lending are removed
	Ceilings on commercial banks' lending are also removed
October 1993	The BOT requires commercials banks to declare the MLR and MRR
	Exchange Rate and Capital Control Reform
July 1989	*First Round*: The government allows the public to lend in foreign funds as well as making outflows as dividend, interest or principle repayments.
May 1990	BOT allows commercial banks to process on purchases of foreign currency without prior approval and limit on capital outflows for loan repayment were increased.
April 1991	*Second Round*: BOT allows public purchasing and selling of foreign exchange without further approval
May 1992	The government allows the public to received payment and investment in foreign currencies and also permitted to transfer these funds abroad. The BOT allows the commercial banks to withdraw and use their funds more freely.
January 1994	*Third Round*: BOT increases the limit of Thai baht to be taken out of Thailand from 250,000 baht to 500,000 baht. The amount permitted to transfers for overseas investments also increased from US$5 million to US$10 million
	Establishment of New Financial Institutions
March 1993	The BIBF is established with an objective to reduce the cost of finance and enhance capital inflows into the financial system.
February 1994	The EXIM bank is established to provide financial support for the export sector.
January 1995	The offshore banking was expanded when the government granting a total of 59 licenses for financial institutions to operate out side Bangkok.
December 1996	Granting 7 new foreign banks to operate as offshore banking.

Index